Hamilton County Tennessee

EARLY ENTRY TAKERS BOOK

1824–1897

WPA RECORDS

Heritage Books
2024

HERITAGE BOOKS

AN IMPRINT OF HERITAGE BOOKS, INC.

Books, CDs, and more—Worldwide

For our listing of thousands of titles see our website
at
www.HeritageBooks.com

A Facsimile Reprint
Published 2024 by
HERITAGE BOOKS, INC.
Publishing Division
5810 Ruatan Street
Berwyn Heights, MD 20740

Originally published
September 15, 1837

— Publisher's Notice —

Pages 112-125 are missing in the Grantee section.

In reprints such as this, it is often not possible to remove
blemishes from the original. We feel the contents of this
book warrant its reissue despite these blemishes and
hope you will agree and read it with pleasure.

International Standard Book Number
Paperbound: 978-0-7884-8909-9

HAMILTON COUNTY

ENTRY TAKER'S BOOK
1824-1835

NEW INDEX

(NOTE: Page numbers in this index refer to those of the
"original book" from which this copy was made. These numbers are carried on the left hand margin of this copy.)

(A)

	(Page)
Adams, Simon	31
Agee, James	147-188
Archer, William	176
Arnel, James	177
Aulder ——	94

(B)

Back Valley Hollow	71
Baker, Solomon	164
Barnes, Isaac	147
Beck, David	2-45-89
	90-169
Bell, William	71-74
Benson, Isaac	24
Berry, William	47-67-84
	86-118
Big Soddy Creek	189-191-212
	217-218
Birdwell, George	19-49
	105-156
Bledsoe County, Tenn.	37-141
Board Camp Creek	82-128
	183-212
Bowman's Knob	134
Boydston, Cavenaugh	9
" Thomas	6-16-
Braden, Henry	111-120
	127-128
	168-211
Brimer, James	186
Brock, James	81-151
	162-170
Brown, James	192
" John	3-9-11-15
	21-25-26-28
	29-30-31-32
	40-41-54-77
	95-96-105-114
	121-124-125
	(Cont'd)

	(Page)
Brown, John	138-145-156
	212-158-191-209
" John C.(GOV.)	222
Brown's Island	125-175
Brown, William	97-210
Brush Creek	129
Bryson, Jacob	93
Bunch, James	15-172
	177-181
	46-172-177
Burket, George	195
Burkhart, George	196-198
Burwick, William	196

(C)

Cain Creek	183
Camp Creek	82
Caney Branch Road	181
Cannon, B.B.	179-195-217
" Benjamin B.	199-200-219
" George R.	208-217
Chattanooga	221-223
Cherry, Benjamin	54-59-64
	91-106
	134-158
Chickamauga Creek	6-24-39-46
	65-75-82-93
	97-111-114-
	117-125-127
	128-133-137
	159-160-163
	168-171-172
	177-181-186
	188-193-201
	206-210-211
	218
Chitty, Hardy	13
" Jesse	14

(C cont'd)	(Page)	(CREEKS cont'd)	(Page)
Clark, Isaac	130	McGrow's Creek	176
Clement, Isaac	79-84-184	McInturf's Creek	163
" James	184	Creek, Middle	42-50-163-
" John	184		165-188-197
" Stephen	184		198-219
" William	184	Mill Creek	23-110
Clift ----	212-218		135-138
" William	128-218	Mountain Creek	4-5-17-38
Coleman, Charles	181		59-92-93-122
Congressional Reservation	8-13-14		130-136-138
Conroy, H.	59		148-150-151
Cook, John	43		152-155-158
Cooper's Creek	137-172-177		185-
	178-182	North Chickamauga	127-130
Corbet, E.	68		159-168-200
" Elisha	12	Opossum Creek	55-121-123
Cornet, John	176		144-157-164
Coulter, Thomas	216		184-199-213
Cozby, James	171-209-217		218
" Robert	21-40-77	Rook Creek	81-107
	143-156		131-184
CREEKS		Rocky Creek	55-108
Big Falling Water	134		149-157
Big Soddy	189-191-212		164-190
	217-218		191-192
Board Creek	82		196
Board Camp	82-128	Roger's Creek	190
	183-212	Sale Creek	51-67-83
Brush	129		84-85-86
Cain	183		81-129-131
Chickamauga	6-24-39-46		132-141-142
	65-75-82-93		151-162-170
	97-111-114		196-203
	117-125-127	Shoal Creek	50
	128-133-137	Soddy(Saudy,Sauty)	57-115-128
	159-160-163		134-143-161
	171-172-177		168-200-204
	181-186-188		210
	193-200-201	Standifer Creek	186
	206-210-211	Suck Creek	50-52-136
	218		160-178-187
Cooper's	137-172-177		219
	178-182	Cumberland Mountain	13-24-27-37
Deep Creek	57-203-211		79-119-136
Falling Water	136-140-186		136-137-141
	201-205		156-163-168
Hunter's Creek	83		172-178-184
Laurel Creek	76-79		192-193-194
	119-123		196-199-200
Little Oven Rock House Creek			201-203-204
	128-200		205-216-217
Little Sandy(Soddy) Creek		Cummings, John	106-138
	191-201		158-175-177
	202-209	" Thomas	16-185
McGill's Creek	145-170		

		(Page)			(Page)
Cunningham,	David	61-68-176	Gent ---		184
"	Hugh	69-70	" Josiah		39
		71-167	" William		39-127
"	James	138	Gentry, William		4-5
			Geses Milden(Mill Dam(?)		92
(D)			Gillespie, George		205
		143-149-163	" Thomas		97-206-210
Dallas, ---		186-187	Gorden, John		119
Danner, John L. C.		223	Gray, Edward		132
Deep Creek		57-203	Green, Abraham		80
		211-218	Guy(?) ----		38
Donelson, Stoksley		155-208			
Donnelson, ----		208	**(H)**		
Dunnagan, Benjamin		83-87			
Dunham, ----		17	Hackett, A.		17
Dunn, Peter		217	Hagle, Hardy		144
			Hail, Enoch		53
(F)			Haney, James		134
			Hanna ----		208
Falling Water Creek		134-136	Hanna, Woodford R.		187-207
		140-186	Hartman, Jacob		63-64-66-93
		201-205			136-187-205
FERRIES			Harwell, Job		120
John Brown's		3-9-11-12	Hatfield, James		172-125
		25-26-31-32	Hawkins, S. B.		178-197
		40-54-59-61			202-219
		112-114-124	" Samuel B.		195
		125-158-208	Henly, William		157-202
Hixson's		176-208-209	Henson ----		204
Ross'		126-173	Hickman, William		116-129-132
			Hicksons ---		13-14
Fields, David		40-69-77	Hixson, Ephraim		22-36
		109-132-135	Hixson's Camp, Branch		137
		156-167-173	" William		183
Field's Trace		149	Hixson's Ferry		176-206-209
Finly, James		213	Hixson's Trace		79
Ford, William(Jr. - Sr.)		5-6-7	Holeman, William		188
Foster, Shepherd F.		133	Hopkins, Thomas		163
Frederick, Henry		117	Hopper, John		147-188-211
" John		168	Hopper's Trace		186
Freeman, ----		165	Horse Shoe, The Big		127
" Alexander		167	Howell, John		65-115
Friar, Jeremiah		116	Hughes, Ephraim		200-204
" John		116	" Hezekiah		204-205
			" John		205-210
(G)			Hunter's Creek		83
			Hunter's Gap		56
Gamble, Charles		31-33-37-56	Hunters Trace		117
		142-80-116-118	Hunter, William		78
Gann, Uriah		140	Hurricane Fork		136
General Assembly		6-8-13-14	Hutchison's Improvement		39
		37-39-68			
		140-160	**(I)**		
		161	Inlow, John B.		53

(J)   (Page)

Jack, Robert	203-216	
Jackson, Major A.	137-169	
" Thomas	137	
James, Thomas	34-53-58	
	90-113-143-	
	169-174	
" , William	18-142-162	
Johnson ---	68-88-91	
	138-180-206	
	138	
" Andrew, Gov.	221	
" Benjamin	51-60-80	
" Daniel	44	
" James	118	
" Joshua	18-20-27	
	30-36-167	
Jones, Benjamin	56	
" D.	118	
" Daniel S.	78-210	
" Elizabeth	79	
" James	142-179	
" Jeremiah	95-121	
	143-189	

(K)

Keeney ---	136	
" James	92-122-146	
	143-150	
	151-152	
	155	
" .	93	
" John	5-6-7-17	
	62-93-138	
	158-159	
Keeney's Trace	136	
Kelley, Alexander	27-168	
Kelley's Turnpike	20-42-62	
	107-112	
	165-166	
Knoxville, Tenn.---Title page.		

(L)

Lauderdale ---	122	
" Robert	148-151-159	
" William	5-6-7-38	
	62-66-92	
	93-150	
	152-159	
Laurel Creek	75-79	
	119-123	

Lawhorn, David W.	190-192	
Layman, George	107	
Lea, James	188	
Lee, James	116	
Lennox, Nathan	15	
Lewis, Henry	76	
Lick Branch	141	
Little Oven RockHouse Creek	128-183	
Little Soddy Creek	187-189	
	191-201	
	202-207	
	209-218	
Lookout Mountain	49	
Lovelady, John	77-133-156	
	173-182	
Lusk's Camp	87	
Lyon, Archibald Overton	160-161	

(M)

Marion County, Tenn.	160-219	
Martain, Patrick	132	
McClung ---	11-172	
	176-208	
	209-217	
McClure ---	123	
McGill's Creek	145-170	
McGill, William	37-116	
McGrew's Creek	17	
McLemore, Andrew Jackson	160-161	
McNutt, Thomas	117	
McRee ---	212-218	
" Robert	128-209	
	218-219	
McSpadan ---	144	
McVey ---	166	
" John	52	
Mead, Samuel B.	125-126	
	127	
Middle Creek	42-50-163	
	163-165	
	188-197	
	198-219	
Milliken, Cornelius--Title page.		
	8-9-10-11--12	
	13-15-16-17	
	18-20-21-22	
	23-to 36 incl.	
	37-to 63-incl.	
	63-66-68-73-75	
	76-77-78-79-81	
	(Milliken cont'd)	

(Milliken cont'd)	(Page)
	to 95 incl. 98
	104-107-109
	110-111-112
	114-115-117
	to 128 incl.
	130-137 incl.
	165-166-167
	180-185-223
Mill Creek	23-110-135-138
Miller, Henry	141

MILLS

Guyses' Mill	38
Mill on Mill Creek	23-110
Pounding Mill, The	17
Qualls' Mill	42-166
Smith's Mill	210

Mitchell, Andrew	94-143
	157-199
" James	16-185
" James C.	6
" John	39 to 44 incl.
	46 to 55 incl.
	56-57-60-61-62
	63-65-66-73-75
	76-77-78-81 to
	89 incl.-92-93
	94-95-98-106
	107-109-110
	111-112-114
	115-118-123
	incl.---125
	126-127-128
	130-137-incl.
Montgomery, Lewis	197
Moore, Thomas A.	143-176
More, James	203
Moss, Arnati	107-112
" Arnold	163-166
" James	167
Mountain Creek	4-5-17-38-54
	59-92-93-122
	130-136-138
	148-150-151
	152-155-185
Mountain Creek Ridge	59-64-66-
	91-106-130
Mountain Creek Road	138-158
Mountain Creek Valley	15-16-17-62-
	63-69-70
Moyers, John	189-210-218
Murdock, Eliott H.	31-32
Mullins ---	128
Murfreesboro	1-6-8-13-14
	37-39-49

(N)	(Page)
Nashville	140-160-161
Norman, W. C. & Co.	222
North Carolina	155
North Chickmauga Creek	39-97-127
	130-159-168
	193-216-217

(O)

Ooltewah Island	142-179
Opossum Creek	55-94-95-98
	101-102-103-
	104-121-123
	144- 157-164
	184-199-213
	213-218
Oven Rock House Creek	200
Owen, Mr.	188

(P)

Pafford, James	211
Parker, E.	215
" Elisha	2-58-89-90
	169-215(?)
Patterson, Alfred	108-191
Picket(or Ricket)	137
Pikeville,	37
Poe ---	204-207
" H.	194
" Easten	168-199-204
Poe's Road	201-207-218
Posey, Benjamin	55
Pounding Mill, The	17
Pullman Place	60
Putnam	
	13-22-
	27-36

(Q)

Qualls, James	42-112
	165-166
Qualls' Mill	166
Qualls' Trace	132

(R)

Rawlings ---	203
" Ahasel	106-149
	156-168-179
Read (&Reed) George	76-83-87
	123-142-179
Reed, Thomas	85
Reede, Stephen	83
Reservations	
James Brown's Reservation	192
	(Cont'd)

(Reservations cont'd)   (Page)   (Page)

John Brown's Reservation
       21-28-29-30   Valley Road   9-10-12-15
       40-41-49-77   18-25-26-54
       105-143-156   59-61-88-110

Congressional Reservation   124-130-176
       8-13-14   209-215
       37-49-70   Witt's Turnpike   162

David Fields   4-23-40-69-77   Fields' Trace   149
       109-132-135   Gesses Trace   186-187
       156-167-173   Hixson's Trace   79

Reynolds, Jacob   201-203-207   Hopper's Trace   186
   "   James H.   200   Hunter's Trace   47-117
Rhea County   208   Keeney's Trace   136
Rhenolds, David   114   Old Trail, Putman's to Hixson's
Richards, William   72-73   13-14-22-36
Richey, John   133   Roaring Fork   37-56-73-74
Richmond, Jonathan   104   132-142-196
   "   John   164   Roberts, George B. 178-182
   "   Martha   131   "   James   82-181
Ricket(or Picket) ---   137   Robin Hoods Barn   95
Rider, George W.   221   Rock Creek   81-107-151
Riddle, Terry   99-100-101   131-184-216
       102-103-144   Rocky Creek   43-44-55-99-
       155-158-184   100-102-103
                           108-149-157

RIDGES & MOUNTAINS   164-190-191
   Boman's Knob   134   192-196
   Mountain Creek Ridge 59-64-66   Rogers Creek   190
       91-106-130   Rogers ---   151
   Robin Hood's Barn(ridge) 95   Rogers' Rock House 13(?)-182-
   Valley Ridge   5-10   Rogers, Alford M.   171
   Cumberland Mountain 13-24-27-37   "   E.   36
       79-119-136   "   Elisha   22-122-146
       137-141-156   147-148-151
       163-168-172   155-158-204
       178-184-192   "   William   11-145-223
       193-194-196   "   William W.   211
       199-200-201   Roilston(or Boilston) Thomas 176
       203-204-205   Rose, Frances   33
       216-217   Rosses Ferry   19-34-58-109
   Lookout Mountain   49   113-126-173
Ritchmond, John   157   Rosses Improvement   88
Roads, Traces & Trails   "   Island   126
   Brown's Ferry Road   158   Runnels, Jacob   211
   Kelley's Turnpike 20-42-62   Russell ---   151-182
       107-165   "   George   29-49
       166   105-223
   Mountain Creek Road 138-158   James   107
   Poe's Road   201-207-218   James B.   145
   Poe & Henson's Turnpike 204   John   37-116-142
   Turnpike Road granted to   145-179
   Gamble, Shelton & Witt 80   Samuel R. 84-86-91-
                          (Cont'd)

(Page)

Russell, Samuel (Cont'd)   106-131
   132-135
   152-173

(S)

Sale Creek   37-51-56-67 -72
   73-74-76-78-80
   83-84-85-86-87
   116-117-118-129
   131-132-141
   142-151-162
   170-196-203

Sciveley, Absolem   132
"   Daniel   62-69
   71-107

Sequatchie Valley   13-51-67
   136-204

Shelton, Chrispian   56-80
   118-142

Shirley, Thomas   175
Simmerman, Henry R.   25-26-143
   173-174
   182-187
   205-215
   217

Simpson, Paschel   196
Singleton, James   157-216
Shoal Creek   50
Skillern, Anderson   141
Smith's Mill   210
Smith, Alexander   112
"   Henry L.   142-145-146
   147-158
"   James   23-24-32
   109-110-132
   135-138-173
   176-182-217
"   Jesse   91-112-124
   206-209
"   Joseph   141
"   Latan   163-168
"   Middleton   176
"   William   10-88-207
Snapp, John   6-64-66
Soddy Creek   13-14-57-116
   128-134-143
   161-168-189
   191-200-204
Spicer, Thomas W.   223
Standifer Creek   186
Stringer ---   12-68-88-91-
Stephens   138-180-206
Stephens Will   118

(Page)

Stringer, William H.   3-20-23-25
   26-40-110
   112-135(?)
   138-143-167
   173-174
   180(?)-182
   215-216
Stump, Christopher   160-161
"   Frederick   161

Suck, The   23-125-175
Suck Creek   13-50-52-136
   160-178
   187-219
Sullivan, John   213
Sutton ---   168-218
"   Buck   57
"   Jesse   140-

(T)

Taber, Heckbeth   173
Talliaferro's San Mill   219
"   John   165-167-180
   197-198-215
   216-219(?)
Taylor, William   190
Tennessee River   1-2-8-13-14-15
   19-25-28-31-33
   34-36-37-40-48
   31-50-52-53-54
   58-88-105-107
   112-124-125-126
   127-142-143
   167-169-176
   177-179-182
   206-209-215
   160-163-165
Tennessee State of   1 to 11 incl.
   13 to 52 incl.
   56-57-58- 60
   62-63-65-66
   68-to 95 incl.
   98 to 159 incl.
   162 to 172 incl.
   175 to 222 incl.
Tennessee Valley   3-24-37-51
   57-40-51-67
   68-106-138
Tiptons Line   162
Tipton, William   215
Trewhitt, Judge   221
Tumbling Shoals   165-175

		(Page)				(Page)
Tygart,	Nathan H.	183	Walker,	Charles		161
			"	Jesse		188-192-193
	(V)					194-195
						217
Valley Ridge		5-10	Washington (Tenn.)			9-11-12-25-
Valley Road		9-10-12-15-18				26-54-59-61-
		25-26-54-59-61				114-124
		88-110-124-130				176
		176-209-215	Waterhouse	---		77-91-
Van Dyke	---	223				124-156
Varner,	James	123				169
Varner,	Madison	210-212	"	E.		180
			"	E. G.		45-89-90
	(W)					105-113
			"	Richard		34-35
Waddel,	Seth	194				180(?)-216-
Waldens Ridge		5-15-22-24-27	"	Richard G.		1-2-3-20-21
		36-37-38-39-43				28-29-31
		44-46-47-51-57				32-33-35
		incl. 60-65-67				40-41-48
		71-76 incl. 78				49-50-56
		79-82-83-84-92				110-143
		-102 incl. 107				174
		111-114-115-116	Webb,	Meredith		172
		117-119-120-122	"	Thomas		172
		125-127-129-132	Williams	---		167
		133-134-136-137	"	George		20-165
		140-152-incl.				166-167(?)
		155-156-157-159				180
		164-incl. 168-170	"	George W.		171-177
		171-172-175-177	Winton,	John		1
		178-180-190-inc.	Witt,	John		56-80
		192-196-incl.-				118
		198-213-incl.				142
		216-217-218	Witt's Turnpike			152

(End of "Original Book" Index.)

NEW INDEX

(Beginning of Transcript Book.)

(NOTE: Page numbers in this index refer to those
of the original "Transcript Book" from which this
copy was made. These numbers are carried on the
left hand margin of this copy.)

(A)		(Page)
Adair,	James	256
"	James A.	257
"	Stephen	249-250
Allen,	M. R.	357
Anderson, A. L.		359
Anderson's Turnpike		320
Askew,	Elisha	295-296-298-361

(B)

Badger,	Samuel	244
"	William	243-244
Barker,	Henry	391
Bear Branch (Creek)		295-296-361
Beck ---		322
" H. C.		387-388-389
Bell,	Joseph	276
Bias,	J. G.	384
Big Soddy Creek		297-325
Billingsly, Jacob		265-269
"	James	270
Blacknall,	F. G.	318-330
		332-335 incl.
		366-368 incl.
		376-381-382
Bledsoe County, Tenn.		331-334-352
		354-356-365-472
Bolton,	Peter	259
Braden,	Henry	295-313
Btison,	Samuel	313
Brown ---		324
"	John	307-325
"	John, Sr.	308
"	John, Jr.	297-301-308-325
Brown,	John's Reserv.)	328-380
Bruster(Brewster) William		231-235
Bunch,	William	297-299
Burdin,	Elijah	257
Burnet,	John	363
Burt,	Nash	365-366-367
		356-370-371
		372-373-374
		375-376-378
		379-380-382

(C)		(Page)
Cain Creek		388
Cannon ---		296
"	B. B.	346-347
		361-370
"	Benjamin	225-226-227
		228-229-231
		232-233-234
		235-236-274
		296-301-303
"	G. B.	344-345-346
"	G. R.	344-346-348
		349-351-365-367
"	George R.	297-301-309-322
		328-244-245-247
Carr,	William	307
Carrick,	Hugh L.	233-234
"	James M.	230
"	John A.	232-233
"	Moses M.	230
"	Samuel V.	229
"	Seth L	233
Carrol,	James	272
"	John J.	292
Caryell,	Lewis S.	240
Chattanooga		292-294-317-356
Chattanooga Company, Ltd.		392
Chattanooga Creek		293
Chickamauga Creek		298-304-308
		211-313-345-370
Chickamauga Island		362
Churchill ---		359
Clark,	B. F.	360
"	Darius	254
"	Davids	253
Clements, Aaron		284
Clenny, James		283
Clift ---		323
Clift & McRee		323-360
Clift,	M. H.	287
"	William	226-291-307
		312-316-360
		364-383-386
		387

	(Page)		(Page)
Cline, George	250	Rocky Creek	226-308-344
Coffee, John	301-304		366-372
Coleman, Charles	287-290	Sale Creek	287-305-360
Collins, Ann	248	Shoal Creek	225-257
Connor, J. C.	326	Soddy Creek	262-301-307
Connor's Green	384		308-334-337
Connor, James C.	314		344-372
Coop Creek	358	Standifer Creek	360
Cornett ---	322	Suck Creek	304-308-309
Cornwell, Thomas	236-246		363-384-389
Coundry, Judson	359	Taylor's Mill Creek	259
Cowart ---	322	Crow, Tion	389
" John	292-294	Crozier, Joseph	246
Cox, Monroe	282	Cumberland Mountain	226-273-286-289
Cozby, ---	309-313-314-		292-296-298-302
	324-344-355		305-306-310-311
	372		312-314-316-323
" Robert	306		334-337-339-344
Crawford, Lillie	283		346-347-348-354
CREEKS			349-355-356-360-361
Big Soddy Creek	297-325		364-367-368-370
Cain	388		373-374-376-385
Chattanooga Creek	293	Cummings, John	387
Chickamauga Creek	296-304-308	Cunningham, William	302-308-325
	311-315-330		355-358
	346-370-385		
Coop Creek	358	(D)	
Falling Water Creek	259-288-305	Dallas(Tenn.)	227-247-290
	306-315----		359
Little Possom Creek	358	Dallas to Jasper Road	290
Little Soddy Creek	355-358-365	Davis, William	293
Lookout Creek	323	Deakins ---	304-306
McGills Creek	275-308-331	Dickens, Absolem	295
	352-359	Dilton, Hannah	254
McInturff's Creek	388	Divine, John L.	356
Middle Creek	225-286-287	Doak ---	332-333-
	325-350-388		378-379
Mill Creek	258	" S. M.	387
Mountain Creek	298-310	(E)	
North Chickamauga Cr.			
	225-226-274-292	Eagland, Ayelsy	249-253
	295-296-302-303	Eastland, Robert	231-232
	306-312-314-317	" Thos.	229-230
	326-330-332-333		231-232
	344-345-346-347		233-254
	355-361-362-368		235
	370-371-373-378	" Thomas B.	227-228
	379-388-392		236
Opossom Creek	284-319-325	Edwards, James S.	330
	344-372	Elens Jonathan	252-253
Owens Creek	351-352		
Rolls Creek	385	(F)	
Roaring Creek	344-372		
Rock Creek	308-331	Falling Water Creek	259-288-304
Rock House Creek	318		305-306-315

	(Page)
FERRIES	
Brown's Ferry	328
John Cowart's Ferry	292
Johnson's Ferry	359
Fletcher, George	358
Ford ---	322
Ford's Gap	306
Former, Lewis	308
Fouts, John	310
Foust Gap	310
Franklin, Jerry	280
Freeman, Joseph	238-239
Frye ----	347
Fryer ----	345-368
	371

(G)

Georgia (State)	323
Glenn, James	281
" Robert M.	277-278
" William	280-281
	282
Gothard, James	309-350
Grayson, Henry	389
Grayson's Gap	365
Green, Ashley	243
" Levi	326
" O. S.	384-389

(H)

Hale ---	392
Haley ---	363
Hall, Doctor	274-275-276
	277-278-279
	280-281-282
	283
Harrison (Tenn.)	323
Hart ---	352
Hartsman, Jacob	310
Hatt, Asahel	266-270-271
Hawkins ---	303
Hawkins S. B.	272-273
	334-341
" Samuel B.	338-339
	374-375
Heifner, Thomas	275-276
Helton ---	290
" Peter	259-260
Henderson, James	264-268
	269
"	317
" R.	307-308
	(Cont'd)

	(Page)
Henderson, R.(Cont'd)	309-311
	312-315
	315-316-317
" Richard	317
Hickman ---	305
Hixson ---	392
" Ephraim	294-300
	304-301
" Houston	301
" Washington	303-316
" William	318-356
	365
" William C.	305
" Wilson	304
Holland, B. F.	391
Hopper ---	304
" James	295
Hopper's Trace	295
Hughs, Ephraim	296-319-
	324
" Hezekiah	296-318
	356-365
Hunter, Samuel H.	326-327
Hyatt, John	290

(I)

Igou, Samuel	237-239-
	249 incl.
	258-271
	incl.-305
	308
Indian Boundary	360

(J)

Jack, Robert	320
Jasper, (Tenn.)	290
Johnson ---	347-348
	376-382
" H.	391
" Henry	392
" John	326
" Joshua	327-328-344
	345-355-358
	371-373-380
" Johnson, R.T.	273
" William	332-333-337
	(?)-331
	332 (?)
Johnson's Ferry	259
Johnston, Joseph	253
Jones, Daniel	324

		(Page)			(Page)
Jones,	Henry	381-382			305-306-312
					314-315-319
(K)					332-335-338
					348-349-357
Kelly,	Daniel	271			358-364-367
"	John	271			369-375-376
Kesterson,	Able	357			378-379-382
Kinsman,	Henry	247			385
Knowles,	Hiram	251-252	Marion & Hamilton Turnpike		314
(L)			Mason,	Walker	329
			Massa,	Pleasant	255-256
Lamon,	James	383-384	Mathis,	David	261
		385-387	McCallen,	George	241-242
Lane,	J. A.	227-229-230	"	Samuel	242-245
		231-232-233	McCalln(or McCallie's)Mill		256
		234-235-236	McClung	---	324-330
"	Jacob A.	226-229-231-248			344-355
		249-250-251	McClung & Comby		324-344-372
		252-253-254	McClung,	Charles	309
		255-256-257	McCracken,	Samuel	246-247
"	Turner, Sr.	236	McCrary,	T. M.	323-325
"	Turner, Jr.	236	McGill's Creek		225-308
Layman,	Thomas	359			351-352
Levi,	George	309			359
Lewis,	John	284-285	McInturff's Creek		388
		286-287	McKenzie,	S. A.	360-361
		288-289			362-363
		290	McNabb,	R. L.	364-365-366
Lick Branch(Creek)		305			367-368-370
Little,	Harmon	275			371-372-373
"	Mary	278			374-375-376
"	Sampson	275			378-379-380
"	Simpson	274			381-382
Little Possom Creek		356	McRee,	Robert C.	225-226-323
Little Soddy Creek		355-358-365			360(?)-388
Lombert	Charles	239	Middle Creek		225-286-287
Lomerick,	P. R.	326			326-350-388
Long	---	363	Mill Branch		301
Lookout Creek		323	Mill Creek		358
Lookout Mountain		323-326	Miller	---	305
Luster	---	325	"	Michael	265-266-270
(M)			MILLS		
			S. H. Hunter's		326
Marcum,	James	263-264	McCalln's(or McCallie's)		356
		267-268	Taliaferro's		284
"	Robert	263-267	Waylen's		259
		268	Minnis	---	384
Marion County (Tenn.)		227-231 incl.	"	J. A.	326-384(?)
		235-236-237	"	John A.	314-320
		239-240-241			321-330
		242-245-246	Mitchell,	David	234
		248-249-250	More	---	322
		263-265-266	Moses	---	383
		267-273-273	Moss,	Arnold	255
		274-275-276	Mountain Creek		298-310
(Cont'd)		277-278-281			

	(Page)			(Page)
Murphy, B. L.	259-260		(R)	
		Rawlings, Asahel	298-314-318	
(N)		Reaves, Isaac	241	
		" Joseph	240-241	
Newbold, Anthony	244-245	Reilly, J. M.	363	
Newman, Alexander	264-265	Rells Creek	385	
	268-269	Reynolds, Jacob	345-371	
North Chickamauga Creek		Rhea County	294-309	
	225-226-274-292		310-345	
	295-296-302-303			
	306-312-314-317	ROADS, TRACES, TRAILS		
	326-330-332-333	Anderson's Turnpike	320	
	344-345-346-347	Brown's Trace	298-310	
	355-361-362-368	Cozby's Trace	303-313-314	
	370-371-373-378	Dallas to Jasper Road	290	
	379-388-392	Hopper's Trace	295	
(O)		Johnson's Ferry to Dallas Road		
			359	
Oldham, Nicholas	228-229	Marion & Hamilton Turnpike	314	
Opossom Creek	284-319-323	Poe's Turnpike Road	297-299	
	344-372		311-316	
Owen Creek	331-352		359(?)	
(P)		Trace-Tenn. River to Heltons Cabin		
			290	
Packett(Puckett)	348	Walker's Turnpike Road	352-354	
Painter, Jennet(or Janet)	242-243	Wild Cat Trace	311	
" Juanna	247	Roaring Creek	344-372	
Parke ---	323	Roberson, Isaac	352-354-359	
Parks ---	308	" Sally	279-280	
" Lewis	308	" Samuel	356-365	
Parks, Thomas	226	" Samuel W.	354	
" William	226	Roberts ----	315	
Patterson, Lewis	350	" Charles	239-240-242	
Pearsons, Elizabeth	323	" Emerson	305-383	
Pendergrass, N.	308	" William	262	
Peterson, John	282-283	Robertson, Samuel R.	352	
Philips, John	245	Robinson, Isaac	331	
" Joseph	245	Rock Creek	306-308-331	
Pickett, Allen	383	Rock House Creek	302-306-318	
Poe, Easten	302-327(?)	Rocky Creek	309-344-360	
	353-387		372	
Poe's Turnpike Road	297-299-	Rogers, Elisha	298-310-314	
	311-316		318-355-358	
	327-359(?)	" E. F.	390-391-392	
Puckett ---	347-348(?)	" James	310	
	376	" John	309	
" A. G.	306-332-333-337	" Joseph	315-383	
	338-361-368-381	" Ransom	392	
	382	" William	315-318	
Puncheon Camp Branch	304		326	
(Q)		Roneyls, Anderson	356	
		Roton, John	252	
Qualls, Robert	305	Round Knob, The	307-384	

	(Page)		(Page)
Salo Creek	297-305	Sparkman, Bryan	257
	360	" William	254-255
Sargent, John	250	Spicer, Thomas	311
Sawyer, George	304	Stanley ---	384
Scarby ----	326	Stratton --	389
Scarlet, Moses	279	Stringer ---	382
Schoolfield, David	237	" William H.	384
Scively, Daniel	318	Suck, The	309-329
Sciveley's Gap	299-300	Suck Creek	284-286-303
	310		329-303
Solcer ---	392		384-389
" A.	383		
" Absalom	315	(T)	
Sequatchie County	365		
" Valley	284-389	Taliaferro ----	236
Shelton, C. E.	354	" John	225
Shepherd, Lewis	389	Taliaferro's Mill Creek	284
Shoal Creek	225	Teague, J. E.	263
Shoemaker	346-370	Tennessee River	237-247-263
Shrewsbury, Albin	278-279		274-290-291
Simmerman	296-322		293-294-303
" Henry R.	258-260		307-311-317
Simpson, James	274-275		322-325-328
	276-277		329-356-357
	278-279		359-362-380
	280-281	Tennessee (State)	225-226-259-260
	282-283		261-272-273
" Sally H.	277		274-284-285
Sims, P. D.	388		291-315-incl.
Smallman, James L.	250-251		316-324 incl.
Smith ---	322		326-368 incl.
" Ellen	276-277		370-378 incl.
" Hannah	280-281		380-392 incl.
" Hezekiah	238-240-241	Tennessee Valley	303
	242-243-244	Thatcher, William	350
	245-246-247	Throop, B. H.	266-270-
" J. G.	264-265		271
	266-311	Todd, Mary Ann	248-249
" J. L.	336	Threwhitt, D. C.	355-358
" James	262-300-304	Tumbling Shoals	291
	328-380	Tunnell, N. J.	273-274
" Jesse	323	" Robert	258-259
" Joseph G.	237-263-267	" Wm. C.	273
	268-269-270		
	271-334-335	(V)	
	339-340-341		
	342-345	Van De Griff's Gap	309
" Layton H.	388	Vandergriff, Gilbert	302-306
Smith's Reservation	313		308-324
Snodgrass, David	235	Varner --	297-301
" James	235	" Lewis	325
Soddy Creek	262-301-307	" Madison	297-301
	308-324-327		324
	344-372		
Soddy Island	307		

S

(W)	(Page)		(Page)
Walden's Ridge	225-226-257-259	Watkins ---	358
	260-261-262-273	Wayland, James C.	260-261
	284-285-289-292	" John H.	261
	294-295-297-316	Waylans Mill Creek	259
	-incl. 318-320	Weaver ----	313
	-327 incl. 329	White, Allen	260-261
	-330-334 incl.		293-294
	337-335-341-344	" Robert	294
	345-349 incl.	" Woodson P.	234-235
	351-354-355-356	Whitehead ---	322
	358-359-360-361	Wild Cat Trace	311
	363-364-365-366	Wilder ---	339
	367-368-370-374	Williams, G. W.	237
	-incl. 376-381	" George W.	285-291
	-incl. 383-385-392		299-300
Walker, Allen	307	" Samuel	300-316
" Charles C.	355		385
" George	362	" Samuel & Co.	316-364-385
" Jesse	262-292-300	Winton Island	330
	304-308-313	Wiltse, J. S.	365-366-367-368
	315-317-325		370-371-373-374
	326-353-354		375-376-378-379
	355-358-363		380-382-392
" John	362	Wyont, Michael	270
Walker's Turnpike Road	352-354		
Warner, Joseph, Jr.	245-246 (?)	(Y)	
Warren, John	230-231	Yarnell, ----	309
Waterhouse, R. G.	328	York Spring	319

(End of Transcript Book Index.)

"ORIGINAL INDEX"

ENTRY TAKERS BOOK
1824-1235

(NOTE: Pages are in numerical order in this book, but
entry numbers are not. After every act of the legisla-
ture with reference to this land, entry numbers began
with "one". Pages are from 1 to 225 incl.
The following Index is as near as possible an exact
copy of the "Original Index."

Alphabetical Index
of the Enterors names
Number of Entry
Quantity of Acres
called for in each entry
Whether Preference or
General
With References
To the Pages
On which each Entry
Is Recorded

The State price of land entered in this Office is 12½ cents per acre. The Official fees are for Receiving and Recording each and every Entry $0.75 and for Issuing a Certified copy .25.

Commissions on all moneys received are paid over every Three months to the Agents of the Banks of the State of Tennessee or if there should be no Banks agent In the County, then to the President and Directors of said Banks at Knoxville (Two percent)

****

Enterors	No.	Acres		General Entry		Page
Boydston, Cavanaugh	1	190		"	"	9
Birdwell, George	11	50	Ballot	"	"	19
Berry, William	40	50		"	"	47
Beck, David	38	100		"	"	45
Bunch, William	39	64		"	"	46
Bunch, William (James in Book)	31	50		"	"	75
Bell, William						
2						
Richards, William	28	100		"	"	72
Bell, William	30	100		"	"	74
Berry, William	23	300		"	"	67
Bunch, James	31	50		"	"	75
Brock, James	40	50		"	"	81
Beck, David	50	135		"	"	89
Bryson, Jacob	60	50		"	"	98
Brady, Henry	75	100		"	"	111
Braden, Henry	90	200		"	"	120
" "	91	100		"	"	120
" "	103	640		"	"	127
" "	104	300		"	"	128
Brown, John	122	10		"	"	138
Clark, Isaac	107	100		"	"	130
Corbet, Elisha	4	186	Ballot	"	"	12
Chitty, Hardy	5	50		"	"	13
" Jesse	6	50		"	"	14
Cummings, Thomas	8	8		"	"	16
Corby, Robert	13	100		"	"	21
" "	32	40		"	"	40
Cook, John	36	82		"	"	43
Cherry, Benjamin	15	80		"	"	59
" "	9	100		"	"	54
Cunningham, David	17	50		"	"	61

Enterors	:	No.	:Acres:		:	General Entry	:Page	:
Cherry, Benjamin	:	20	: 25 :		:	" "	: 64	:
Cunningham, Hue	:	26	: 25 :		:	" "	: 70	:
Clemmont, Isaac	:	38	: 200 :		:	" "	: 79	:
Charry, Benjamin [	:	76	: 50 :		:	" "	:111	:
Geo. Will.]	:		: :		:			:
Cunningham, James	:	121	: 25 :		:	" "	:138	:
Coulter & Jack	:	127	:1000 :		:	" "	:215	:
Cannon, B. B.	:	84	: 200 :		:	" "	:195	:
	:		: :		:		:	:
Dunegan, Benjamin	:	42	: 300 :		:	" "	: 83	:
	:		: :		:		:	:
Frederick, Henry	:	86	: 100 :		:	" "	:117	:
Fryer, Jeremiah	:	85	: 321 :		:	" "	:116	:
	:		: :		:		:	:
Gentry, William	:	4	: 80 :	R. Pref.	:	" "	: 4	:
Gamble, Charles	:	23	: 50 :		:	" "	: 31	:
" "	:	25	: 6 :		:	" "	: 33	:
" "	:	29	: 77 :		:	" "	: 37	:
Gent, William	:	31	: 50 :		:	" "	: 39	:
Gamble, Charles	:	11	: 50 :		:	" "	: 56	:
Green, Abraham	:	39	: 100 :		:	" "	: 80	:
	:		: :		:		:	:
Harwell, John	:	21	: 50 :	Prof.	:	" "	: 65	:
Hail, Enoch P.	:	7	: 100 :		:	" "	: 53	:
Hartsman, Jacob	:	19	: 27 :		:	" "	: 63	:
" "	:	22	: 27 :		:	" "	: 66	:
Hunter, William	:	35	: 50 :		:	" "	: 78	:
Hartman, Jacob	:	55	: 160 :		:	" "	: 93	:
Hickman, William	:	84	: 100 :		:	" "	:116	:
Harwell, John	:	82	: 50 :		:	" "	:115	:
Hickman, William	:	111	: 50 :		:	" "	:132	:
Senior & Junior	:		: :		:		:	:
" "	:	107	: 200 :		:	" "	:129	:
	:		: :		:	" "	: 53	:
Inlow, John B.	:	8	: 100 :		:		: 18	:
	:		: :		:	" "	: 20	:
Johnson, Joshua	:	10	: 50 :		:	" "	: 27	:
" "	:	12	: 58 :		:	" "	: 30	:
" "	:	19	: 50 :		:	" "	: 44	:
" "	:	22	: 200 :		:	" "	: 51	:
" Daniel	:	37	: 50 :		:	" "	: 51	:
" Benjamin	:	3	: 50 :		:	" "	: 60	:
" "	:	4	: 50 :		:	" "	: 78	:
" "	:	16	: 150 :		:	" "	: 79	:
Jones, Daniel S.	:	36	: 50 :		:	" "		:
" "	:	37	: 150 :		:	"	: 95	:
" Jeremiah [	:		: :		:" "	"		:
Brown, John]	:	57	: 200 :		:		: 96	:
" Jeremiah & [	:		::		:	" "	:113	:
Brown, John]	:	58	: 50 :		:	" "		:
James, Thomas	:	80	: 50 :		:			
	:		: :		:			

Enterors	: No.	:Acres:	: General Entry	:Page :
ane, Elizabeth	: 37	: 150 :	" "	: 79 :
orden(?) John	: 98	: 100 :	" "	: 119 :
ones, Jeremiah) & John Br.)	: 92	: 100 :	" "	: 121 :
eeny, John	: 7	: 50 :	" "	: -- :
" "	: 9	: 8 :	" "	: 17 :
" "	: 18	: 25 :	" "	: 62 :
auderdail, William	: 5	: 123 :	" "	: 5 :
enox, Nathan	: 7	: 100 :	" "	: 15 :
auderdail, William	: 30	: 10 :	" "	: 38 :
ewis, Henry	: 33	: 100 :	" "	: 76 :
ovelady, John	: 34	: 25 :	" "	: 77 :
auderdel, William	: 54	: 25 :	" "	: 92 :
illiken, Cornl.	: 24	: 31½ :	" "	: 68 :
itchell, Andrew	: 56	: 50 :	" "	: 94 :
oss, Arnate	: 69	: 25 :	" "	: 107 :
ead, Samuel B.	: 102	: 100 :	" "	: 127 :
" "	: 100	: 100 :	" "	: 126 .
" "	: 101	: 100 :	" "	: 126 .
" "	: 99	: 600 :	" "	: 125 .
c.Vey, John	: 6	: 50 :	" "	: 52 :
osey, Benjamin	: 10	: 100 :	" "	: 55 .
arker, Elisha	: 14	: 50 :	" "	: 58 .
" "	: 51	: 150 :	" "	: 90 .
atterson, N. Alfred	: 71	: 50 :	" "	: 108 .
ualls, James	: 35	: 2 :	" "	: 42 .
" "	: 79	: 50 :	" "	: 113 .
" "	: 78	: 25 :	" "	: 112 .
ogers, William	: 3	: 190 :	" "	: 11 .
" Elisha	: 14	: 90 :	" "	: 22 .
ussell, George	: 21	: 100 :	" "	: 29 .
ead, George	: 32	: 250 :	" "	: 76 .
ichard, William	: 28	: 100 :	" "	: 72 .
oberts, James	: 41	: 100 :	" "	: 82 .
ead, Stephen	: 43	: 200 :	" "	: 83 .
ussell, Sam. R.	: 44	: 168¾ :	" "	: 84 .
eede, Thomas J.	: 46	: 605 :	" "	: 85 .
ussell, Samuel	: 47	: 90 :	" "	: 86 .
" "	: 52	: 37½ :	" "	: 91 .
" James	: 70	: 25 :	" "	: 107 .
henolds, David	: 81	: 25 :	" "	: 114 .
ead, George	: 93	: 150 :	" "	: 123 .
ogers, Elisha	: 93	: 100 :	" "	: 122 .
usel R. Samuel	: 110	: 43¾ :	" "	: 132 .
" R. Samuel	: 109	: :	" "	: 131 :

Enterers	No.	Acres		General Entry	Page
Richmond, Martha &	108	200		" "	131
Rogers, Elisha &	--	--		" "	147
S. Smith ()					
Snapp, John	6	120	Prefference		6
Smith, William	2	205		General Entry	10
" James	15	54		" "	23
" "	16	90		" "	24
Simmerman, Henry R.	17	51		" "	25
" Henry R.	18	51		" "	26
Smith, James	24	50		" "	32
Sutton, Buck	12	50		" "	57
" "	13	80		" "	57
Scively, Daniel	25	25		" "	69
" "	27	25		" "	71
Smith, William	49	50		" "	88
Springer, William	73	25		" "	110
Smith, James	74	25		" "	110
" "	72	50		" "	109
" Alexander	77	100		" "	112
" Jesse	96	25		" "	124
" "	97	25		" "	124
" Laton	--	--		Page 163	32
					E. No.
Turkenet, George	5	50		General Entry	52
Tipton, William	83	100		" "	115
Vey, John Mc.	6	50		" "	52
Varner, James	94	50		" "	123
Waterhouse, Richard G.	1	90	Preferred		1
Ditto Ditto	2	100	Preferred		2
Ditto Ditto	3	160	Resident		3
Waterhouse, Richard G.	20	152		" "	28
Waterhouse, Richard, Junior	26	101		" "	34
Ditto Do.	27	50		" "	35
Waterhouse, Richard G.	33	70		" 2 "	41
" "	34	52		" "	41
" "	41	56		" "	48
" "	1	320		" "	49
" "	2	320		" "	50

Beginning of "Original Transcript Book" Index.
1835-1897

Page	Enterer	Acres	No.	Locator
249	Adair, S.	5000	183	J. A. Lane
295	Askew, E.	1000	272	Enterer
298	" E.	---	277	"
359	Anderson, A. L.	2000	370	"
269	Billingsley, J.	5000	221	J. E. Smith
276	Bell, J. W.	"	235	Jas. Simpson
297	Bunch, C.	"	275	Chas. Coleman
297	Brown, Jno. et al	"	276	Enterer
301	Brown, J. J. et al	"	284	"
307	Brown & Carr	2000	295	"
313	Brison Saml	300	313	"
325	Brown & Varner	2000	326	"
359	Bolton, Peter	5000	389	"
391	Barker, Henry	9	411	------
231	Bruster, Wm.	5000	146	"
243	Badger "	"	171	Smith, H.
244	" Samuel	"	172	" "
257	Burden E.	3000	198	Lane, J. A.
265	Billingsley, J.	5000	213	Smith, J. G.
232	Carrick, J. A.	5000	149	---
233	" S. L.	5000	150	---
233	" H. L.	"	151	
238	Cornwall, Thos.	"	160	
240	Coryell, S. L.	"	164	Smith, H.
246	Crozier, Jos.	"	176	" "
248	Collins, A.	"	181	Lane, J. A.
253	Clark, D.	"	191	"
256	Cline, Geo.	"	196	"
256	" J.	"	197	Enterer
272	Carroll, J. B.	"	227	"
272	" "	"	228	Jas. Simpson
282	Cox, M.	"	247	"
283	Clenny, Jas.	"	249	"
283	Crawford, W.	"	250	Enterer
284	Clement, A.	150	251	Enterer
291	Clift, Wm.	200	265	"
296	Cannon, B. B.	1000	273	"
299	Coleman, C.	5000	279	"
301	Coffee, J.	500	283	"
302	Cunningham, Wm.	300	285	"
303	Cannon, B. B.	5000	288	"
306	Cozby, R.	300	293	Locator
307	Clift, Wm.	100	296	"
309	Cannon, G. R.	5000	301	"
314	Cannon, J. C. (Conner)	"	310	"
322	Cannon, G. R.	1600	322	"

Page	Enterer	Acres	No.	Locator
306	Corby, R.	300	293	"
307	Clift, Wm.	100	296	"
309	Cannon, G. C.	5000	301	"
314	Cannon, J. C. (Conner)	"	310	"
322	Cannon, C. R.	1600	322	"
327	Connor, G. R.	500	329	"
328	" " "	1	330	"
328	" G. R.	50	331	"
344	" " "	150	349	"
344	" " "	5000	350	"
345	" " "	1000	351	"
346	" " "	500	352	"
347	" " "	2000	353	"
348	" " "	5000	354	"
229	Carrick S. V.	"	142	"
229	" W. M.	"	143	"
230	" J. M.	"	144	"
349	Conner, G. R.	5000	355	"
351	" " "	"	358	"
360	Clark, B. F.	"	372	"
364	Clift, Wm.	3000	376	"
385	" J. Wm.	4800	406	"
387	Cummings, Jno.	----	407	Lamon, James
387	Clift, Wm. et al	500	408	Enterer
254	Dilton, H.	5000	192	Lane, J. A.
295	Davis, W. M.		268	Enterer
227	Eastland, T. B.	5000	138	Lane, J. A.
227	" Thos.	"	139	Enterer
231	" Thos.	"	147	"
249	Eagland, A.	"	182	Lane, J. A.
252	Elens, J.	"	189	" " "
330	Edwards, J. S.	1	333	Enterer
238	Freeman, J.	5000	161	"
280	Franklin, J.	"	243	Simpson, Jas.
308	Farmer, L.	"	298	Parks, Lewis
232	Glenn, Wm.	5000	148	Enterer
243	Green, A.	5000	170	Smith, H.
277	Glenn, R. M.	5000	238	Simpson, Jas.
281	Glenn, Jas.	5000	245	" "
281	Glenn, Wm.	5000	246	" "
309	Gothard, Jas.	280	300	Simpson, Jas.
384	Green, O. S.	225	405	Enterer
389	Green, O. S.	60	410	"
311	Henderson, R.	3000	305	Enterer
317	"	300	314	"

: : Page	:	Enterer	:	Acres	:	No.	:	Locator
: 318	:	Hughes, H.	:	500	:	317	:	Enterer
: 319	:	" A.	:	322	:	318	:	"
: 326	:	Hunter, S. H.	:	25	::	327	:	"
: 356	:	Hughes, H. et al	:	100	:	363	:	"
: 259	:	Hilton, P.	:	640	:	302	:	Murphy, B. M.
: 260	:	" "	:	150	:	204	:	White, A.
: 264	:	Henderson, Jas.	:	100	:	211	:	Smith, J.G.
: 266	:	Hatt, A.	:	640	:	216	:	" " "
: 270	:	" "	:	4000	:	224	:	" " "
: 275	:	Heifner, Thos.	:	5000	:	234	:	Simpson, Jas.
: 290	:	Hyatt, J. B.	:	"	:	264	:	Enterer
: 294	:	Hixon, E.	:	100	:	270	:	"
: 295	:	Hopper, Jas.	:	500	:	271	:	"
: 296	:	Hughes, Hez.	:	700	:	274	:	"
: 302	:	Hixon, W. C.	:	5000	:	287	:	"
: 304	:	" E.	:	1000	:	289	:	"
: 304	:	" W.	:	300	:	290	:	"
: 253	:	Johnston, J.	:	5000	:	190	:	Lane, J. A.
: 273	:	Johnson, R. S.	:	"	:	229	:	Tunnell, N. J.
: 324	:	Jones, D. S. et al	:	500	:	325	:	Enterer
: 330	:	Jack, R. G. et al	:	5000	:	334	:	"
:: 381	:	Jones, H. S.	:	300	:	402	:	"
: 392	:	Johnson, Henry	:	500	:	412	:	"
: 247	:	Kinsman, H. I.	:	5000	:	178	:	Smith, H.
: 251	:	Kelly, D.	:	5000	:	186	:	Lane, J. A.
: 251	:	Knowles, H.	:	"	:	187	:	" " "
: 271	:	Kelly, J.	:	"	:	225	:	Smith, J. G.
: 357	:	Kesterson, Ab.	:	"	:	365	:	Enterer
: 357	:	" "	:	"	:	366	:	"
: 228	:	Lane, J. A.	:	5000	:	140	:	Enterer
: 236	:	" T. Sr.	:	"	:	156	:	"
: 236	:	" T. Jr.	:	"	:	157	:	"
: 239	:	Lombert, Chas.	:	"	:	163	:	"
: 274	:	Little, S.	:	"	:	232	:	Simpson, Jas.
: 275	:	" H.	:	"	:	233	:	" "
: 278	:	" M.	:	"	:	239	:	" "
: 284	:	Lewis, John	:	"	:	252	:	Enterer
: 285	:	" "	:	"	:	253	:	"
: 285	:	" "	:	"	:	254	:	"
: 286	:	" "	:	"	:	255	:	"
: 286	:	" "	:	"	:	256	:	"
: 287	:	" "	:	"	:	237	:	"
: 287	:	" "	:	"	:	258	:	"
: 288	:	Lewis, Jno.	:	"	:	259	:	"
: 288	:	" "	:	"	:	260	:	"
: 289	:	" "	:	"	:	261	:	"
: 289	:	" "	:	"	:	262	:	"
: 290	::	" "	:	"	:	263	:	"

Page	Enterer	Acres	No.	Locator
309	Levi, Geo.	500	299	Enterer
326	Lemerick, P. R.	180	328	"
234	Mitchell, D. L.	5000	152	"
255	Moss, A.	"	194	Lane, J. A.
255	Massa, P.	"	195	" " "
261	Mathis, D. H.	"	205	Allen, W.
263	Marcum, R.	"	209	Smith, J. G.
263	" J.	"	210	" " . "
265	Miller, M.	"	214	" " "
267	Marcum, R.	"	217	" " "
267	" J.	"	217	" " "
268	" J.	"	219	" " "
269	Miller, M.	"	222	" " "
314	Minnis, J. A.	"	309	" " "
320	" J. A.	"	319	" " "
320	" J. A.	"	320	" " "
321	" J. A.	"	321	" " "
329	Mason, W.	200	332	" " "
241	McCallen, Geo.	5000	167	Enterer
242	" Sam	"	168	"
246	McCracken, Jos.	"	176	Smith, H
246	" Sam	"	177	" "
323	McRae, R. C.	"	323	" "
388	" " "	500	409	Enterer
244	Newbold, A.	5000	172	Smith, H.
264	Newman, Alex.	"	212	" J. G.
268	" "	"	220	" " "
228	Oldham, N.	"	141	Enterer
226	Parks, Thos.	"	136	"
226	" Wm.	"	137	"
242	Painter, J.	"	169	Smith, H.
245	Philips, Jos.	"	175	" "
247	Painter, J.	100	179	" "
282	Peterson, Jno.	5000	248	Simpson, Jas.
323	Pearson, E.	"	324	Enterer
332	Puckett, A. G. W.	"	335	"
333	" " " " " et al	"	336	"
337	" " " " "	"	337	"
338	" " " " " "	"	338	"
350	Patterson, L.	2900	356	"
361	Puckett, A. G. W.	200	373	"
305	Qualls, Jas.	640	292	Enterer
239	Roberts, Chas.	5000	162	Enterer
240	Reaves, Jos.	"	165	"
241	" I.	"	166	"

Page	:	Enterer	:	Acres	:	No.	::	Locator
252	:	Rotan, Jno.	:	5000	:	188	:	Lane, J. A.
262	:	Roberts, W. C.	:	640	:	207	:	Enterer
279	:	Roberson, S.	:	3000	:	242	:	Jas. Simpson
298	:	Rogers, E. }	:	1600	:	278	::	Enterer
298	:	Rawlings, A. }	:		:		:	"
310	:	Rogers , E.	:	1000	:	302	:	"
305	:	Roberts, E.	:	25	:	291	:	"
310	:	Rogers E. }	:	1600	:	303	:	"
310	::	" Jas. }	:		:		:	
315	:	" Wm.	:	5000	:	311	:	"
315	:	" Jas. et al	:	---	:	312	:	"
318	:	" E.	:	1000	:	316	:	"
331	:	Roberson, I.	:	5000	:	334	:	"
352	:	" S. W.	:	"	:	359	:	"
354	:	" I.	:	"	:	361	:	"
356	:	Roncyls, A.	:	7	:	364	:	"
363	:	Riley, J. M. et al	:	2000	:	375	:	"
383	:	Roberts, E.	:	---	:	404	:	"
392	:	Rogers, Ransom	:	500	:	412	:	"
	:		:		:		:	
285	:	Snodgrass, D.	:	5000	:	154	:	Enterer
235	:	" D. et al	:	5000	:	155	:	"
237	:	Schoolfield, D. et al	:	100	:	158	:	"
250	:	Sargent, J.	:	5000	:	184	:	Lane, J. A.
250	:	Smallman, Wm.	:	"	:	185	:	" " "
254	:	Sparkman, Wm.	:	"	:	193	:	" " "
257	:	Sparkman, B.	:	"	:	199	:	" " "
258	:	Simmerman, H.	:	640	:	200	:	Enterer
276	:	Smith, Ellen	:	5000	:	236	:	Simpson, Jas.
277	:	Simpson, S. H.	:	"	:	237	:	" "
278	:	Shrewsbury, A.	:	"	:	240	:	" "
279	:	Scarlett, M.	:	"	:	241	:	" "
280	:	Smith, H.	:	"	:	244	:	" "
311	:	Spicer, T. W.	:	"	:	304	:	Smith, J. G.
315	:	Selcer, Ab.	:	600	:	312	:	Enterer
339	:	Smith, J. G. et al	:	5000	:	339	:	"
339	:	" " "	:	"	:	340	:	"
340	:	" " "	:	"	:	341	:	"
340	:	" " "	:	"	:	342	:	"
341	:	" " "	:	"	:	343	:	"
341	:	" " "	:	5000	:	344	:	"
342	:	" " "	:	5000	:	345	:	"
342	:	" " "	:	5000	:	346	:	"
343	:	" " "	:	5000	:	347	:	"
343	:	" " "	:	5000	:	348	:	"
	:		:		:		:	
248	:	Todd, M.	:	5000	:	180	:	Lane, J. A.
259	:	Tunnell, R.	:	640	:	201	:	Enterer
266	:	Throop, B. H.	:	5000	:	215	:	Smith, J. G.
270	:	" E. H.	:	"	:	223	:	" "

Page	Enterer	Acres	No.	Locator
273	Tunnell, W. C.	5000	230	Tunnell, N. J.
274	" N. J.	4000	251	Enterer
350	Thatcher, W. C.	1800	357	"
302	Vandergriff, G.	2000	286	Enterer
306	" "	2000	294	'
297	Varner, M.	5000	276	Locator
	" Lewis	---	276	Locator
230	Warren, Jno.	5000	145	Enterer
234	White, W. P.	"	153	"
237	Williams, G. W.	250	159	"
245	Warner, Jos.	5000	174	Smith, H.
260	Wayland, J. C.	"	203	Murphy, B. M.
262	Walker, J.	1000	208	Enterer
271	Wyontt, M.	5000	226	Smith, J. C.
292	Walker, J.	640	266	" "
292	White, A.	5000	267	" "
294	" R. M.	"	269	White, Allen
299	Williams, G. W.	"	280	Enterer
300	" Sam	"	281	"
300	Walker, J.	1000	282	"
308	" J.	5000	297	"
313	" J.	2000	307	"
316	Williams, Saml.	4000	313	Clift, Wm.
317	Walker, J.	500	315	Enterer
353	" C. C.	4500	360	"
355	" J.	500	362	"
355	" J. et al	320	363	"
358	" " "	320	367	"
358	" G. & J.	200	368	"
362	" " "	1½	374	"
365	Wiltse, J. S. et al	1000	377	"
366	" " "	5000	388	"
367	" " "	"	369	"
368	" " "	"	390	"
368	" " "	2000	391	"
370	" " "	500	392	"
371	" " "	1000	393	"
372	" " "	5000	394	"
373	" " "	100	395	"
374	" " "	5000	396	"
375	" " "	"	397	"
376	" " "	"	398	"
378	" " "	"	399	"
379	" " "	"	400	"
380	" " "	50	401	"
382	" " "	1818	403	"

HAMILTON COUNTY

ENTRY TAKER'S BOOK
1824-1835

(NOTE: Pages 1 through 224, 1824-1835, were copied from "original book." Beginning on page 225
through page 392, 1835-1897, copied from "Transcript
Book.")

Opened at the place of holding Courts in said County for Preference Entries on the 1st Monday in April, 1824.

            ****

In pursurance of the provisions of an act of the General Assembly of November, 1823.

                ENTITLED AN ACT

To establish offices for receiving entries for the vacant lands in the
several Counties in this State lying north and east of the Congressional
reservation line and North of Tennessee River.

                          Cornelius Millican
                          Entry Taker

The State price of land entered in this Office is 12½ cents an acre.

The Official fees are for Receiving and Recording each and every Entry
$0.75 and for issuing a certificate copy .25.

Commissions on all moneys received are paid over every Three months to
the Agents of the Banks of the State of Tennessee or if there should be
no Banks agent in the County then to the President and Directors of Said
branch Banks at Knoxville. (Two percent)

PAGE 1
            : State of Tennessee, Entry takers office of Hamilton
No. 1   : County,No. One — Richard G. Waterhouse Enters Ninety
Richard G. Water-: acres of land in Said Clunty On the North side of Tenn-
house 90 Acres : essee River adjoining his forty five acre tract Grant-
Prefered Entry : ed to him by the State of Tennessee by Grant No.18811
            : Beginning on a Black Oak marked 45 corner to said Grant
Location Rec.   : Thence north with a line thereof East Ninety six poles
and this   : to two Box Elders marked 45 On the river bank thence
Entry made : up the meanders of the Tennessee river North thirty
5th April   : five East Thirty six poles to a Sycamore marked J. W.
1824   : corner to Joun Wintons 1000 acre tract of Grant No.
            : 301 thence with a line of the same North twenty three
Recd. for   : East one hundred and thirty five poles. Thence a di-
the State : rect line to the beginning.
$11.25   :
            :   Richard Waterhouse, Locator

: Fees of Office $1. paid
: Certificate copy Issued and delivered to the Enteror
: 5th April, 1824.
:

PAGE 2
:
No. 2   : State of Tennessee
Richard G.Water-   : Entrytakers Office of Hamilton County.
house, 100 Acres   : Richard G. Waterhouse enteres one hundred Acres of
Preferred Entry   : land in said county Including the Improvement where
                        : Elisha Parker now lives and adjoining lines with David
Location Received: : Beck and said Waterhouse Grant No. 18808 for 150 acres.
& this Entry   : Beginning on a Box Elder on the bank of Tennessee riv-
made 5th April,   : er marked F. corner to said Grant. Then with lines
1824   : thereof North 42 poles to a Sweet Gum marked E.W. 50
                        : then West 100 poles to a Post Oak at the foot of the
Received for the   : hill corner to David Beck. Thence with his lines N.
State $12.50   : Sixty five East 108 poles to a Post Oak Blak Oak and
                        : Spanish Oak his corner. Then with his line North 210
                        : poles to a Black Oak in a hollow. Thence East 36 poles
                        : to Tennessee River and down the meanders of the same
                        : to the beginning.
                        :   Richard G. Waterhouse
                        :
                        :
                        : Certificate Copy Issued and delivered to the Enteror
                        : 5th April, 1824.
                        : Fees of Office $1. paid
                        :

PAGE 3
                        :
                        :
No. 3   : Richard G. Waterhouse Enters One hundred and Sixty Acres
Richard G.Water-   : of land In Hamilton County In the State of Tennessee
house, 160 Acres   : lying on each side of the Road leading down Tennessee
Resident Prefer-   : Valley to John Brown's ferry on Tennessee river In-
red   : cluding the place where William H. Stringer now lives.
                        : Beginning on a Spanish Oak and White Oak marked W. H.
Location Received: : S. twenty eight poles below his house thence South
and this Entry   : Sixty East Seventy poles thence North thirty East two
made 5th April,   : hundred & twenty six & a half poles. Thence North
1824   : Sixty West crossing the Valley one hundred and thir-
                        : teen and a fourth poles thence South thirty West two
Recd. for the   : hundred twenty six and a half poles. Thence to the
State $20.00   : beginning.
                        :   Richard G. Waterhouse
                        :
                        :
                        : Certificate Copy Issued and delivered to the Enteror
                        : 5th April, 1824
                        : Fees of Office $1. paid
                        :

PAGE 4   :
                        :
No. 4   : William Gentry Enters Eighty Acres of land In Hamilton
William Gentry   : County In the State of Tennessee Lying on both sides
80 Acres Resident: : of Mountain Creek including part of the Improvement
Preferred   : where he now lives. Beginning on a White Oak and

Location Received : Entry made 5th : April, 1824 : : Received for the : State $10.00 : : : : :	Dogwood on the East side of Said Creek on a line of David Fieldses Reservation. Thence with said line West crossing said creek One hundred and sixty poles Then North Eighty poles along the side of a hill then East One hundred and sixty poles then South to the beginning. William Gentry Certificate copy Issued and Delivered to the Enterer 5th April, 1824. Fees of Office $1. paid

PAGE 5

No. 5 : William Lauder- : dail, 123 Acres : Prefference Entry : : Location Received : and the Entry made : 17 April, 1824. : : Received for the : State $15.37½ : : : : : : : : : : : : : : :	William Lauderdale enteres one hundred and twenty three Acres of Land in Hamilton County beginning on the South W. Side of Waldens Ridge North west corner on a post oak and a Black oak Running South Eighty one East ninety six poles on a conditional line Des- ignated By a committee appointed Between John Keeny and William Lauderdail to a Black Walnut on the East Side of mountain Creek thence south Eighty East 58 poles to a White oak along a Conditional Line Desig- nated By the Said Committee Between William Lauder- Dail and William Ford Senr. thence south thirteen west along the meanders of the Valley Ridge a natural Boundary one hundred and twenty five poles to a white oak on William Gentry's line thence west along his line one hundred and Seventy poles to a stake north twenty nine East and with the meanders of the moun- tain one hundred poles to a post oak thence north forty five poles to the Beginning Including one hun- dred and twenty three acres. William LauderDail Certificate Copy Issued and Located Delivered to the Enterer 17th April, 1824. Fees of office paid $1.00

PAGE 6

No. 6 : John Snapp, 12 : Acres prefference : Entry by assignee : of : Thomas Boidston : & : William Ford : : : :	John Snapp assignee of Thomas Boidston and William Ford Enters one hundred and twenty acres of land in Hamilton County as an Occupant Claim in pursuance of an act of Assembly passed at Murfreesborough the 22nd day of November 1823. Beginning of said land on a White Oak between the South West Corner of William fords femce and A Cabbin formerly occupied By William Ford Jun. from thence to a marked walnut Corner of William Lauderdail (and?) John Keeny thence Between William ford and John Keeny to a marked white Oak from thence Between last mentioned to a White Oak

: and sweet gum at the foot of the mountain thence a-
: long the foot of said mountain to the We— Line from
: the mouth of Chickamaugy thence East with said Line
: to a Stake and post oak Corner James C. Mitchell
: thence south to a Black oak marked J. C. M. Corner
: to said Mitchell thence Ea— to Hickry on the point
: of a Ridge and Corner to the Said J. C. Mitchell
: thence along the side of a Ridge to a stake thence
: west to the Beginning

John Snapp, assignee of
Thomas Boidston and
William ford Locator

: Certificate Copy Issued and delivered to Enterer
: 19th of April, 1824.
: fees of office paid $1.00

PAGE 7

No. 7
John Keeny, 50
Acres Prefference
Entry

Location Received :
and this Entry
made 29th June,
1824

Received for the :
State $6.25

: John Keeny Enters fifty acres of Land in Hamilton
: County beginning on a Black Walnut in William Lauder-
: dail line Running north fifteen degrees East ninety
: poles to a marked white oak that the Committee mark-
: ed Between William ford and John Keeny thence along
: a conditional Line made by the Committee to A sweet
: gum and white Oak marked By them near the foot of
: the Mountain then along the meanders of the mountain
: of the mountain to a post oak and Black Oak William
: Lauderdail's north west corner thence south Eighty
: one Degrees East to the Beginning Including the Im-
: provement where said John Keeny now lives Including
: fifty acres.

John Keeny, Locator

: Certificate Copy Issued and Delivered to the Enterer
: the 29th of June, 1824
: fees of Office $1.00

PAGE 8

: State of Tennessee
: Entry Taker's Office of Hamilton County Opened at the
: place of Holding Courts in Said County for General
: Entries on the first Monday of July, 1824.
: In pursuance of the provisions of an Act of the Gen-
: eral Assembly of the State of Tennessee passed at
: Murfreesborough the 22d day of November, 1823 en-
: titled An Act To establish offices for receiving En-
: tries for the vacant lands in the several Counties
: in the State lying North and east of the Congressional
: reservation line and north Tennessee River

Cornelius Milliken
Entry Taker

(This was the second Act of General Assembly and numbers begin with one again. Pages are all in numerical order. At the end of the first three months period they began with No. 1 again)

PAGE 9

No. 1
Cavenaugh Boydston:
190 Acres General
Entry By Ballet

Location Received
and this Entry
made 5 July, 1824

Received for the
State $23.75

State of Tennessee { Cavanaugh Boydston Enters one
                  { hundred and ninety acres of
Hamilton County   { Land lying on both sides of the
                   Valley Road Leading from washington to Brown's ferry Bounded as follows Viz: beginning on a post oak on the aforesaid Line Running thence S. 28 W. one hundred and forty five poles to a Black Oak thence S. 62 E. one hundred and twenty two and a half poles to a stake thence N. 28 E. two hundred and thrity poles to a stake on the said line thence with Said line to the Beginning.

                         Cavanaugh Boydston

Fees of office paid $1.00
Certificate Issued and Delivered to the Enterer the 13th ? day of July 1824

                         Cornelius Millican
                         Entry Taker for
                         Hamilton County

PAGE 10

No. 2
William Smith
205 Acres General
Entry

Location Received
and this Entry
made 5th July,
1824

Received for the
State $25.62½

State of Tennessee William Smith Enters two hundred & five acres of Land In Hamilton County Lying on both Sides of the Valley Road Below the west line of 20000 Acre Grant Beginning on a post oak and Black oak trees marked M standing in said west Line of the 20000 Acre grant at the foot of the Valley Ridge on the East Side of said Valley Road thence west with the Line of the said 20000 Acre Grant 140 poles to a smal hickory on the side of a ridge on the west side of said Road thence S. 25 W. 225 poles then S. 65 E. 140 poles and thence to the Beginning.

                         Wm. Smith

Fees of office paid $1.00
Certificate Copy Issued and Delivered to the Enterer this 5 Day of July, 1824

                         Cornelius Milliken
                         Entry taker for
                         Hamilton County

PAGE 11

No. 3
William Rogers
190 Acres General
Entry

State of Tennessee }
Hamilton County }

William Rogers Enters one
hundred and ninety acres of
Land lying on both Sides of the
Road Leading from Washington
to Brown's Ferry Beginning on a post oak and Black
oak on the Due West Line of the twenty thousand acre
Survey Claimed by McClung and others Running thence
S. 28 ? W. two hundred and forty five poles to a
black Oak thence 62 E. one hundred twenty two and a
half poles to a stake thence N. 28 E. to a stake on
the aforesaid Due West Line thence with said Line to
the Beginning.

Location Received
and this Entry
made 5th July,1824

Received for the
State $23.75

William Rogers

Entry Made Void

Fees paid $1.00
Certificate Copy Issued and Delivered to the Enterer
July 13th ? 1824

Cornelius Millican
Entry taker for
Hamilton County

PAGE 12

No. 4
Elisha Corbet
&
C. Millikin
186 Acres Joint En-
try By ballet

State of Tennessee }
Hamilton County }

Elisha Corbet & Cornelius Milliken Enters one hundred and
Eighty six acres of Land in
said County on both sides of
the Valley Road Leading from Washington to Brown's
ferry sixty poles west of Sd Road Beginning at a
Black Oak thence Running S. 28 W. two hundred and
forty five poles to a stake supposed to be on or
near Stringer's Line thence South Sixty two East one
hundred and twenty two and a half poles to a stake
thence N. 28 E. two hundred and forty five poles to
a post oak thence North (page torn----) Sixty two
west one hundred and twenty two and a half poles to
the Beginning.

Location Received
and this Entry
made 5th July,1824

Received for the
State $23.25

Elisha Corbet
Cornelius Milliken, Locator

Certificate Copy Issued and Delivered to the Enterers
this 5th day of January 1825

Cornelius Milliken
Entry Taker for
Hamilton County

PAGE 13

No. 5
Hardy Chitty, 50
Acres General
Entry

Location Received
and this Entry
made 5th July,
1824

Received for the
State $6.25

State of Tennessee | purseant to the provisions of an act of the general assembly

Hamilton County | of the State of aforesaid passed at Murfreesborough on the 22 of November, 1823 Entitled an act to Establish offices for Receiving Entrys for the vacant Lands in the several Countys In this State Lying north and E. of the Congressional Reservation Line and north of Tennessee River hardy Chitty Enters fifty acres of land Lying on Waldens Ridge of Cumberland mountain Beginning at a Black oak and pine trees standing near the Rock House near Suck Creek a branch of Soddy Creek and near the old trail leading from putmans to Hickson's in Sequachee Valley running 80 poles then North eastwardly 100 poles thence N. westwardly 80 poles thence South westwardly 100 poles to the Beginning.

Hardy Chitty

Fees of office paid $1.00
Certificate Copy Issued and Delivered to the Enteror
July 13th ? 1824

Cornelius Milliken
Entry taker for
Hamilton County

PAGE 14

No. 6
Jesse Chitty, 50
Acres General
Entry

Location Received
and this Entry
made 5th July
1824

Received for the
State $6.25

State of Tennessee | Surveyors Fourth District In pursuance of an act of the

Hamilton County | general assembly of the State of Tennessee passed at Murfreesborough on the twenty Second Day of November 1823 Entitled an act to Establish offices for receiving Entrys for the vacant Lands in the Several Counties in this State lying north and East of the Congressional Reservation line and north of Tennessee River — Jesse Chitty Enters fiffty acres of Land lying on Waldens ridge on the waters of Soddy Creek Beginning at a Black Oak Tree on the North East Side of the old trace leading from putmans to Hixsons in Sequachee and ---- on the North East side of a branch Running thence Eastwardly one hundred and Seven poles thence northwardly Seventy five poles Including a small Branch Thence Westwardly 107 poles to the said trace thence along said trace Southwardly to the point of beginning.

Jesse Chitty

Fees of office paid $1.00
Certificate Copy Issued and Delivered to the Enterer
July the 13th, 1824.

Cornelius Millican
Entry taker for
Hamilton County

PAGE 15

No. 7
Nathan Lenox
100 Acres General
Entry

Location Received
and this Entry
made 5th July,
1824

Received for the
State $12.50

State of Tennessee | Nathan Lennox Enters one hun-
dred Acres of Land lying in a
Hamilton County | Small Valley west of the Valley
Road Leading to John Brown's
Ferry on Tennessee River and East of the Mountain
Creek Valley Beginning on a post oak Running thence
S. 64 E. forty five poles to a stake thence N. 26 E.
One hundred and Eighty poles to a stake thence N.64
W. ninety poles to a Stake thence S. 26 W. ninety
poles to a Stake thence S. 26 W. one hundred and
Eighty poles to a stake thence S. 64 E. forth five
poles to the Beginning.

Nathan lennox

Fees of office paid $1.00
Certificate Copy Issued and Delivered to the Enteror
July the 13th 1824.

Cornelius Millican
Entry taker for
Hamilton County

PAGE 16

No. 8
Thomas Cumings
8 Acres General
Entry

Location Received
and this Entry
made 5th July,
1824

Received for the
State $1.00

State of Tennessee | Thomas Cummings Enters Eight
Acres of Land lying on Moun-
Hamilton County | tain Creek Valley bounded as
follows to wit: Beginning on
stake the N. E. Corner of James Mitchell Land at
present occupied by Thomas Britston Running thence
with the Due West Line E. 30 poles to a stake thence
along the Ridge to Mitchels Line to a stake 80 poles
thence with Said Mitchells line to the Beginning.

Thomas Cummings

Fees of office paid $1.00
Certificate Copy Issued and Delivered to the Enteror
July the 13th 1824.

Cornelius Milliken
Entry taker for
Hamilton County

PAGE 17

No. 9
John Keeny, 8
Acres General
Entry

Location Received
and this Entry
made 5th July,
1824

Received for the
State $1.00

State of Tennessee | John Keeny Enters Eight acres
of Land lying on a branch of
Hamilton County | Mountain Creek and lying in
the Mountain Creek Valley bound-
ed as follows to wit, Beginning on a poplar above the
pounding mill Thence Running E. 60 poles to a stake
on a line of Dunhams a purchase made by Said Dunham
of A —— Hackett thence along his line Down the Valley Crossing the Branch fifty poles to a stake thence
a Direct Course to the Beginning.

John Keeny

Fees of office paid $1.00
Certificate Copy Issued and Delivered to the Enterer
July 14, 1824.

Cornelius Milliken
Entry taker for
Hamilton County

PAGE 18

No. 10
Joshua Johnson, 50
Acres General
Entry By Ballot

Location Received
and this Entry
made 5th July,
1824

Received for the
State $6.25

State of Tennessee | Joshua Johnson Enters fifty
Acres of Land on a place known
Hamilton County | by the name of William James
Improvement on the East Side
of the Valley Road Beginning on a poplar & white oak
in the fork of the Spring Branch Running thence W.
36 E. 32 poles to a stake thence N. 53 W. 128 ?
poles to a Stake thence S. 36 W. 64 poles to a Stake
thence S. 53 E. 128 poles to a Stake thence N. 36 E.
32 poles to the Beginning.

Joshua Johnson

Fees of office paid $1.00
Certificate Copy Issued and Delivered to the Enterer
July 5, 1824.

Cornelius Milliken
Entry taker for
Hamilton County

PAGE 19

No. 11
George Birdwell
50 Acres General
Entry By Ballot

State of Tennessee | George Birdwell Enters fifty
acres of Land lying on the North
Hamilton County | Side of Tennessee River about
two miles Below Rosses ferry
Bounded as follows Beginning on an ash on the Bank
of Tennessee River Running thence west to the foot

Location Received
and this Entry
made 5th July,
1824

Received fees for
the State $6.25

: of the Bluff thence with the meanders of said Bluff
: a natural Boundary two hundred and — to a stake at
: the foot of the Bluff thence East to the bank of the
: River thence meandering the River to the Beginning
:
: George Birdwell
:
: Fee of office paid $1.00
: Certificate Copy Issued and Delivered to the Enter-
: ors July 5, 1824
:

PAGE 20

No. 12
Joshua Johnson &
William H. Stringer:
58 Acres Joint
General Entry
By Ballot

: State of Tennessee } Joshua Johnson and William H.
: } Stringer Enters fifty Eight
: Hamilton County } Acres of Land lying on Each
: Side of Co. Co. Kellys turn-
: pike Road and bounded as follows to wit, Beginning
: at a post oak a Corner of Richard G. Waterhouses
: land at present occupied by George Williams thence
: running with the Said Line of Richard G. Waterhouse
: S. 60 poles to A. white Oak thence 62 E. 156 poles
: to a white oak thence N. 60 poles to a Black Oak
: thence S. 62 W. 157 poles to the Beginning.
:
: Joshua Johnson
: Wm H. Stringer
:
: Fees of office paid $1.00
: Certificate Copy Issued and Delivered to the Enteror
: July 14, 1824.
:
: Cornelius Milliken
: Entry taker for
: Hamilton County

PAGE 21

No. 13
Robert Cozby
100 Acres General
Entry

Received for the
State $12.50

Location Received
and this Entry
made this 5th
July, 1824

: State of Tennessee, Robert Cozby Enters one hundred
: acres of Land in hamilton adjoining John Browns Re-
: servation Beginning on the Lower side of said Reser-
: vation at Richard G. Watterhouses Corner then north
: along Watterhouses line 178 poles then East 89 poles
: then south 178 poles to the line of said Reservation
: then west with the same 89 poles to the Beginning.
:
: Robert Cozby
:
: Fees of office paid $1.00
: Certificate Copy Issued and Delivered to the Enterer
: July 14th, 1824
:
: Cornelius Milliken
: Entry taker for
: Hamilton County

PAGE 22

No. 14
Elisha Rogers, 90
Acres General
Entry By Ballet

Location Received
and this Entry
made 5th July,
1824

Received for the
State $11.25

State of Tennessee } Elisha Rogers Enters ninety
acres of Land lying on Walden's
Hamilton County } Ridge said land lying on the S.
west side of a small trace lead-
ing from putmans across said Waldens Ridge to Ephrain
Hixsons and said piece of land running so as to Include
a cave spring and a pond and the same lying about two
miles from putmans Bound as follows to wit, Beginning
on a Chesnut Immediately under the top Clift of said
Waldens Ridge thence South 40 W. 70 poles to a stake
thence North 50 west 120 poles to a stake Thence N.
40 E. 120 poles to a stake thence S. 50 E. 120 poles
to a stake thence a Direct line to the Beginning.

Elisha Rogers

Fees of office paid $1.00
Certificate Copy Issued and Delivered to the Enteror
July the 13th, 1824

Cornelius Milliken
Entry taker for
Hamilton County

PAGE 23

No. 15
James Smith, 54
Acres General
Entry

Location Received
and this Entry
made 5th July,
1824

Received for the
State $6.75

State of Tennessee } James Smith Enters Fifty four
acres of Land lying on the E.
Hamilton County } side of David fields reservation Beginning on a Black oak
and a hickorry on the South Side of the Road leading
past the Suck between William H. Stringers and the
mill on the mill Creek Running thence south with said
line thirty two poles to a stake thence S. 80 E. Sixty six poles to a stake thence North thrity two poles
to a Hickory Corner of said Smiths three acre tract
on the North side of said Road thence North one hundred poles to a stake thence N. 80 W. Sixty six poles
to the aforesaid Reservation line thence South with
said line one hundred poles to the Beginning.

James Smith

Certificate Copy aforesaid and delivered to the Enterer July 14th, 1824.

Cornelius Millican
Entry taker for
Hamilton County

PAGE 24

No. 16
James Smith, 90
Acres General
Entry

Location Received
and this Entry made
5th July, 1824

Received for the
State $11.25

State of Tennessee / James Smith Enters ninety
acres of Land lying on Waldens
Hamilton County / Ridge a part of Cumberland
Mountain nearly opposite Isaac
Bensons ? in Tennessee Valley on the waters of Chickamauga Beginning on a Black oak and Hickory running
South 45 West one hundred poles to a stake thence N.
45 West one hundred and twenty poles to a Stake
thence North 45 East one Hundred and twenty poles to
a stake thence South 45 E. one hundred and twenty
poles to a stake thence a Direct line to the Beginning.

James Smith

Certificate Copy Issued and Delivered to the Enteror
July the 14th, 1824.

Cornelius Millican
Entry taker for
Hamilton County

PAGE 25

No. 17
Henry R. Simmerman
51 Acres General
Entry

Location Received
and this Entry
made July 5th, 1824

Received for the
State $6.37½

State of Tennessee / Henry R. Simmerman Enters 51
acres of land lying on the
Hamilton County / Valley Road leading from Washington C. H. to John Browns
ferry on Tennessee River and said Land lying between
William H. Stringers and John Browns ferry and bounded as follows to wit - Beginning on a red oak South
20 West 50 poles from the head of a spring on said
Road running thence South 70 East 32 poles to a stake
thence North 20 East 128 poles to a stake thence N.
70 West 64 poles to a stake thence South 20 West 128
poles to a stake thence south 70 East 32 poles to the
Beginning.

Henry R. Simmerman

Certificate Copy Issued and Delivered to the Enteror
July 14th, 1824.

Cornelius Millican
Entry taker for
Hamilton County

PAGE 26

No. 18
Henry R. Simmerman
51 Acres General
Entry

State of Tennessee / Henry R. Simmerman Enters 51
acres of land lying on the Val-
Hamilton County / ley Road leading from Washington C. H. to John Browns ferry

Location Received
and this Entry made
th July, 1824

Received for the
State $6.37½

on Tennessee River and the said land lying between
William H. Stringer and John Brown's ferry and
bounded as follows to wit - Beginning on a black
gum on said Road thence North 60 West 32 poles to a
thence South 30 West 128 poles to a stake thence S.
60 E. 64 poles Crossing said Road to a stake thence
North 30 E. 128 poles to a stake thence North 60.32
poles to the Beginning.

Henry R. Simmerman

Certificate Copy Issued and Delivered to the Enteror
July 14th, 1824.

Cornelius Millican
Entry taker for
Hamilton County

PAGE 27

No. 19
Joshua Johnson, 50
Acres General En-
try by Ballot

Location Received
and this Entry made
th July, 1824

Received for the
State $6.25

State of Tennessee) Joshua Johnson Enters Fifty
) Acres of land on Waldens Ridge
Hamilton County) a part of Cumberland Mountain
below the upper clift of said
Mountain Beginning at a white Oak at the foot of the
afforesaid Clift Running N. 36 E. along the foot of the
said Clift thirty five poles then crossing a spring
branch thence with the foot of said clift, Crossing
a new Road leading from putmans to Alexander Kellys
one hundred and twenty poles to three post oaks thence
S. 54 E. Sixty six poles to a black oak and Black gum
thence S. 36 W. one hundred and twenty poles to a
stake thence N. 54 W. sixty six poles to the beginning.

Joshua Johnson

Fees of office paid $1.00
Certificate Copy Issued and Delivered to the Enteror
July the 13th, 1824.

Cornelius Milliken
Entry taker for
Hamilton County

PAGE 28

No. 20
Richard G. Water-
house, 152 Acres
General Entry

Richard G. Waterhouse Enters 152 acres of land In Hamilton County, State of Tennessee On the north side of
Tennessee River Beginning on a Maple blased ash on
the River bank opposite the lower end of an Island
and bluff of Rocks on the south side of the River
Corner to his 150 Acre tract of Grant No. 18808
thence with a line of the same North 64 poles to a
small post oak marked A Corner to said Grant and 50

Location Received
and this Entry made :
this 6th July, 1824 :

Received for the :
State $19---00 :

poles more to an Oak marked B on a Ridge thence
west Crossing several branches and drains 215 poles
thence South 85 poles to a Hickory and red oak on
the bank of a branch Corner to John Brown's Reservation thence with a line thereof sixty poles to a
Hackberry on the River bank Corner to said Reservation thence up the River as it meanders to Beginning.

Richard Waterhouse

Fees of office $1.00 paid
Certificate Copy Issued and Delivered to the Enterer this 6th July, 1824.

Cornelius Milliken
Entry taker for
Hamilton County

PAGE 29

No. 21
G. Russell, 100 :
Acres General Entry :

Location Received :
and this Entry made :
July 6th, 1824 :

Received for the :
State $12.00 :

George Russell Enters one hundred Acres of Land In
Hamilton Cty State of Tennessee on the south side
of John Brown's Reservation Beginning on Sd Reservation line at the Corner of Richard G. Waterhouses 200 acre Survey Bounded By lines of Sd. Survey
and Sd. Reservation line running according to law
for Complement.

G. Russell

fees of --- (office ?) paid $1.00
Certificate Copy Issued and Delivered to the Enterer July 6, 1824.

Cornelius Milliken
Entry taker for
Hamilton County

PAGE 30

No. 22
Joshua Johnson, 200 :
Acres General
Entry :

Location Received :
and this Entry made :
6th July, 1824 :

Received for the :
State $25.00 :

State of Tennessee ⟩ Joshua Johnson Enters two
⟩ hundred acres of land lying
Hamilton County ⟩ above John Brown's Reservation line on Tennessee River
Bounded as follows to wit Beginning on two Black
oaks on the west side of the River hill Running
thence west on the aforesaid Reservation line 130
poles to a poplar on a side of a Swamp thence S.
16 West along said Swamp 110 poles to a Hickory
Sweetgum on the Side of a large pond thence South
27 E. 150 poles along said pond to a stake thence
East 120 poles to a stake on the Side of the River
hill thence North along said hill to the Beginning.
Joshua Johnson

Fees of office paid $1.00
Certificate Copy Issued Delivered to the Enteror
July 13, 1824.

Cornelius Milliken
Entry taker for
Hamilton County

PAGE 31

No. 23
Charles Gamble, 50
Acres General Entry

Location Received
and this Entry made
8 July, 1824

Received for the
State $6.25

State of Tennessee | Charles Gamble Enters fifty
acres of land lying on Tennes-
Hamilton County | see River above John Brown's
ferry bounded as follows to wit
Beginning at a poplar and white oak at the foot of a
Ridge opposite the lower End of an Island Thence N.
eighty five east Seven poles to a mulberry on the a-
foresaid River Bank thence down said River to two
Hacberry trees on the bank of said river marked with
a W on each tree and marked for Corner trees and on
the largest one of said trees is marked with a fig-
ure thirty the same supposed to be Richard G. Watterhouses Corner trees thence with said supposed line
of Richard Waterhouse passing a large forked poplar
marked W. H. and continuing with Said line supposed
to be Richard G. Watterhouses line as aforesaid to
a small Beech marked R. W. a small Distance below
Simon Adams thence with said line supposed to be
Richard G. Waterhouses line to a black oak near a
mount with a grave on the same above Eliath H. Murdocks field thence North forty poles to a stake
Thence a Direct line to the Beginning.

Charles Gamble

fees of office paid $1.00
Certificate Copy Issued and Delivered to the Enter-
or July 14th, 1824.

Cornelius Milliken
Entry taker for
Hamilton County

PAGE 32

No. 24
James Smith, 50
Acres General Entry

Location Received
and this Entry made
8th July, 1824

State of Tennessee | James Smith Enters fifty
acres of land lying in the
Hamilton County | bend above John Brown's ferry
bounded as follows to wit Be-
ginning at a stake South sixty four poles to a black
Oak near a mount with a grave on the same marked for
a corner tree Supposed to be Richard G. Watterhouse
Corner thence with said line supposed to be Richard
G. Watterhouse line as aforesaid passing through

Received for the
State $6.25

Elliot Murdocks field thence continuing with said
line supposed to be Richard G. Watterhouse line as
aforesaid Down the River one hundred and twenty
Eight poles to a stake Thence North Sixty four poles
to a stake thence a Direct line to the Beginning.

James Smith

fees of office paid $1.00
Certificate Copy Issued and Delivered to the Enter-
or July 14th, 1824.

Cornelius Millican
Entry taker for
Hamilton County

PAGE 33

No. 25
Charles Gamble, 6
Acres General Entry

Location Received
and this Entry
made 8th July,
1824

Received for the
State $ .75

State of Tennessee } Charles Gamble Enters Six acres
of land on Tennessee River be-
Hamilton County } tween two Entrys made By Richard
G. Watterhouse the same occupied
at present by Frances Rose Beginning on a Sweet Gum
a corner tree to Richard G. Watterhouse lower Entery
thence a Direct line to said Richard G. Watterhouse
Corner on his upper Entry thence with that line to a
Stake on the River bank thence Down the River to a
stake a corner of Richard G. Watterhouse lower Entry
thence a direct line to the Beginning.

Charles Gamble

fees of office paid $1.00
Certificate Copy Issued and Delivered to the Enter-
or July 14th, 1824.

Cornelius Milliken
Entry taker for
Hamilton County

PAGE 34

No. 26
Richard Waterhouse
101 Acres General
Entry

Location Received
and this Entry
made July 10th
1824

Received for the
State $10.62½

Richard Watterhouse Enters one hundred & one acres
of land in Hamilton County one a branch that Empties into Tennessee River a small Distance below
Rosses Ferry Including the Spring and improvement
where Thomas James now lives Beginning at a post
oak and Black oak on the East bank of said branch
in the line of Richard G. Watterhouses General Entry No. 20 for 152 Acres Running North one hundred
and Eighty poles then west ninety poles Then South
180 poles to the line of said 152 acre tract then
with a line thereof East to the Beginning.

Richard Waterhouse

fees of office paid $1.00
Certificate Copy Issued and Delivered to the Enterer July 10th, 1824.

> Cornelius Milliken
> Entry taker for
> Hamilton County

PAGE 35

No. 27
Richard Waterhouse
50 Acres General
Entry

Location Received
and this Entry made
July 10th, 1824

Received for the
State $6.25

Richard Waterhouse Enters fifty acres of Land in
Hamilton County State of Tennessee on Thomas James-
es Spring Branch adjoining his 101 Acre Entry No.
26 Beginning at the South west Corner of said Entry No. 26 on the line of Richard G. Waterhousees
152 Acre Entry No. 20 then North with the line of
Sd. Entry No. 26 Eighty poles then west one hundred poles then south Eighty poles and East 100
poles to the Beginning.

> Richard Waterhouse

fees of office paid $1.00
Certificate Copy Issued and Delivered to the Enterer July 10th, 1824.

> Cornelius Milliken
> Entry taker for
> Hamilton County

PAGE 36
No. 28
Joshua Johnson, 100
Acres General Entry

Location Received
and this Entry
made July 14th,
1824

Received for the
State $12.50

State of Tennessee } Joshua Johnson Enters one
hundred acres of land lying
Hamilton County } on Waldens Ridge North of
Tennessee River and being on
the south west side of the trace leading from putmans to Ephraim Hixsons Bounded as follows Beginning on two Chesnuts in the head of a Cave spring
twelve poles south west of a pond on the top of
said Ridge Running north 50 W. 120 poles along E.
Rogerses line to a stake thence south westwardly
170 poles to a stake thence south Eastwardly to
the top Clift of the said Ridge a natural Boundary
along the top of said Ridge to the Beginning.

> Joshua Johnson

Fees of office paid $1.00
Certificate Copy Issued and Delivered to the Enterer July 14, 1824.

> Cornelius Milliken
> Entry taker for
> Hamilton County

PAGE 37

No. 29
John Russell,
William McGill
&
Charles Gamble, 77
Acres General
Entry

Location Received
and this Entry
made this 11th day
of August, 1824

Received for the
State $9.62½

State of Tennessee | In pursuance of an act of the
General Assembly of the State
at Murgreesborough on the 22d
Hamilton County | Day of November 1823 entitled
an Act to Establish offices for receiving Entrys for
the vacant lands in the several Counties in this
State lying north and East of the Congressional Reservation line and north of Tennessee River, John
Russell, William McGill and Charles Gamble Enters
Seventy Seven acres of land in said County on Waldens
Ridge of Cumberland Mountain on the Roaring fork of
Sale Creek about two and a half miles from Tennessee
Valley Including an Improvement at the place known
by the name of Lusks Camp Beginning at a black oak
and white oak trees standing in the point between a
branch and the Roaring fork of Sale Creek North East
of said Creek and South west of a small trace leading
from said Creek in Tennessee Valley twards Pikeville
in Bledsoe County running thence North 45° East 111
poles to a stake thence North 45° west 111 poles to
a stake South 45° west 111 poles thence a Direct line
to the beginning.

Charles Gamble, Locater

fees of office paid $1.00, 14th July, 1824.

PAGE 38

No. 30
William Lauderdale
10 Acres General
Entry

Location Received
and this Entry
made Aug. 11, 1824

Received for the
State $1.25

State of Tennessee | William Lauderdale Enters ten
acres of land in Said County
on the North Branch of the
Hamilton County | head of Mountain Creek Begin-
ning on a Black oak the North Corner about three poles
above Guyses mill house on Said Creek Thence Running South 50 East along the meanders of a spur of
Waldens Ridge a Natural Boundary fifty three poles
to a stake thence west 30 poles to a stake thence
South West 53 poles to a stake from thence a Direct
line to the Beginning.

William Lauderdail, Locator

fee of office paid $1.00

PAGE 39

No. 31
William Gent, 50
Acres General
Entry

William Gent Enters fifty acres of Land pursuant to
an act of the General Assembly of the State of Ten-
nessees passed at Murfreesboro the 22nd of November
1823 beginning on a stake on Waldens Ridge on the
waters of North Chickamaugy Creek Running East -

Location Received
and this Entry
made this 21st of
August, 1824

Received for the
State $6.25

wardly on the breaks of a Ridge thence North to a
Chesnut thence west to a black oak thence South so
as to Include Hutchicsons Improvement and to the beginning.

Josiah Gent, Loc.

Certified Copy issued and delivered to the Enterer.
Fees of office paid $1.00.

Cornelius Milliken, E - taker
By his Dupty
John Mitchell

PAGE 40

No. 32
Robert Cozby, 40
Acres General
Entry

Location Received
and this Entry
made this 10th
March, 1825

Received for the
State $5.00

State of Tennessee, Robert Cozby enters forty acres
of land in Hamilton County neare the Tennessee Valley Road between William H. Stringers and John
Browns Ferry on Tennessee River. Beginning at two
post oaks and a Black Oak on the West side of a
Rockey Ridge near Tennessee River between John Browns
and David Fields Reservation Running thence West
thirty four poles to Richards G. Waterhouses line
thence along Said Waterhouses line South 20° East
thirty poles thence with Said Waterhouses line South
one hundred & seventy poles thence with a line of
said Waterhouses Survey East twenty five poles to
Said Cozby survey of one hundred acres Entry No. 13
thence with the line of Said Cozby Survey north
Eighty fore poles thence East forty five poles a-
long the End line of Said Cozbys one hundred acre
Survey thence a direct line the point of beginning,
10th March, 1825.

Robert Cozby, Locator

Fees of office paid $1.00
Certified Copy Issued and Delivered to the Enterer
March 10, 1825.

Cornelius Milliken
Enter taker,
By his Deputy
John Mitchell

PAGE 41

No. 33
Richard G. Water-
house, 70 Acres
General Entry

Richard G. Waterhouse enters 70 acres of land in the
County of Hamilton and State of Tennessee adjoining
his two tracts of ten and 45 acres as per Grants No.s
18812 & 18811 Beginning at a Black Oak marked 45
corner to his 45 acre tract thence with a line of
the same South 150 poles to the line of his 10 acre
tract thence with the same West passing a sweet Gum

Location Received
and this Entry made:
this 12th May,1825 :

Received for the
State $8.75

and Poplar corner to said 10 acre tract 75 poles ,
then North 150 poles, then East 75 poles to the beginning.

Richard G. Waterhouse

Fees of office $1.00 - Paid
Certificate Copy Issued and delivered to the Enterer 12 May, 1825.

Cornelius Milliken
Entry taker
by his Deputy
John Mitchell

PAGE 41

No. 34
Richard G. Water-
house, 52 Acres
General Entry

Location Received
and this Entry
made 12th May,
1825

Received for the
State $6.50

Richard G. Waterhouse enters 52 acres of land in
Hamilton County State of Tennessee adjoining his
172 acre tract Grant No. 9703 - Beginning on the
of the river ridge on the line of John Browns Reservation Thence with the same East 150 poles to
a Hickory and Red Oak corner to said Reservation
and to said 172 acre tract Thence with a line of
the latter North 85 poles to a Spanish Oak, Black
Gum and Post Oak on the top of said ridge Corner
to said 172 acre survey thence West 45 poles then
to the Beginning.

Richard G. Waterhouse

Fees of office $1.00 paid
Certificate Copy issued and delivered to the Enterer 12 May, 1825.

Cornelius Milliken
by his Deputy
John Mitchell

PAGE 42

No. 35
James Qualls, 2
Acres, General
Entry

James Qualls Enters 2 acres of Land in the County
of Hamilton and State of Tennessee lying on each
Side of Middle Creek including a mill Seat Built
by said Qualls Beginning on a dogwood on the East
side of Said Crick and supposed to be near Qualls
line of 15 acre tract and near Kelley's turnpike
roade and running N. 20 poles to a Stake at the
foot of a Clift thence West 16 poles to a Stake
thence Sout 20 poles down said creek to a stake
thence to the beginning.

James Qualls
Fees of office $1.00 Paid

Certificate copy issued and delivered to the Entrier
13th July, 1825

Cornelius Milliken
by his deputy
John Mitchell

PAGE 43

No. 36
John Cook, 82
Acres General
Entry

Location Received
and this Entry
maid this 6th
July, 1825

Received for the
State $10.25
On No. 3rd Entry
and no land found

State of Tennessee — John Coock Enters eighty two acres of Land in Hamilton County Lying on Waldens Ridge on the waters

Hamilton — July 6, 1825

of Rocky Crick beginning on a chesnut Tree running North fifty five East one hundred and Sixty poles to a Stake thence eastwardly eighty two Poles to a stak thence Southwardly one hundred and Sixty Poles to a stak thence to the Beginning.

John Cook

Fees of office $1.00 Paid
Certificate Copy Issued and Delivered to the Enterer July 6th, 1825.

Cornelius Millican
Entry taker
by his Deputy
John Mitchell

PAGE 44

No. 37
Daniel Johnson
50 Acres genneral
Entry

Location Received
and this Entry
mad this 6th
July, 1825

Received for the
State $6.25
on General Entry
No. 3rd where
this was, no land
found

Hamilton County — Daniel Johnson Enters fifty acres of land in Hamilton County lying on Waldens Ridge on the waters of Rockey Crick Beginning on a Black

July 6th, 1825

Oak tree Running South Eighty Poles to a stak thence westwardly one hundred poles to a Stake thence Northwardly eighty poles to a stak thence to the Beginning.

Daniel Johnson

fees of office $1.00 paid
Certified Copy Issued and Delivered to the Enterer.

Cornelius Milliken
Entry take
By his Deputy
John Mitchell

PAGE 45

No. 38
David Beck, 100
acres General
Entry

State of Tennessee, Entry taker of Hamilton County.
David Beck Enters 100 acres of Land in said County adjoining the tract where he now Lives Beginning on a Spanish Oak and Black oak near a line of R. G.

Location Received :   Watterhouses Land thence north one hundred poles
and this Entry   :   thence East 200 poles to R. G. Watterhouses Line
made this 23rd of :   thence with said Line to a post oak and Black oak,
August, 1825   :   Spanish oak Corner to Sd. tract and to the Land where
                  :   Said Beck now lives thence with the line of the same
Received for the :   South 65 West so as to Include 100 acres then to the
State $12.50   :   Beginning
                  :
                  :   David Beck
                  :
                  :   fees of office paid $1.00
                  :   Certified Copy Issued and Delivered to the surveyor
                  :   this 23rd, 1826.
                  :
                  :   Cornelius Milliken
                  :   Entry Taker

PAGE 46

No. 39   :   State of Tennessee | William Bunch Enters 64 Acres
William Bunch, 64 : | of Land in Hamilton County and
Acres General   :   Hamilton County | State of Tennessee on Waldens
Entry   : | Ridge near a small branch one
                  :   of the tributary streams of Chickamauga Beginning on
Location Received :   a possimon running Southwardly down said branch 100
and this Entry   :   poles then Eastwardly 100 poles thence Northwardly
made this 12 of :   100 poles thence westwardly 100 poles to the begin-
October, 1825   :   ning -- Running so as to include said Bunches im-
                  :   provement.
Received for the :
State $8.00   :   William Bunch
on N 3 entry   :
and no land found :   Fees of office paid $1.00
                  :   Certified Copy Issued and Delivered to the Enterer.
                  :
                  :   Cornelius Milliken
                  :   Entry taker for Hamilton Co.
                  :   By his Deputy
                  :   John Mitchell

PAGE 47

No. 40   :   William Berry, Enters fifty acres of Land in Hamilton
William Berry, 5 :   County & State of Tennessee on Waldens Ridge lying on
Acres General   :   each side of Hunters trace Bounded as follows Begin-
Entry   :   ning on a black oak and running North eastwardly one
                  :   hundred poles thence south Eastwardly 80 poles thence
Location Received :   southwestwardly 100 poles thence to the Beginning.
and this Entry   :
made this 4 of   :   William Berry
October, 1825   :
                  :   fees of office paid $1.00
Received for the :   Certificate copy Issued and delivered to the enteror
State $6.25   :   this the 4 October, 1825.

Cornelius Milliken
Entry taker
by his Deputy
John Mitchell

PAGE 48

No. 41
Richard G. Watter-
house, 56 Acres
General Entry

Location Received
and this Entry
made this 12 of
October, 1825

Received for the
State $7.00

State of Tennessee | Entry takers office, Richard
                   | G. Waterhouse enters 56 acres
Hamilton County | in said County on the north
                   | side of Tennessee River Begin-
ning at a poplar and sweet Gum marked W. corner to
his ten acre tract thence with a line thereof South
64 poles to a Hickory corner to said 10 acre tract
thence East 20 poles to an ash tree marked K corner
to said 10 acre tract on the river bank thence down
the meanders thereof 186 poles to a white oak corner
to his 100 acre tract there with a line of the same
West 136 poles to a Black oak ina Hollow corner to
said 100 acre tract then North to the line of his
70 acre entry no. 33 thence with the same East to
the Beginning.

                              Richard G. Waterhouse

fees of office paid $1.00
Certified coppy Issued and delivered to the enterer
this 12 October, 1825.

                              Cornelius Milliken
                              by his Deputy
                              John Mitchell

PAGE 49

No. 1
Richard G. Water-
hourse, 320 Acres
State price one
cent per acre

Location Received
and this Entry
med this 5th
January, 1826

Received for the
State $3.20

State of Tennessee | Entry Takers office provisions
                   | of an act of the general as-
Hamilton County | sembly of the State of Tennes-
                   | see passed at Murfreesborough
3 December, 1825 supplementary to a act or title an
act to establish offices for receiving entrys for the
vacant land in the several Countyes in this State
lying North and east of the congressional reservation
line and North of the Tennesse river passed 22 of
November, 1823.
  Richard G. Waterhouse Enters 320 Acres of Land in
said county opposit the Lookout Mountain Beginning
at two hackberry trees marked W on the bank of Tennessee corner to his 50 acre tract of grant No.
18810 thence with a line of the same W 135 poles to
a post & white oak corner to said tract thence with
another line thereof sout 35 poles to a sweet gum
& post oak marked xx corner to the sgim thence with
the closing line of his 200 acre tract of grant No.
23623 N. 55° W. 265 poles to a sycamore marked W at

the upper end of a lake beginning corner to said
Grant then with the different lines thence N. 50°
W. 7 poles N. 55° E. 31 poles N. 20° W. 20 poles
N. 15 W. 60 poles N. 20 W. 82 poles to the lower
end of the lake thence East 70 poles to a black oak
the beginning corner of George Russells 100 Acre
tract of Grant No. 9700 thence reversing his lines
which will be South 43 poles thence East 105 poles
to a small Black oaks. Then North 153 poles to a
Black Oaks his corner on the line of John Brown's
Reservation thence with Said line East to Tennessee River and down said river excluding George
Birdwells 40 acre tract of Grant 9701 to the beginning Entered 5th day of January 1826.

R. G. Waterhouse

Fees State price one cent per acre - $3.20
Entry taker fee -   1.00
                          Amount - $4.20

Cornelius Milliken
by his deputy
John Mitchell

PAGE 50

No. 2
Richard G. Water-
house, 320 acres
general Entry
State price one
cent per acre

Location Received
and this Entry
made this 5th
January, 1826

Received for the
State $3.20

State of Tennessee | Entry takers of of office by
                   | virtu of an act passed 3 Dec-
Hamilton County | ember 1825 Supplemental to an
                   | act passed 22 November 1823 by
the legislatures of the State of Tennessee.
Richard G. Waterhouse Enters 320 acres of Land in
said County Beginning at the foot of t — Mountain
on a large Spanish oak and marked B cor — to his
121 Acre tract of Grant No. 18809 thence with a
line thereof South 11 poles to two Black Walnuts
marked R. A. his corner on the bank of Tennessee
River thence down the meanders of Said river being
a Natural boundary passing the mouth of Shoal creek
Middle Crick Suck Crick and several small branches
in all 1600 poles then leaving the River at Right
angles to the foot of the Mountain thence the foot
thereof as a natural boundary with the various
courses of the saim to the beginning Entered 5th
January, 1836.

Richard G. Waterhouse

Fees to the State — $3.20
Entry taker fees —   1.00
                   Amount — $4.20
Cornelius Milliken
Entry taker for Hamilton Co.
John Mitchell, Deputy

PAGE 51

No. 3
Benjamin Johnson
50 Acres General
Entry

Location Received
and this Entry mad
this 5th January,
1826

Received for the
State $0.50

State of Tennessee — Benjamin Johnson Enters fifty
acres of Land in Said County
Hamilton County — on Waldens ridg and lying on
the waters of Sail ? Creek
Beginning on a black oak tree on the North side of
the road leading from Sequachey to Tennessee Valley
running thence Eastwardly 80 poles thence acording
to law for complement.

Benjamin Johnson

fees of office paid $1.00
Certified copy issued and delivered to the entryer
this 5 January, 1826.

Cornelius Milliken
Entry taker
by his Deputy
John Mitchell

PAGE 51

No. 4
Benjamin Johnson
50 Acres General
Entry

Location Received
and this entry
made this 6th
January, 1826

Received for the
State $0.50

State of Tennessee — Entry takers office Benjamin
Johnson enters 50 acres of
Hamilton County — Land in said County on Waldens
Ridge and the waters of Sail
Creek — Beginning on a black oak running thence West
100 poles thence South 80 poles thence East 100 poles
thence North 80 poles to the Beginning.

Benjamin Johnson

Fees of office paid $1.00
certified copy issued and delivered to the entryor
this the 6 January, 1826.

Cornelius Millican
Entry taker
by his Deputy
John Mitchell

PAGE 52

No. 5
George Terkinett
50 Aces General
Entry

Location Received
and this Entry
made this 9
January, 1826

Received for the
State $0.50

State of Tennessee — Entry Takers office, George
Turkeynett Enters 50 Acres of
Hamilton County — land in said County on Waldens
Ride on the Waters of Sail
Creek Beginning on a Black oak tree running then E.
thence North thence West thence to the Begining.

George Turkeynett

Cornelius Milliken
Entry taker by his Deputy
John Mitchell

Fees of office paid $1.00
Certified Copy Issued and Delivered to the Enterer
the 9th January, 1826.

PAGE 52

No. 6
John McVey, 50
Acres General
Entry

Location Received
and this Entry
made this the 2
January, 1825

Received for the
State $0.50

State of Tennessee | Entry takers office, John Mc-
Vey Enters fifty acres of Land
Hamilton County | in said County and on Waldens
Ridge Beginning at a black oak
corner to his 25 acre tract with a line of the same
Westwardly 200 poles crossing Suck Creek then Northward 50 poles meandering suck creek then Eastwardly
200 poles then southwardly 40 poles to the beginning.

John McVey

Fees of office paid $1.00
Certified copy Isued and delivered to the entryor
this 20 January, 1826.

Cornelius Millikin
Entry taker
by his Deputy
John Mitchell

PAGE 53

No. 7
Enoch P. Hail
and
John B. Inlow
100 Acres Genneral
Entry

Location Received
and this Entry
mad this 24th
January, 1826

Received for the
State $1.00

State of Tennessee | Enoch P. Hail and John B. Inlow
Enters one hundred acres of
Hamilton County | Land Situate in Hamilton Coun-
ty and on Wallens Ridge Begin-
ning on a hickory thence westwardly thence south –
wardly thence Northwardly for complement so as to
include a Spring that Rises and Sinks to in Clude
a good Body of Land to the best advantage.

Enoch P. Hail
John B. Inlow

Fees of office $1.00
Certified Copy issued and delivered to the Enterer
this 24th January, 1826.

Cornelius Millikin
Entry taker for Hamilton Co.
by his Deputy
John Mitchell

X Return made up to this No. 7

PAGE 53

No. 8
John B. Inlow

State of Tennessee, Hamilton County, John B. Inlow
Enters one hundred Acres of Land Situate in Hamilton

100 Acres General
Entry

Location Received
and this Entry
mad this 24 January
1826.

Received for the
State $1.00

County and on Wallens Ridge Beginning on a hickory
thence Eastwardly thence Northwardly a Crosing a
Crick thence Westwardly thence to the Beginning Including a sertan Spring.

John B. Inlow

Certified Copy Issued
Fees of Office paid $1.00
Received for the State $1.00

Cornelius Milliken
Entry taker for
Hamilton County
By his Deputy
John Mitchell

this 24 January, 1826

PAGE 54

No. 9
Benjamin Cherry
&
Cornl Mittiken
100 acres General
Entry

Location Received
and the Entry made
27th of February
(January) 1826

Recsived for the
State $1.00

State of Tennessee, Hamilton County Benjamin Cherry
and Cornelius Milliken Enters one hundred acres of
Land Lying in said County in a small Vally West of
the Valley Road Leading from Washington to John
Brown's ferry on tennessee River and East of Mountain Creek Valley Beginning on a post oak Running
thence S. 64 E. forty five to a stake thence N. 36
E. one hundred and Eighty poles to a stake thence
N. 64 W. ninety poles to a stake thence S. 26 W.
one hundred and Eighty poles to a Stake thence S.
64 E. forty five poles to the Beginning.

Benjamin Cherry
Locatore

fees office paid $1.00
Received for the state $1-
Certified Copy Isued and Delivered to the Enterer
this 26th of Febuary 1827.

Cornelius Milliken
Entry taker for
Hamilton County

PAGE 55

No. 10
Benjamin Posey
100 Acres at one
cent per acre

Received for the
State $1.00

Benjamin Posey Enters one hundred acres of land in
Hamilton County Beginning on two Chesnuts on the
North side of the dividing Ridge between opossom
and Rocky creeke running North sixty East one hundred poles to a dogwood on the north side of the
south fork of Rocky creek thence South thirty East
Crossing said Creeke to a blackoak one hundred

an sixty poles thence south sixty West one hundred
poles to a pine thence a Strait line one hundred and
sixty poles to the Beginning making one hundred acres.

Benjamin posey

Fees for the State $1.00
Fees of office $1.00 March 1st 1826

Cornelius Milliken
Entry taker for
Hamilton County
by his Deputy
John Mitchell

PAGE 56

No. 11
Charles Gamble,
Chrispin E. Shelton
and John Witt
50 Acres General
Entry

Location Received
and this Entry
made this the
12 April, 1826

Received for the
State $0.50

State of Tennessee | Entry Takers Office, Charles
| Gamble, Crispin E. Shelton and
Hamilton County | John Witt Enters fifty acres of
| Land lying on the side of Waldens
Ridge West of the Roaring fork of Sale Crick and
where the Road from Benjamin Joneses to Hunters gap
runs up said ridge bonded as follows to wit Beginning
at a Chesnut Oak Tree & Dogwood Sappling on the South
Sid of the road on a Spur of Said Ridg Running thence
North westwardly ninety poles thence South Westwardly
ninety poles and thence North eastwardly No. North
Eastwardly ninty poles to the point of beginning.

Charles Gamble
Chrispin E. Shelton
John Witt

Fees of office paid $1.00
Certified copy isued and delivered to the entryor
this the 12 April 1826

Cornelius Milliken
Entry taker for
Hamilton County
by his Deputy
John Mitchell

PAGE 57

No. 12
Buck Sutton, 50
Acres General
Entry

Location Received
and this Entry
made this the
20 March 1826

State of Tennessee | Entry Takers office Buck Sut-
| ton Enters fifty acres of
Hamilton County | land in Hamilton County and
| on Waldens Ridge & on the wat-
ers santy or small Greek known by the name of Deep
Creek Beginning on a black oak running thence Northwardly one hundred poles to a stake thence westwardly
80 poles thence Southwardly 100 poles thence to the
beginning.

Received for the
State $0.50

Buck Sutton

fees of office paid $1.00
Cirtified copy issued and delivered to the entryor
this 20th March 1826.

Cornelius Milliken
Entry Taker
by his Deputy
John Mitchell

PAGE 57

No. 13
Buck Sutton, 80
Acres General
Entry

Location Received
and this Entry
made this the 20th
March 1826

Received for the
State $0.50

State of Tennessee | Entry Takers Office Buck Sutton Enters Eighty acres of
Hamilton County | Land in Hamilton County lying on Waldens Ridg and on
the south side of Deeps Creek or the waters of
Sauty. Beginning on a black running thence Northeast one hundred and sixty poles thence Eighty
poles westwardly thence Southwardly one hundred
and sixty poles thence to the Beginning.

Buck Sutton

Fees of office paid $1.00

Cornelius Milliken
Entry taker for
Hamilton County
by his Deputy
John Mitchell

PAGE 58

No. 14
Elisha Parker, 50
Acres General
Entry

Location Received
and this Entry
made this 12 April
1826

Received for the
State $0.50

State of Tennessee | Entry takers office Elsha
Parker Enters 50 Acres of
Hamilton County | Land in Hamilton Countyand
North of Tennessee River
Near Rosses Ferry Beginning a Read Oak marked P
running South 25 Poles to a Line of Thomas Jamases
S - ier thence East with said line 25 poles to
the Corner at a Post Oak thence South with said
Line 225 Poles to a White Oak & Red Oak - thence
X East with a line of Richard G. Waterhouses 60
poles to the top of a Ridge to a Post oak marked
B thence South 40 Poles with said line to a Post
marked A thence East 40 Poles with a line of said
Parkers 50 Acre tract to a Spanish oak thence N.
250 Poles to a Stake thence west to the Beginning.

Elisha Parker

Fees of office paid $1.00
Certified Copy Isued and delivered to

Cornelius Millikin
Entry Taker for
Hamilton County
By his Deputy
John Mitchell

PAGE 59

No. 15
Benjamin Cherry
General Entry

Location Received
and this Entry
made this 10th
April, 1826

Received for the
State $00.80

Benjamin Cherry Enters Eighty acres of Land in hamilton County in a small valley East of Mountain
Creek and west of the Valley Road Leading from Washington to John Brown's ferry beginning in a post oak
marked thus M Running Eastwardly Down a wet weather
Branch thirty five poles to a stake thence South -
wardly along a Ridge 160 poles to a stake thence
westwardly 80 poles Crossing said Valley to a stake
thence northwardly 160 poles along the mountain Creek
Ridge to a Stake thence forty five poles Down the said
Ridge to the Beginning so as to Include 80 acres
April 16, 1826.

Benjamin Cherry
Locator

fees of office paid $1.00
Certyfyd Copy Issued and Delivered to the Enteror
this 27th of Nov. 1826

Cornel Milliken
Entry taker for H. County
per H. Conroy?

PAGE 60

No. 16
Benjamin Johnson
150 acres General
Entry

Location Received
and this Entry
mad this 15th
Aprile, 1826

Received for the
State $1.50

State of Tennessee Entry Takers Office, Benjamin
                    Johnson Enters 150 Acres of Land
Hamilton County   in Hamilton County on Waldens
                    Ridge known by the name of the
pullum place where said Johnson now resides begining
on a White Oak on the East Side of S_id Johnson 30
Acre tract runing thence Westwardly thence Northwardly thence Eastwardly then to the Begining.

Bengamin Johnson
Aprile 15th, 1826

Fees of office paid $1.00
Received for the State $1.50

Cornelius Millikin
Entry Taker for Hamilton Co.
By his Deputy
John Mitchell

PAGE 61

No. 17
David Cunningham
50 Acres at one
cent per acre

Location received
and this Entry
made this 11th of
July, 1826

Received for the
State $00.50

David Cunningham Enters fifty acres of Land in Hamilton County on the East Side of the Valley Road
leading from Washington to John Browns Ferry. Beginning on a large post oak about Six poles Southwardly from Said Cuninghams hundred Acre Survey
runing Eastwardly Sixty fiv poles to a stake thence
Northwardly one hundred and thirty poles to a stak
thence westwardly Sixty five poles to a Stak on the
East side of Said Cuninghams Said Hundred acre
tract of Land thence with the Line of Said tract
to the Beginning so as to in Clude fifty acres.
June the 15, 1826.

David Cuningham, Locator

Received for the State $00.50

Cornelius Millican
Entry Taker for Hamilton Co.
by his Deputy
John Mitchell

PAGE 62

No. 18
John Keny, 25 Acres
at one Cent per
Acre

Location Received
and this Entry
mad the 11th July
1826

Received for the
State $00.25

John Keny Enters twenty five Acres of Land in Hamilton County and State of Tennessee in Mountain
Crick Valley Beginning on a post oak corner to a
tract of Land Entered by William Lauderdale now
occupied by Daniel Scivley runing thence Westwardly thirty eight poles to a Stake on a Natural
Boundary thence along Said Natural Boundary Northwardly ninety eight poles crossing the Kelley turnpike road to a Stake thence thirty eight poles
Eastwardly to said Keneys occupent Entry line and
and from thence with Said line to the Beginning so
as to include twenty five Acres, June the 24th,
1826.

John Keney, Location

Fees of office paid $1.00
Received for the State $00.25
Cornelius Millikan Entry taker for Hamilton County
by his Deputy, John Mitchell.

PAGE 63

No. 19
Jacob Hartman, 27
Acres one cent
per acre

State of Tennessee | Jacob Hartman Enters 27 Acres
| of Land in Said County and in
Hamilton County | Mountain Creek Valley Beginning
on two Poplers Corner to Said
Hartmans 107 Acre tract Runing thence North 55° W.
40 poles to a Stake thence N. 35 East 106 poles to
a Stake thence South 55 E. 40 poles to pine Corner

Location Received and this Entry made this -- July 1826	to his 107 Acre tract then west with a line of the Same to the Beginning.

Jacob Hartman

<table><tr><td>Received for the State $00.27</td><td>fees of office paid $1.00
Certified Copy Delivered to the Enterer.
Received for the State $00.27</td></tr></table>

Cornelius Milliken

Entry taker for Hamilton County By his Deputy
John Mitchell

PAGE 64

No. 20
Benjamin Cherry
25 Acres General
Entry

Location Received and this Entry mad this 20th July, 1826

Received for the State $00.25

Benjamin Cherry Enters twenty five acres of Land in Hamilton County on the west side of the mountain Creek Ridge Beginning on a chestnut tree on the line of a tract of Land Entered By John Snapp now occupied by Jacob Hartman on the north Side of a small branch Running with Said Line forty two and a half poles Southwardly to a Stake thence forty two and a half poles Eastwardly to a stake on the Ridge thence eighty five poles Northwardly so as to include the head of a spring to a stake forty two and a half poles down the said Ridge westwardly to the said hartmans Line and from there forty two and a half poles Strait line to the Beginning so as to include twenty five acres June 20th, 1826.

Benjamin Cherry

Fees for the State $00.25
fees of office paid $1.00
Cornelous Millikin Entry taker for Hamilton County by his Deputy.

John Mitchell

PAGE 65

No. 21
John Harwell, 50
Acres at one cent
per acre

Location Received and this Entry mad this 28 August, 1826.

Fees for the State $00.50

State of Tennessee) John Howell Enters 50 acres of Land in said county on Wallens Ridge & on the North fork of Chickamauga. Beginning on a black oak runing thence Northwardly 100 poles to a stak thence westwardly 80 poles thence Southwardly 100 poles thence Eastwardly to the Beginning.

Hamilton County

John Howel

Fees for the state $00.50
fees of office $1.00 July 20, 1826

Cornelius Milliken

Entry taker for Hamilton by his Deputy

John Mitchell

PAGE 66

No. 22
Jacob Hartmann, 27
Acres at one cent
per acre

State of Tennessee	Jacob Hartman Enters 27 acres of Land in Hamilton County Lying on the West Side of the Mountain Crick Ridg a Natural
Hamilton County	

Boundary Begining on a white oak on a line of a tract that was Enterd by John Snapp occupied by Jacob Hartsman Runing 35 poles to the corner of the said Entry and an Entry mad by William Lawderdel and from there along said line 75 poles to a Black oak thence Eastwardly 40 poles oup the Ridg to a Stak from there along a natural boundary one hundred 10 poles to a stake thence to the Begining so as to include 27 acres.

Jacob Hartman

Fees of office paid $1.00
Fees for the State $00.27
Certified Copy Delivered to the Enterer

Cornelius Milliken
Entry taker of Hamilton Co
By his Deputy
John Mitchell

PAGE 67

No. 23
William Berry
300 Acres at one
cent per acre

Location Received
and this Entry mad
this 28th August,
1826

Fees for the State
$3.00

State of Tennessee	Entry takers office, William Berry Enters 300 acres of Land in said county on Waldons Ridge and on the watters of Sail
Hamilton County	

Creeke and on each side of the Turnpike Road leading from Sequachy Valley to Tennessee Valley Beginning on a black oak Running thence North Eastwood 300 poles thence South Eastward 160 poles thence South westward 300 poles thence to the Beginning.

William Berry

Fees of office paid $1.00
for the State $3.00

PAGE 68

No 24
C. Milliken, 31¼
Acres General
Entry

State of Tennessee	In pursuance of an act of Assembly in that Case made and provided, Cornelius Milliken Enters thirty one and a quarter
Hamilton County	

Location Reced and
this Entry made
August 16th, 1826

Received for the
State $ - 31¼

Acres of Land in Hamilton County in Tennessee Valley Beginning on a post oak Corner to an Entry Lately made by David Cunningham thence Running South Eastwardly fifty poles to a stake on Said Cunningham fifty acre Entry line thence South westwardly one hundred poles so as to corner on the line of an Entry By Johnson and Stringer thence North? westwardly the Last? aforesaid line fifty poles so as to Corner on the line of an Entry made by E.Corbet & C. Milliken thence North Eastwardly along the said line to the Beginning so as to Include thirty one acres and a fourth. July 6th Day, 1826.

Cornelius Milliken, Locator

fees for office $1.00
Certified copy Issued and Delivered to the Enterer the 28th day of Febuary, 1827

PAGE 69

No. 25
Daniel Scively &
Hugh Cunningham
25 Acres at one
cent per? cent.

Location Received
and this Entry
made this 28th of
August, 1826

Received for the
State $ -.25

State of Tennessee | Daniel Scively & Hugh Cunningham Enters twenty five acres of Land in said County and in Mountain Creek Valley Beginning on a Walnut and Sycamore and Ironwood on the west of the said mountain Creek Running Eastwardly Sixty seven poles to a white oak Corner to Daniel Scively's land from thence 30 poles Southwardly to the David fields Reservation Line thence along Said line 35 poles westwardly to a white oak and Dogwood Corner to Hugh Cunningham's land where he now lives and from thence northwardly 80 poles to the Beginning so as to include twenty five acres. August 19th, 1826.

Hamilton County

Hugh Cunningham, Locator

fees of office paid $1.00

PAGE 70

No. 26
Hugh Cunningham
25 acres at 1 pr
ct.

Location Received
and this Entry
made this 28th
August, 1826

State of Tennessee | Hugh Cunningham Enters twenty five acres of Land in Said County and in Mounty Creek Valley Beginning on a black oak on the Reservation Line and Corner to the place where he now lives Running Sixty seven poles Northwardly along his line to a Stake thence Sixty poles westwardly to a stake thence Sixty Seven poles Southwardly to the Sd. Reservation line and with said line to the Beginning so as to Include twenty five acres August 19th, 1826.

Hamilton County

Hugh Cunningham, Locator

fees of office paid $1.00

PAGE 71

No. 27
Daniel Scively, 25
Acres at 1 pr. ct

Location Received
and this Entry
made this 28th of
August, 1826

Recd for the State
$ - 25

State of Tennessee | Daniel Scivily Enters 25 acres
| of Land in said County Begin -
Hamilton County | ning on a post oak on a Line
| of Hugh Cunninghams Land Run-
ning along said Scively line 85 poles northwardly to
a stake thence 45 poles westwardly to a stake thence
85 poles Southwardly to a Stake thence 45 pole to
the beginning so as to Include the Mouth of the Back
Valley Hollow. August the 28th, 1826.

Daniel Scivily, Locator

fees of office paid $1.00

PAGE 72

No. 28
William Richards
&
William Bell
100 Acres

Location Received
and this entry mad
this 1st Septen.
1826

Received for the
State $1.00

State of Tennessee | Entry Takers office, William
| Richards & Willaim Bell Enters
Hamilton County | 100 Acres of Land in said
| county and on Wallens Ridge &
on the East of the roaring fork of Sail Creek Beginning on a white pine Runing thence Northwestward
100 poles thence Northeastward 160 poles thence southeastward 100 poles thence to the Begining.

William Richards
William Bell

PAGE 73

No. 29
William Richards
150 Acres General
Entry

Location Received
and this Entry
made this 29
August, 1826

State of Tennessee | Entry takers office William
| Richards Enters 150 Acres of
Hamilton County | Land in said county on Wallens
| Ridge and on the west Side of
the Roaring fork of Sail Crick Begining on a White
pine thence westward 200 poles thence Northward 120
poles thence Eastward 200 poles thence to the Begining.

William Richards

Fees of office paid $1.00
fees for the State $1.50
Cirtified Copy Issued.

Cornelius Milliken
Entry Taker for Hamilton Co.
By his Deputy
John Mitchell

PAGE 74

No. 30 : State of Tennessee⟨ Entry takers office --William
William Bell : ⟩ Bell Enters 100 Acres of land
100 Acres : Hamilton County ⟨ in said County and on Wallens
Genneral Entry : ⟩ Ridge and on the East Side of
: the Roaring fork of Sail Crick Beginning on a white
: Pine tree Running thence Northwestward 160 poles
Location received : thence North Eastward 100 poles thence South East-
and this Entry made: ward 160 poles thence to the Beginning
this 31st :
August : William Bell
1826 :
: Fee of office paid $1.00
:
Recd. for the :
State :
$1.00 :
:
:
:

PAGE 75

No. 31 : State of Tennessee⟨ Entry takers office--James
James Bunch : ⟩ Bunch Enters 50 acres of land
50 Acres : Hamilton County ⟨ in Said County and on Wal-
Genneral Entry : ⟩ lens Ridge and on the Head
: waters of Chick amaga Beginning on a black Oak
: tree Running thence South westward 90 poles thence
Locatio Received : Southeastward 90 poles thence Northeastward 90
and this 31st : poles thence to the Beginning
August 1826 :
this entry : James Bunch
mad :
: Fees of office paid $1.00
:
Recd. for the Sta : Cornelius Milliken
State $00.50 : Entry taker of Hamilton County by his
: Deputy John Mitchell
:
:
:
PAGE 76 :
No. 32 : State of Tennessee⟨ Entry Takers office--George
George Read : ⟩ Reed Enters 250 acres of Land in
250 Acres : Hamilton County ⟨ said county and on Waldens Ridge
General Entry : ⟩ and on lorel(?) Creek one of the
: forks of Sail Creek Beginning on a white oak runing
: thence North Eastwardly so as to include 250 acres.
Location Received :
and this entry : George Read
made this 26th : Fees of office paid $1.00
day of Septem- : Cirtified copy issued and
ber 1826 : delivered to the entryor

Received   :   Cornelius Millikon
for the   :   Entry Take for Hamilton County by his Deputy
State   :   John Mitchell
$2.50   :

PAGE 76   :

No. 53   : State of Tennessee Entry Takers office--Henry Lewis
Henry Lewis :   Enters 100 acres of land in said
100 Acres   : Hamilton County   county and on Waldens Ridg and
General   :   on Lorrel Creoke one of the head
Entry   : forks of Sail creek beginning on a black oak runing
          : so as to include 100 acres.

Location Re- :   Henry Lewis
ceived and : fees of office paid $1.00
this entry : cirtified copy issued and delivered to the enteror.
mad this 26th :
day of September: Entry taker for
1826   :   Hamilton County
Received for :   by his Deputy
the State $1.00 :   John Mitchell

PAGE 77   :
No. 34   :
John Lovelady : State of Tennessee John Lovelady Enters twenty five
25 Acres   :   Acres of land in said County Be-
Gener 1   : Hamilton County   tween John Brown's Reservation
Entry   :   and David fields Reservation
          : beginning on a post oak on Waterhouses line thence
          : Running with said Line Sixty four poles Southwardly
Location   : to a Stake on or near Robert Cozbys line thence East-
Received and : wardly along Cozbys line Sixty fon poles to a stake
this Entry : thence Northwardly Sixty four poles to a stake and
made this 10th : from thence to the Beginning so as to include twenty
October 1826 : five acres
          : October the 9th 1826

Received for :   John Lovelady
the State $--25 :   Locator

          : FEES OF OF ICE paid $1.00
          :   Cornelius Millikan
          : Entry taker for Hamilton County
          : Certified Copy Issued and Delivered
          : to the Enteror

PAGE 78   :

No. 38   : State of Tennessee William Hunter Enters 50 Acres
William Hunter :   of Land on Waldens Ridg in said
50 acres   : Hamilton County   county on the watersof Sale
General   Creok Beginning on a Black oak

Entry	Running thence Eastwardly 100 poles thence Northwardly 80 poles thence Westwardly 100 poles thence to intersect with said Hunters Lines to the Begining.
Location received This Entry made this 28th October 1826	William Hunter Fees of office paid $1. Cornelius Milliken Entry Taker For Hamilton County by his deputy John Mitchell
Received for the State $0.50	

PAGE 78

No. 36 Danuel S. Jones 50 Acres General Entry	State of Tennessee — Daniel S. Jones Enters 50 acres in said County on wallens Ridg on the waters of Sale Creek Beginning on a Black oak marked D.J. Corner to said Jones Twenty acre Entry, and Running thence Northwestwardly one hundred poles thence Southwardly Eighty poles. Thence Eastwardly one hundred poles thence to the Beginning.
Location received and This Entry made this 28th October 1826	Hamilton County
Received for the State $-50	D. S. Jones Locator Fees of office paid $1. Certified Copy Issued and Delivered to the Enterer. Cornelius Milliken Entry Taker For Hamilton County by his Deputy John Mitchell

PAGE 79

No. 37 Elizabeth Jones 150 Acres General Entry	State of Tennessee — Elizabeth Jones Enters one hundred and fifty acres of Land in Sai Said County and on waldens Ridge of Cumberland mountain on both sides of Hixsons trace adjoining the flat Rock Beginning on a post oak Running Eastwardly 150 poles to a stake Southwardly 160 poles to a stake thence northwardly 150 poles to a stake thence Eastwardly 160 poles to the Beginning so as to Include one hundred and fifty acres.
Location received and this entry made this 28th October 1826	Hamilton County
Received for the State $1.50	Elizabeth Jones Locator October 25th 1826 fees of office paid $1.00 Cornelius Milliken Entry taker for Hamilton County

PAGE 79

No. 38
Isaac Clement
200 Acres
General
Entry

State of Tennessee }
Hamilton County } Isaac Clements enters two hundred acres of Land in Hamilton County on wallens Ridge of Cumberland mountain about a quarter of mile west of Hixons trace Beginning on a Black gum above the head of A Branch the waters of Laurel Creek Running southwardly 150(?) poles to a stake then westwardly 250 poles then according to law for compliment so as to include 200 acres
Oct. 25th 1826

Isaac Clement
Locator

Fees of office paid $1-00

Cornelius Milliken
Entry taker for Hamilton County

PAGE 80

No. 39
Abraham Green
100 Acres
General Entry

Location
Received and
entry
made this
22th of October
1826

Received for the
state $1.00

State of Tennessee }
Hamilton County } Abraham Green Enters one hundred acres of Land in Said County lying on the mountain and waters of Sale Creek and on Each side of the turnpike Road granted Gamble Shelton and Witt. Including the Improvement where he now lives Beginning on three white oak s west Corner to Benjamin Johnsons 150 acres Entry and Running S. 86 W 90 poles to a black Oak and Spanish Oak Thence N 4° W crossing a small Branch at 45 poles poles and another twice at 53 poles and said Road 158 poles in all 178 poles to a white oak thence N 86 E 90 poles to a stake thence S 4° E 18 poles to a Spanish oak North Corner to said Johnsons Entry Thence with a line of the same to the Beginning S 4° E 160 poles to the Beginning.

Abraham Green
Enteror

PAGE 81

No. 40
James Brock
50 acres
General
Entry

Location
Received
and this ---
made this
11th day of
November
1826

State of Tennessee }
Hamilton County } James Brock Enters 50 acres of land in said County and on the North fork of rock creek about one quarter of a mile above said fork Beginning on a maple and pine marked with a day and date Running Northward 100 poles to a stake thence westward 80 poles thence Southward 100 poles thence Eastward 80 poles to the Beginning

James Brock

Received for the : fees of office paid $1.00 Cirtified copy issued
state : and delivered to the entryor the 11 November 1826
$0.50 :
: Cornelius Milliken
: Entry taker for Hamilton County by his Deputy
:
: John Mitchell
:
:

PAGE 82 :
:
No. 41 :
James Roberts : State of Tennessee) James Roberts 100 acres of
100 Acres :) land in Said County on Wal-
Genneral : Hamilton County (lens Ridg on Board Camp &
Entry : Chickamoga Cricks, Begin-
Location : ning at a white oak Black o k and Spanish oak
Received and : Tres Standing on a Bluff on the East Side of B
this Entry : Board Camp and in the fork between Board Camp
made 12th : & Chickamoga Cricks, Beginning North 130 poles
November : thence South 130 poles thence west 130 poles to
1826 : the beginning.
:
: James Roberts
Received for : Fees of office paid $1.00
the : Certified Copy issued and delivered
State : to the order of the Enteror 9th January 1827.
$1.00 :
: Cornelius Milliken
: Entry taker by his Deputy
: John Mitchell
:
:

PAGE 83 :
:
No. 42 : State of Tennessee) Benjamin Dunagan enters 300
Benjamin : (Acres of land in said county
Dunagan : Hamilton County (on Wallens Ridg and on the
300 acres : west side of Hunters Creek
General Entry : onoof the forks of Soil Crick Beginning on a white
Location re- : oak Running thence Southward to a line of George
ceived and : Reads thence Northward with Said Read's line thence
this Entry : according to law for compliment
made this :
18th November : Benjamin Dunagan
1826 : Fees of office paid $1.00
: Certified Copy isued and Delivered to the Enterer.
Received for :
the State : Cornelius Milliken
$3.00 : Entry taker for Ham-
: ilton County by his
: Deputy
: John Mitchell

PAGE 83
No. 43
Stephen Reade
200 acres
of land
General Entry

Location re-
ceived and
this Entry
18th November
1826

Received by
the State
$2.00

State of Tennessee| Stephen Reade Enters 200 acres of
| Land in said county on Wallens
Hamilton County   0 Ridge and the waters of Sail Creeke
| Beginning on a hicory near the
head of a branch runing Northward thence to include Rogerses Rock House in a square or oblong including 200
acres of land.

Styphen Reade

Certified copy issued and delivered to entrior.
Fees of office
paid $1.00   Cornelius Millikin
Entry Taker for Hamilton
County by his Deputy
John Mitchell

PAGE 84
No. 44
Isaac Clement
50 Acres Gen-
eral Entry

Location Re-
ceived and this
Entry made 18th
November 1826

Received for the
State $0.50
Fees $1.00

State of Tennessee| Isaac Clement Enters 50 acres of
| land in said County on Wallens
Hamilton County   X Ridg. and the side of a branch
part of Sail Creek neare the flat
Rock Beginning on a post oak runing thence west of south
60 poles to a stake to the North of west 120 poles thence
Eastward 60 poles thence to the Beginning
Isaac Clement
Certified Copy Isued and delivered to the Enterer.

Cornelius Milliken
Entry taker of Hamilton County by his Deputy
John Mitchell

PAGE 84 No. 45
Samuel R. Russel
168¾ acres
General Entry

Location Re-
ceived and
this entry
27 November1826

State tax $1.68¾

Fees of office
paid $1.00

State of Tennessee| Samuel R. Russel Enters one hun-
| dred and sixtyeight acres and three
Hamilton County   I quarters of land lying on the Moun-
tain in said County and on the wat-
ers of Sail Creeke Begining on a black oak and two ches-
nuts on the line of William Berrys 300 acre entry
marked S. R. and Running N. 19 E. 142 P. thence No.71
W. 190 P. thence S. 19 W. 142 P. thence a direct line
to the Beginning.
Samuel R. Russel
Enterer
Certified Copy Isued and delivered to the Enterer
Cornelius Milliken
Entry taker, by his Deputy
John Mitchell

PAGE 85
No. 46
Thos. J. Reed
605 Acres
General
Entry

State of Tennessee| Thomas J. Reed enters 605 acres of
| land on the Mountain in said Moun-
Hamilton County   I tain in said county on the waters of
sail Creeke Beginning on two Black
oaks marked T.J.R. on the North side of a small Branch

said creek and runing S 30 E crossing said branch at 10 poles and another at 80 poles in all 220 poles to a white oak thence S. 60 W crossing a branch at 29 poles and another at 380 poles in all 440 poles to spanish oak thence North 30 W. Crossing a branch at 87 poles in all 220 poles to a stake thence n. 60 E. 440 poles to the Beginning.

Location received and this Entry mad this 27th November 1826

T. J. Reed
Enteror

Received by the State $6.05

fees of office paid 1.00
Certified Copy Isued and Delivered to the Enterer
Cornelius Milliken
Entry taker for Hamilton County by his Deputy
John Mitchell

PAGE 86

No. 47
Samuel R.
Rusel 90 Acres
General Entry

State of Tennessee} Samuel R. Rusel Enters 90 Acres
of Land on the mountain in Said
Hamilton County } County on the waters of Sale
Crick Beginning on a poplar and
Hickory on a Steep Hilside on the west side of Said Crick Marked S. R. an Running N 72 W 13 poles thence

Location Received and this Entry mad this 28th November 1826

S. 13 W. 170 poles to a line of Wm. Bereys 300 acre Entry thence S. 72 E. 85 poles thence N. 18 E. 170 poles thence N. 72 west to the Beginning

S. R. Rusel
fees of office $1.00 paid.-
Cortified copy Isued and Delivered to the Enterers

Received for the State $00.90

Cornelius Milliken

Entry taker for Hamilton County by his Deputy
John Mitchell

L

PAGE 87

No. 48
Benjamin
Dunagan
300 acres
General
Entry

State of Tennessee} Benjamin Dunagan Enters 300
acres of Land on the Mountain
Hamilton County } including his former 300 acre
entry in said county and on the
waters of Sail Creek beginning on a hicory and white oak marked B.D. on the east side of a hill and running N. 61 E. crossing a forke of Sale Creek at 158 poles in all 200 poles to a black oak thence S. 29 E. running into said creek at 150 poles and out

Location Received and this entry mad8 this 28 November 1826

again at 154 poles and crossing it at 205 poles in all 240 poles to a hicory and dogwood thence S. 61 W. crossing a branch at 114 in all 200 poles to a stake thence N. 29 W. to a line of George Reeds 250 acre entry thence according to law to the Beginning

Received   :   B. Dunagan
for the   :   Enterer
State   : fees of office $1.00 paid
$3.00   : Certified Copy Isued and Delivered to the enterer
                        :   Cornelius Milliken
                        : Entry taker for Hamilton County by his Deputy
                        :   John Mitchell
                        :
PAGE 88   :
                        :
No. 49   : State of Tennessee William Smith Enters fifty acres
William Smith   :   of Land in Said County on both
50 acres   : Hamilton County   Sides of the path that Leads from
General Entry   :   the Valley Road to Rosses Im-
                        : provment on Tennessee River Beginning on a poplar Corner
Location Re-   : to an Entry made by Stringer and Johnson Running South
ceived and   : wardly 67 poles to a stake thence Eastwardly 120 poles
this Entry   : TO a stake thence Northwardly 67 poles to a stake on
made   : the aforesaid S.J. line and from thence along the said
November 28th   : line to the Beginning So as to Include fifty acres.
1826   : November 27th 1826
                        :
                        :   William Smith
Received for the: Locator
State $--50   :
                        : fees of office paid $1.00
                        : Certified Copy Isued and Delivered to the Enterer
                        : February ---- 1827
                        :   Cornelius Milliken
                        :   Entry taker for
                        :   Hamilton County
                        :
                        :
PAGE 89   :
                        :
No. 50   : State of Tennessee David Beck Enters 135 acres of
David Beck   :   land in Said County Including his
135 Acres   : Hamilton County   former entry of 100 acres No. 38
General entry   :   Dated 23 August 1825 adjoining
                        : the Lands of said Beck and others Beginning on a Span-
                        : ish oak and Black Oak near the Corner to Elisha Park-
Location   : er and R. G. Watterhouses and Running N. 100 poles
Received   : to a Post oak thence E. 249 poles to a black Jack and
and this   : Post Oak on Said Watterhouses Line thence with the
Entry   : same S. 50 poles to a Black oak Spanish oak and Post
made this   : oak Corner to the tract on which Said Beck now lives
4th of   : thence with a line of the same S. 65 W. to a Corner
December   : of R.G. Watterhouses 50 acre tract then W. to the
1826   : Beginning.
                        :
                        :   David Beck
                        :   Enterer
                        : Fees of office paid $..00

Received   : Certified Copy Isued and Delivered this 4th of
for the   : December, 1826
State
100.36   :
       :   Cornelius Milliken
       :   Entry taker for
The 100 acres :   Hamilton County
her to fore
paid for

PAGE 90

No. 51   : State of Tennessee | Elisha Parker Enters 150 acres of
Elisha Parker : | land In said County adjoining the
150 acres : Hamilton County | landon which he now lives and others
General Entry :   Beginning on a Spanish Oak and
      : Black Oak Corner to David Beck and Running N. with said
      : Becks line passing his Corner at 100 P. in all 150 P
Location : to a Post oak thence W. 102 P to a line of the tract
Received : on which Thomas James now lives thence with said line
and this : S. 104 P to a Red Oak and Spanish Oak Corner to the
Entry made : same then with R.G. Watterhouses line E to a Post Oak
this 4th : on a hill marked B Tjence with another line of the same
of December : tract south to a Post Oak Corner to said Parker Thence
1826   : with Said Parkers line E. to the Beginning.

      :   Elisha Parker
Rec'd. for :   Enterer
the State
$1.50   : fees of office paid $1.00
      : Certified Copy Isued and Delivered to the Enterer
      : this 4th of December, 1826

      :   Cornelius Milliken
      :   Entry taker for Hamilton County

PAGE 91

No. 52   : State of Tennessee | Samuel R. Russell Enters $37\frac{1}{2}$ acres
S. R. Russell : | of land in Said County adjoining
$37\frac{1}{2}$ acres : Hamilton County | Benjamin Cherry's 80 acre Entry Begin-
General. :   ning on a black Jack on a line of
Entry   : said Cherry's Entry and on the top of Mountain Creek
      : Ridge and Running S 33 W 108 P then S. 57 E 56 P then
Location Re- : N. 33 W 108 P then N. 57 W. to said Chery's line then
ceived and : with Said Cherry's lines to the Beginning.
this Entry
made this :   S. R. Russell
4th of December :   Enterer
1826   : fees for office paid $1.00
Received for : Certifyd Copy Issued and Deliveredto the
the state : Enterer this 4th of December 1826
$.37\frac{1}{2}$:   Cornelius Milliken
      :   Entry taker for Hamilton County

PAGE 91 :
:
No. 53 : State of Tennessee} Jessee Smith enters fifty acres
Jesse Smith : of land in said County adjoining
50 acres : Hamilton County } South Side of a fifty acre Entry
General Entry : that was made By Johnson and
: Stringer Beginning thence 125 poles to a State and
: near watterhouses Line and N. W. and N. W. of the
Location : Beginning then S. Sixty four poles to a stake from th
Received : thence S. Eastwardly 125 poles to a Stake and from
and this : thence a straight line Sixty four poles to the Begin-
Entry made : ning So as to Include fifty acres.
this 4th of : fees of office paid $1.00
December :
1826 : Jesse Smith
: Locator
: Certified Copy Issued and
Received for : Delivered to the Enterer
the State : Settled up with Cornelius Milliken
$-30 : this Day up to No.53 and page 91.
:
:
:
PAGE 92 :
:
No. 54 :
William Lauder : State of Tennessee} William Lauderdel Enters 25 acres
del. 25 Acres : of land in said County and on one
General Entry : Hamilton County } of the head Branches of Mountain
: Creek near the foot of Gallen's
: Ridg and including his former entry of 10 Acre Begin-
Location : ning on a black oak tree on the North east Side of
Received : Geses Mildam(?) running south 35 E along a Spur of
and this Entry : Wallens Ridg a natural Boundery 66 poles to James Kenys
mad this 8th : line thence along said line 60 poles thence North 35
December : west 66 poles to a stak thence to the Beginning.
1826 :
: William Lauderdale(?)
: FEES OF OFFICE $1.00 paid
Received for : Certified Copy Delivered
the State : to the enterer
$0.45 :
: Cornelius Milliken
: entry taker for Hamilton
: County his Deputy
: John Mitchell
:
:
:
PAGE 93 :
:
No. 55 : State of Tennessee} Jacob Hartsman ' William Lauderdel
Jacob Hartman : } Enters 160 acres of land in said
& : Hamilton County } county Lying on the North side of
William Lauder : Mountain Creek at the foot of
del 160 acres : Gallons Ridg Beginning on or neare John Kenys west
General Entry : corner a West line Runing from Chickamaga Crick Runing

Location Received and this Entry mad 12th December 1826	North 35 west 80 poles to a stak thence North 29 East 300 Poles Crosing Several Spurs of Wallens Ridg a natural Boundary thence South 35 East to James S. Keneys and William Lauderdale Division line thence with Said line to the Beginning

Jacob Lauderdel
William Lauderdel

Received
for the
State
$1.00

Fees of office $1.00 paid
Certified Copy Deliver to
the enterer.

Cornelius Milliken
Entry Taker for Hamilton County by his Deputy
John Mitchell

P GE 94

No. 56
Andrew
Mitchell
50 Acres
Genneral
Entry

State of Tennessee } Andrew Mitchell Enters 50 acres
of land in said County on Wallens
Hamilton County } Ridg and on the south Side of
oposom Creek and including the Aulder
Spring Begining on a Spanish oak tree runing thence
North eastward 80 poles thence South Eastward 100 poles
thence to the Beginning.

Location
Received and
this Entry
mad this
12th December
1826

Andrew Mitchell

Fees of office $1.00 paid
Certified Copy Deliver to
the enterer

Cornelius Milliken
Entry taker for Hamilton
County by his Deputy

John Mitchell

Received
for the
State
$100.50

(Note)
Settled with the Bank agent to---
8th Jany. 1827 and up to No. 56

John Mitchell

PAGE 95

No. 57
Jeremiah Jones
and John Brown
200 acres
general
entry

State of Tennessee } Entry Takers office--Jeremiah Jones
and John Brown Enters two hundred
Hamilton County } acres of Land on Wallens Ridge on
the West Fork of oposom Creeke Be-
ginning at a maple on the Bank of said Creek and Running westwardly to a large Poplar Tree on the foot of
a Ridge known by the name of Robinhoods barn thence
southwardly thence eastwardly & northwardly for complement.

Location
received

Jeremiah Jones & John Brown

and this
Entry made
this 15th
January
1827

: Fees of office
: Cirtifyed Copy Delivered to the enterers

Cornelius Milliken
Entry taker for Hamilton
County By his Deputy
John Mitchell

Received for
the State
$2.00

PAGE. 96

No. 58
Jereriah Jones
&
John Brown
50 acres
general entry

: State of Tennessee, Entry takers office of Hamilton Coun-
: ty Jere iah Jones and John Brown enters fifty acres of
: land on Wallens Ridge at a white oak standing at or near
: the head of a spring and running Eastwardly to opossom
: creek thence up said creeds as it meanders to the mouth
: of t e spring Branch thence up the spring branch to the
: beginning

Location
Received and
this entry
made this
15th January
1827

: Jeremiah Jones and
: John Brown

: Fees of office $1.00
: Certified Copy Delivered to
: the Enterers.

Cornelius Milliken
Entry taker for Hamilton
County By his Deputy
John Mitchell

Received for
the State
$0.50

PAGE 97

No. 59
William Brown
50 Acres
General Entry

: State of Tennessee Entry takers office--William Brown
:   enters 50 acres of land in said
: Hamilton County   county on each side of North
:   Chickamaga and in a Cove of Wallens
: Ridg Beginning on a white oake and Black oak trees a
: corner of Thos. Gillaspies tract of land where s id

Location
received and
this entry mad
this 22nd
January
1827

: creek leaves said Ridge running Northward with said
: Gillaspies line to a spur of said Ridg thence up said
: Creek along the Spur of the Ridg to whare the Creek
: falls off of the Ridg then crossing the Creek then
: with the meanders of the Ridg down the Creek to the
: Beginning.

: William Brown

: Fees of office paid $1.00

PAGE 98

No. 60
Jacob Bryson
50 acres
general
Entry

Location
received and
this entry
made this
30 January
1827

Received
for the
State
$0.50

State of Tennessee : Jacob Bryson enters 50 acres of
land in said county on the South
Hamilton County : east side of Wallens Ridg on the
North side of the West prong of
opossom Creek Beginning on a black oak marked J.B. -
running Northward 120 poles to a black oak marked
J. thence eastward 60 poles to what is called the
short ridge thence Southward 120 poles thence to the
Beginning.

Jacob Bryson

Fees of office paid $1.00
Certified Copy Deliver to the Enterer

Cornelius Milliken
Entry taker for Hamilton County
By his Deputy
John Mitchell

PAGE 99

No. 61
Terry Riddle
fifty acres
General
Entry

Location
Received
and this
Entry made
this 2nd
Day of Feb.
1827

Rec'd for
the State
$-50

State of Tennessee : Terry Riddle Enters fifty acres
of Land in Said County and on
Hamilton County : Waldens Ridge on the riddle fork
of Rocky Creek Beginning on a
top of a Clift Bank to said Creek Running Southwardly
120 poles to a stake and from thence 60 poles westwardly to a stake and from thence 120 poles northwardly
to a stake and from thence a straight line to the
Beginning so as to Include Fifty acres
february the 2nd, 1827

Terry Riddle
Enterer
Rec'd for the state $1.00

PAGE 100

No. 62
Terry Riddle
100 acres
General Entry

State of Tennessee : Terry Riddle Enters one hundred
acres of Land in said Countyand
Hamilton County : on Walden Ridge on the South
fork of Rocky Creek beginning
on the South Side of Said Creek on a white oak and
Maple Running Northwardly ninety poles to a stake
thence westwardly one Hundred and Eighty poles to a
stake thence Southwardly ninety poles to a stake

Location Received and this 2nd Day of February 1827	thence a straight line to the Beginning so as to include one hundred acres.
	
	February the 2nd, 1827
	
	     Terry Riddle
	     Enteror

Recd. for the State $1.00	Recd. for the state $1.00

PAGE 101

No. 63 Terry Riddle 100 acres General Entry	

State of Tennessee) (Terry Riddle Enters one Hundred Acres of Land in Said County on Hamilton County (the East side of Walden's Ridge Beginning on the south Bank of the South fork of Oposam Creek on a pine and white Oak at the foot of said Ridge Running Southwardly with the meanders of the foot of said Ridge one hundred and Eighty poles to a stake thence westwardly up the Side of said Ridge ninety poles to a stake thence northwardly one hundred and Eighty poles to a stake thence a straight Line to the Beginning So as to Include one hundred acres February the 2nd 1827

Location Recd. and this Entry made 2nd Day of February 1827

     Terry Riddle
Received for the state $1.00   Enteror
fees of office paid $1.00

PAGE 102

Terry Riddle
50 Acres
General
Entry

State of Tennessee) Terry Riddle Enters fifty acres of land South and Middle fork of Hamilton County (opossam Creek Beginning on a white oak at the foot of Waldens Ridge known By George T. Gillespies Corner Running northwardly Sixty poles to a stake thence westwardly 60 poles to a Stake thence southwardly 120 poles to a stake thence Eastwardly Sixty poles to a stake at the foot of the said Wallens Ridge thence with the meanders of the foot of said Ridge to the Beginning so as to include fifty acres February the 2nd Day 1827

     Terry Riddle
     Enteror
fees of office paid $1.00

PAGE 103

No. 65
Terry Riddle

State of Tennessee) Terry Riddle Enters fifty acres of land in said County Beginning on a Dogwood at the foot of Waldens Ridge Between Opos-

Hamilton County

50 acres
General Entry

: SAM AND ROCKY Creeks near the dividing Ridge Running no
: northwardly on hundred and twenty poles to a stake
: thence westwardly up the side of said Ridge Sixty
: poles tl a stake thence southwardly one hundred and

Location Re-
ceived and
this Entry
made this
2nd February
1827

: twenty poles to a stake thence a straight line to the
: beginning so as to Include fifty acres February the
: 2nd, 1827

                      Terry Riddle
                      Enteror

: fees of office paid $1.00

Recd. for
the State
$--50

PAGE 104

No. 66
Jonathan Rich-
mond
200 Acres
General Entry

: State of Tennessee｜ Jonathan Richmond Enters two Hun-
:   ｜ dred acres of Land in said County
: Hamilton County ｜ Beginning on a Chestnut Oak on
:   the south side of Opossam Creek
: Running Eastwardly 223 poles to a stake thence south-
: wardly 126 poles to a stake thence westwardly 226
: poles to a stake thence a straight line to the Be-

Location
Received and
this Entry
made this
2nd Day of
February
1827

:: ginning so as to Include two Hundred acres

                      Jonathan Richmond
                      Enteror

: fees of office paid $1.00
: Certifyd Copy Issued and
: delivered to the Enteror
: August 20th Day, 182--- (1827(?)

Recd. for the
State $2.00

                    Cornelius Milliken
                    Entry taker for Hamilton County

PAGE 105

No. 67
George Birdwell
&
George Russell
one hundred
&
six and a fourth
acres
General Entry

: State of Tennessee｜ George Birdwell and George Rus-
:   ｜ sell enters one hundred and sic ac
: Hamilton County ｜ acres and a fourth of Land in Said
:   County on the North side of Tennes-
:   see River Beginning at two Black
: Oaks Location to George Russells grant of No. 9700
: in a line of John Brown's Reservation thence with a
: line of said Russells Grant, to a small Black oak
: corner to said grant, thence Contining the same
: course untill it strikes a line of R.G. Watterhouses
: Entry of 320 acres thence sd. line to a Vorner of
: George Birdwells Grant No. 9701 thence with the lines
: of the same as it meanders to the Banks of Tennessee

Location Recd. and this Entry made this 26 Day of February 1827	River thence up the River as it meanders to John Browns Reservation Line Thence with said line to the Beginning.
	George Birdwell
	George Russell
	fees office paid $1.00
Received for the State $1.06½	

PAGE 106

No.68 John Cummings & Benjamin Cherry enters 62½ acres of land General Entry	State of Tennessee] John Cummings and Benjamin Cherry Enters Sixty two acres and a half Hamilton County] of land in said County and adjoining the tract that Samuel R. Russol entred in a small valley and Mountain Creeke Beginning on a black oak on the top of Mountain creeke Ridge Running South westwardly 144 poles to a stake from thence 72 poles S. Eastwardly to a stake from thence N. Eastwardly 144 poles to a stake on or near Russels line and from thence a strate line of 72 poles to the Beginning so as to include 62½ acres
Location Reveifed and this entry made this 28 February 1827	John Cummings and Benjamin Cherry locators
	fees of office paid $1.00
Received for the State 62½ Cts.	A certified Copy issued and delivered to Benjamin Cherry one of the above locators, the 23d Day of January 1828
	John Mitchell, D.S. by Asahel Rawlings

PAGE 107

No. 69 Arnate Moss fifty acres General Entry	State of Tennessee] Arnate Moss Enters 50 Acres of Land in said County on the north Hamilton County] side of Tennessee River and on Kelleys turnpike Road on the side of Waldens Ridge Beginning on a white oak near a large Spring Corner to said Mosses 15 acre tract Running thence Eastwardly with the line of the same 120 poles to a stake thence northwardly 67 poles to a stake thence westwardly 120 poles then stake thence westwardly 120 poles thence to the Beginning.
	May the 18th Arnate Moss, Locator 1827

PAGE 107

No. 70
James Russell
&
George Layman
twenty five
acres
General Entry

State of Tennessee⟩ James Russell and George Layman
                    ⟩ enters 25 acres of Land in said
Hamilton County   ⟩ County on Waldens Ridge and on
                       the south west side of the north fo
fork of Rock Creek Beginning on a forked tree(?)
Marked J.R. Running thence south westward 40 poles
thence north Eastwardly 80 poles thence South Eastwardly 50 poles then to the Beginning.

Location
Received and
this Entry
made this
28th May
1827

                        James Russell
                            &
                        George Layman
fees of office paid $1.00
Certified Copy Delivered to the
enterer

Received for
the State
$00.25

                            Cornelius Williken
                            Entry taker for Hamilton
                            County By his Deputy
                            John Mitchell

PAGE 108

No. 71.
Alfred N. Pat-
terson
fifty acres
General Entry

State of Tennessee, Hamilton County Alfred N. patterson Enters fifty acres ten poles of Land lying in
said County on Rocky Creek Bounded as follows: viz.
beginning on a Chestnut Oak and spruce pine on the
first point of the mountain that puts in to the
creek on the South Side thence E. 20 po to a stake
Thence N. 96 po to a Stake Thence W. 90 p to a stake
Thence S 90 poles to a Stake thence E. 70 p to the
beginning

Location
Recd. and
this Entry
made this
28th May
1827

                        A. N. Patterson

fees of office paid $1.00
Certify Issued and Deliveres to
the Enterer

Recd. for the
State $.50

                        (No signature)

PAGE 109

No. 72
James Smith
50 acres
general
entry

State of Tennessee⟩ Entry Takers Office- James Smith
                    ⟩ Enters 50 acres of land in said
Hamilton County   ⟩ county Beginning on a black oak
                       on Fields Reservation line on
the south side of said Reservation in a holler leading from Rosses Ferry road through to where Timothy Hic
Hickson Bilt a house and sunk a well Running thence
west along said line 64 poles to a stake thence
southwardly 128 poles to a stake thence Eastwardly
64 poles to a stake thence to the beginning.

Location		James Smith
Received and	:	Fees $1.00 paid
this entry	:	Received for the State $00--50
made this	:	Copy Issued
14th June	:	
1827	:	
	:	Corneilius Millikin
	:	Entry taker for Hamilton
	:	County by his Deputy
Received for	:	John Mitchell
the State $0.50	:	
0	:	
	:	

PAGE 110

No. 75   : State of Tennessee] Entry Takers office - William
William H. Stringer   ] H. Stringer enters twenty five
25 Acres General: Hamilton County   ] acres of land in said County
Entry   :   lying on both sides of the
                 : valley Road an betwene his 160 acre tract and James
                 : Smith's fifty acre tract Beginning at a Spanish sake
Location   : marked W.H.S. thence S. 60 E. with a line of his 160
Received and   : acre Tract 20 poles to a stake thence south 30 W 50
this entry made : poles to the line of said Smiths Survey thence with
this 15th June   : his line so afrs as to include the said 25 acres to
1827   : the best advantage according to law.
                 :
                 :   William H. Stringer
Received   :
for the   : fees $1.00 paid
State   : Received for the State $00.25
$00.25   :
                 :   Cornelius Millikan
                 :   Entry taker for Hamilton
                 :   County by his Deputy
                 :   John Mitchell

PAGE 110

No. 74   : State of Tennessee] James Smith enters 25 acres of
James Smith   :   ] land in said county lying Both Sides
25 acres   : Hamilton County   ] of Mill Creek and between his 54
general   :   Acre Entry & Richard C. Watter-
Entry   : housees preference Entry of 160 acres now occuped
                 : by William Stringer Beginning on the line of the 54
                 : Acre Entry a black oak on the north side of the Creek
Location   : thence eastward across the Ridge to a stake on Water-
Received and   : houses line thence along the line crossing the Creek
this entry   : to a white oak corner marked R. thence a direct line
made this   : to the corner of his fifty four acre Entry corner
16th June   : thence along the line to the beginning.
1827   :
                 :   James Smith
                 : Fees of office paid $1.00
                 :

Received for the State $0.25

Certified Copy Isued

> Cornelius Milliken
> Entry taker for Hamilton
> Countyby his Deputy
> John Mitchell

Received for the State $0.25

PAGE 111

No. 75
Henry Braden
110 Acres
General Entry

State of Tennessee | Entry takers office— Henry Braden Enters 100 acres of land in said
Hamilton County | county on Wallens Ridge and on the head waters of Chickamoga Creek Beginning on a White oak tree on the North Side of Said creek runing Eastward down said creek 160 poles to a stake thence southward crossing Said creek 100 poles thence west ward 160 poles thence to the Beginning

Location
Received
and this
entry made
this 25th
June, 1827

> Henry Braden

Fees of office $1.00
Received for the State $1.00
Certified Copy

Received for the State $1.00

> Cornelius Milliken
> Entry taker for Hamilton
> County by his Deputy
> John Mitchell

PAGE 111

No. 76
Benjamin
Cherry
and George
Williams
50 Acres
Gen. Entry

State of Tennessee

Benjamin Cherry and George Williams Enters 50 Acres of Land in Said County each Side of Shoal Creek and on the North
Hamilton County | Side of Kelley's turnpik Road in a Gap of Wallens ridg Beginning a pine tree marked B.C. runing thence westward 39 poles crosing said creek to a stake thence Northward 128 poles to a stak thence eastward 64 poles to a stak thence Southward 128 poles to a stak thence 32 poles to the Beginning

Location
Received
and this
Entry made
this
2 July 1827

> Benjamin Chery
> George Williams

Fees of office $1.00
Received for the State $00.50
Certified Copy

Received for the state $0.50

(No signature)

PAGE 112 : State of Tennessee | Alexander Smith enters 100 Acres
: | of land in Said County on each
No. 77 : Hamilton County | side of the Road leading to John
Alexander Smith : | Browns Ferry on Tennessee River
100 Acres : and Joining the tracts of land now occupied by Wil-
Gen. Entry : liam H. Stringer, Cornelsons Milliken and Jesse Smith
: Beginning on a Black Oak Tree on the South Side of a
: Branch on the Side of a high nob running thence
Location Re- : westwardly so as to include the vacant land lying
ceived and : between the above mentioned tracts of land
this Entry : August 8, 1827
made : Fees of office $1.00
this 8th of :   Alexander Smith
August 1827 :
:
:   Cornelius Milliken
Received for :   By his Deputy
the State $1.00 :   John Mitchell

PAGE 112 :
:
No. 78 : State of Tennessee | James Qualls Enters twenty five
James Qualls : | acres of in said County and on the
25 Acres : Hamilton County | North Side of Kelleys turnpike
: | Road beginning on a white oak
Location : Corner to Arnate Mosses Entry Running thence north
and Entry : ward forty two and a half poles thence westwardly eighty
made the : five poles thence southwardly forty two poles and a
27th August : half poles thence Eastwardly Eighty five poles to the
1827 : Beginning so as to Include twenty five acres August
: 10th 1827
:
Fees for :   James Qualls
the State :   Locator
$--25 :
: Fees of office paid $1.00
:
:   (No signature)
:
:
PAGE 113 :
:
No. 79 : State of Tennessee | James Qualls Enters fifty acres
James Qualls : | of Land in Said County Beginning
50 Acres : Hamilton County | on a dogwood just below his mill
: | and on his tract of 15 acres and
Location Re- : Running with Said line 140 poles to a Stake on or
ceived and : near McVey(?) Line thence with Said Line 70 poles
this Entry : westwardly a stake thence northwardly 140 -- so as to
made this : include a small field to a stake and from thence a
27th of August : Straight line to the Beginning So as to Include fifty
1827 : acres
: August 10th, 1827   James Qualls
: fees of office   Locator
: paid $1.00 (No signature)

P   B 113

No. 80 : State of Tennessee] Thomas James Enters 50 Acres
Thomas James :] of land in Said County Beginning
50 acres : Hamilton County] on a post oake corner to Richard
: G. Waterhouses 150 acre Entry
Location : near Rosses Ferry on Tennessee River Runing thence
Received : North 100 poles to a Stake thence West 50 poles to
and this : a Stake thence South 100 poles to Waterhouses line
Entry made : then Eastwardly to the Begining.
this 28th :
of August : Thomas James
1827 :
: Fees of office paid $1.00
: Fees for the Stat $.50 paid
Received for :
the State : Cornelius Milliken
0-50 : Entry taker for Hamilton
: County by his Deputy
: John Mitchell

PAGE 114

No. 81 : State of Tennessee] David Rhenolds Enters 25 Acres
David Rhenolds :] of Land in Said County on Wal-
25 Acres : Hamilton County] lens Ridg on the North side of
: Chickamoga and on the west side
: of the Rode leading from Washington in Rhea County
Location Received To John Browns Ferry aboutt ½ oa a mile from Said
and this entry : Creek one mile from Said Road Beginning on a Spruse
made this 3rd : Pine Runing thence Southwardly 40 poles to a stake
Septem. : thence Eastwardly 50 poles to a Stak thence Northwardly
1827 : ly 40 poles thence to the Beginning So as to include
: a Saltpeter Cave.
:
Received : David Renolds
for the :
State $00.25 : fees of office $1.00
:
: Cornelius Milliken
: Entry taker for Hamiltn
: County By his Deputy
: John Mitchell

PAGE 115

No. 82 : State of Tennessee] John Howell Enters 50 acres of
John Howell :] Land in Said County on Waldens
50 Acres : Hamilton County] Ridge and on Both Sides of a Spring
: Branch beginning on a Black oak tree
Location Re- : runing thence Southwardly 100 poles thence Eastward 80
ceived and : poles thence Northwardly 180 poles thence to the Be-in-
this Entry : ing so as to include his ould improvement

mad this
9th October
1827

: John Howel
: fees of office $1.00 paid
: Received for the State $60.50

Received for
the State
$00.50

: Cornelius Milliken
: Entry taker for Hamilton
: County By his Deputy
: John Mitchell

PAGE 115

No.83
William Tipton
100 Acres

: State of Tennessee   William Tipton Enters 100 Acres
:   of Land in Said County and on Wal-
: Hamilton County   lens Ridg Beginning on a Black
:   oak Corner to his 50 acre Tract Run-

Received for
the State
$1.00

: ing then according to law and to the best advantage
: so as to include 100 acres adjoining his 50 Acre tract

: William Tipton

Location Received
this Entry
mad this
9th October
1827

: Fees of office $1.00 paid
: Received for the State $1.00

: Cornelius Milliken
: Entry taker for Hamilton
: County By his Deputy
: John Mitchell

PAGE 116

No. 84
William
Hickman
&
William
Hickman
110 Acres

: State of Tennessee   William Hickman and William Hick-
:   man Enters 100 Acres of Land on
: Hamilton County   Wallens Rid on the Waters of Sail
:   Creek ajoining the Lands of John
: Russel Charles Gambell and William McGill and James
: Lee Beginning and Cornering on a White oak and Hick-
: ory on or near the west line of John Russell Gambell
: and McGills Seventy Six Acre grant thence North 160
: poles to a stak thence west 100 poles to a stak thence
: South 160 poles to a stak thence a Direct line to the

Location Re-
ceived and this
Entry
mad this 9th
October
1827

: Beginning

: William Hickman
: William Hickman

: Fees of office $1.00
: Received for the Stat $1.00

Received for
the State
$1.00

: Cornelius Milliken
: Entry taker for Hamilton
: County By his Deputy
: John Mitchell

PAGE 116
No. 85

Jeremiah
Frier &
John Frier

Location Received and
this Entry mad
this 9th
October, 1827

Received for
the State $3.20

State of Tennessee] Jeremiah Frier and John Frier
&nters 320 acres of land in
Hamilton County] said County on the waters
of Sandy Beginning on a Saus-
a fras and White oak runing southward 320 poles
thence west 160 to the Beginning

Jeremiah Frier
John Frier
Fees of office $1.00 paid
Received for the State $3.20

Cornelius Milliken
Entry taker for Hamilton
County By his Deputy
John Mitchell

PAGE 117

No. 86
Henry Fredrick
100 acres

Gen. Entry
Location
received and
this Entry mad
this 9 October
1827

State of Tennessee] Henry Fredrick &nters 100 Acres
of Land in Said County on Wallens
Hamilton County] Ridg and on one of the Head
forks of Chickamoga Creek Begin-
ningon a Maple on the North &ast Side of Said Creek
runing Thence North westward 160 poles thence 100
poles Southwestward thence 160 poles South Eastward
then to the Begining

Henry Fredrick

Fees of office $1.00
Received for the State $1.00

Cornelius Milliken
&ntry taker for Hamilton Co.
By his Deputy
John Mitchell

PAGE 117

No. 87
Thomas McNut
50 Acres
General
Entry

Location Received and
this Entry
made this
Received for the
State $-50

Thomas Mcnutt &nters fifty acres of Land lying and
being in the County of Hamilton on the Roaring fork
of Sale Creek Beginning on a Large white pine on
the &ast Side of Said Creek about three quarters of
a mile above where the Road known By the name of
Hunters trace Crosses said Creek Running thence
agreeable to Law So as to Contain fifty Acres.

fees of office paid $1.00
Copny Isd. 22 Oct. 18-- (1827)(?)

(No signature)

PAGE 118

No. 88
James Johnson
150 Acres

State of Tennessee | James Johnson Enters 150 acres
of Land in said County on the mountain
Hamilton County | mountain on the waters of Sail Creek
Creek on the turnpike Road Grant-
ed C. Gamble C. E. Shelton and J. Witt adjoining the
lands of D. Jones Will Stephens and Wm. Bery Beginning on a poplar Stump South East Corner to said Jon-
ses 20 Acre tract and Runing North with a line of the
Same Crossing Said Road pasing the corner to a lin of
Stovenses 50 acre tract on which he now lives thence
with said line East pasing the Corner to a line of
said Berrys 300 acre tract then Reversing said line
to the Beginning corner of said 300 Acre tract thence
Reversing the Closing line of Said tract so as to include 150 acres according to law

Location Re-
ceived and
this Entry mad
the 15th October:
1827

Received for:
the State
$1-50

James Jonson

fees of office paid $1.00
Cirtified copy Delivered to
the Enterer

Cornelius Milliken
Entry taker for Hamilton
County By his Deputy
John Mitchell

PAGE 119

No. 89
John Gorden
100 Acres

State of Tennessee | John Gorden Enters 100 Acres of
land in Said County on Wallens
Hamilton County | Ridge part of Cumberland moun-
tain Near the flat Rock on the
East Side of lorrel Creek and the Said Creek inCluding
his 50 acre Entry enterd by Isaac Clement Begining on a
a post Oak thence Runing North of west 150 poles thence
Eastwardly Round to the beginning so as to inClud 100
Acres aCording to law

Location
Received
and this
Entry mad
this 27
October
1827

John Gorden

fees of office $1.00
fees for the Stat $1.00

Received for
the Stat
50 of this
money on a
former Entry

Cornelius Milliken
Entry taker for Hamilton
County By his Deputy
John Mitchell

PAGE 120
No. 90
Henry Braden

State of Tennessee | Henry Braden Enters 200 acres of
land in said County and on Wallens
Hamilton County | ridge neare the place whare Job

200 acres

Location received and this entry made this 5th November 1827

Received for the State $2.00

Harwell first settled Beginning on a white oak running thence southward far enough to inClude 200 acres in a square or oblong to a stake then Eastward then Northward then to the beginning so as to include a spring.

           Henry Braden
Fees of office $1.00 Paid

           Cornelius Milikin
           Entry taker for Hamilton
           County by his Deputy
           John Mitchell

PAGE 120

No. 91
Henry Braden
100 Acres

Location
Received and this Entry mad this 5 November 1827

Received for the Stat $1.00

State of Tennessee | Henry Braden Enters 100 Acres of Land in Said County and on Wallens Ridg Beginning on a Post oak runing thence South so fare a s to include 100 Acres in a Square or ablong thence eastward then Northward then to the beginning So as to include a Spring

Hamilton County

           Henry Braden
Fees of office $1.00 paid
Received for the State $1.00

           Cornelius Milliken
           Entry taker for Hamilton
           County By his Deputy
           John Mitchell

PAGE 121

No. 92
Jeremiah H.
Jones &
John Brown
Gen. Entry

Location Received and this Entry mad this 26th November 1827

State of Tennessee | Entry takers office--Jeremiah H. Jones and John Brown Enters 100 acres of Land on the Mountain in Said County including their fifty

Hamilton County

Acre Entry ofNo. 58 Dated 15th January 1827 Beginning at the mouth of a Spring Branch that empties in to Opossom Creek and Runing Southwardly 88 poles thence Northwardly to Said Creek thence with the meanders of the Saim to the Beginning.

           J.H. JOnes Enters
           John Brown
Fees of office $1.00 paid

Received for   : Cirtified Copy Delivar
the State   : to the Enterer
$0.50   : Received for the State $.50

               :   Cornelius Milliken
               :   Entry taker for Hamilton County
               :   By his Deputy
               :   John Mitchell

PAGE 122

No. 93   : State of Tennessee| Elisha Rogers Land in said County
Elisha Rogers : S | Bounded as follows Begining on a
100 Acres   : Hamilton County | marked white oakcorner at the
Genneral   :   foot of the Mountain Supposed to
Entry   : be James Denys & Lauderdails Corner Runing thence
               : Southwardly along Lauderdails line 160 poles to s stak
Location Re- : thence Westwardly 100 poles to a stak thence Eastward-
ceived and   : ly 100 poles to the Beginning.
this   :
Entry mad   :   Elisha Rogers
this 2nd   : Fees for the Stat $1.00
December   : Fees of office $1.00 paid
1827   : Certified Copy Isued
               :
Received for :   Cornelius Milliken
the State   :   Entry taker for Hamilton
$1.00   :   County By his Deputy
               :   John Mitchell

PAGE 122

No. 94   : State of Tennessee| Elisha Rogers 100 Acres of Land
Elisha Rogers : | in Said County on the Hend Wat-
100 Acres Gen. : Hamilton County | ers of Mountain Creek Begining on
Entry   : | a Black Oake his(?) corner to
               : William Lauderdales 25 acre Entry on Said Creek Run-
               :   ing thence Reversing Lauderdels Closing line to said
Location Recd. : Keenys line thence with Said line fare anough to in-
and this entry : Clud 100 acres then to wallens Rid then to the Begin-
mad this 4th : ning.
January 1828 :
               :   Elisha Rogers
               : Fees of office $1.00
Received for : Foes for the State $1.00
the State $1.00 : Certified Copy Isued
               :
               :   Cornelius Milliken
               :   Entry taker for Hamilton
               :   County By his Deputy
               :   John Mitchell

PAGE 95

| No. 95
James Varner
50 Acres
gen entry | : State of Tennessee│ James Varner Enters 50 Acres of
: ────────────────│ land lying on the North western ork
: H milton County │ of opposson Creed, Beginnin on a
: pine and runing Westwardly 100
: poles thence Southwardly 80 poles thence Eastwardky
: 100 poles thence Northward 80 poles to the Begining. |

Location re-
ceived this
entry mad
this 21st
January
1928

: James Varner

: Fees of office $1.00 paid
: for the State $0-50 paid
: Certified Copy Delivered to the
: EntereR

R eceived for
the State
$-50

: Cornelious Milliken
: Entry taker for Hamilton County
: By his Deputy
: John Mitchell

PAGE 123

No. 96
George Reed
150 Acres
General
Entry

: George Reed Enters 150 acres land on the waters of
: lorrel Creek Joining said Reeds Lot that McClure
: now lives on beginning on Reads South East Corner on
: a white oak Running West 20 poles thence South 150
: poles thence West 150 thence North to Said Reeds line
: so as to Include 150 acres
: February the 25th 1828

Location Re-
ceived and
this Entry
made this
25th Day of
february
1828

: George Reed

: Fees of office paid $1.00
: Certifyd Issued

: Cornelius Milliken
: Entry taker for Hamilton
: County

Received for
the State $1.50 :

PAGE 124

No. 97
Jesse Smith
25 acres
general
Entry

: State of Tennessee│ Jesse Smith Enters Twenty five acres
: │ of land in daif County on the South
: Hamilton County │ Side of valley Road Leading from
: Washington to John Browns ferry
: on Tennessee River Begining on a Black oak on the
: East End of a fifty acre Entry made By Jesse Smith

Location Re-
ceived and
this Entry
made this
25th Day
of february
1828

Received for
the State
$.25

Running Eastwardly 45 poles to a Stake thence Southwardly 87 poles to a stake thence westwardly 45 p to
a Stake thence Northwardly 87 poles to the Beginning so as to Include twenty five acres

Jesse Smith

Fees of office paid $1.00
Certified Copy Issued and
Delivered to the Enterer
the 23 Day of February
1828

Cornl. Milliken
E. T. H. C.

PAGE 124

No. 98

State of Tennessee Jesse Smith Enters twenty five
acres of Land in Said County on the
Hamilton County South Side of the Valley Road
Leading from Washington to John
Browns ferry on Tennessee River Beginning on a hick-
ory on the west End of a fifty acre Entry made by
Jesse Smith Joining a one hundred and 60 acre Entry
made By Watterhouse Running thence from the Begin-
ning Southwardly 100 poles to a Stake thence East-
wardly 50 poles to a Stake thence Northwardly to Said
Jesse Smiths 50 acre Entry Line thence with Said
Lines to the Beginning So as to Include 25 acres of
Land february 25th 1828

(Blank)

Jesse Smith
Locator

PAGE 125

No. 99
James Hatfield
50 acres
general Entry

State of Tennessee James Hatfield Enters 50 acres
of Land in said county on Wal-
Hamilton County lens Ridge and on the Waters of
Chickamaga Beginning on a Red
oak marded J.H. Running thence Northward thence
Eastward then south then to the Begining.

James Hatfield

Location Re-
ceived and
this Entry
made this
13th March
1828

Received for
the State
$0.50

Received for the State $00.50
Certified Copy Isued

Cornelous Milliken
Entry taker for Hamilton
County by his Deputy
John Mitchell

PAGE 125

| No. 100
Samuel E. Mead
600 acres
general entry | State of Tennessee

Hamilton County | Samuel B. Mead enters six
hundred acres of in said
County lying on Tennessee
River including an Island |

in said river the first above the Suck commonly
called Browns island as being near to John Browns

Location Received and
this entry
made this
26th March
1828

ferry beginning at the lower end of said island
thence meandering the river up then southwardly
around for complement so as to include the above
quantity.of land.
March 26th 1828

Samuel B. Mead

Received
for the
State
$6.00

Fees of office paid $1.00
Certified Copy Isued

Cornelius Milliken
Entrytaker for Hamilton
County by his Deputy
John Mitchell

PAGE 126

No. 101
Samuel B. Mead
100 Acres
general
Entry

State of Tennessee

Hamilton County

Samuel B. Mead enters one hundred acres of land in said county including an island in Tennessee river commonly called

Roses island above Roses Ferry beginin at the uper
end of said island meander down and around so as
to include the above quantity of land.

Location Received and
this Entry
made this
26 March
1828

Samuel B. Mead
Fees of office Paid $1.00
Certified Copy Isued

Cornelius Milikin
Entry Taker for Hamilton
County by his Deputy
John Mitchell

PAGE 126

No. 102
Samuel B. Mead
150 acres
general Entry

State of Tennessee

Hamilton County

Samuel B. Mead enters one hundred and fifty acres of land
on an island on Tennessee River opposite the place of Hold-

ing Court in said county Beginning at the upper end
of said Island on a stake near an old wast field
thence south westwardly around for compliment so

Location Re
ceived and
this entry
made this
26 March
1828   :   as to include a good body of land.

                       Samuel B. Mead

Fees of office paid $1.00
Certified Copy Isued

Received
for the State
$1.50

                       Cornelius Milikin
                       Entry taker for Hamilton
                       County by the Deputy
                       John Mitchell

PAGE 127

No. 103
Samuel B. Mead
100 Acres
general entry   :   State of Tennessee Samuel B. Mead Enters one hundred
                                acres of land in said county includ-
                Hamilton County   ing and island opposite the mouth

Location Re-
ceived and
this entry
mad this
26 March 1828   of North chickumaga creek Beginning at the upper end of said Island on a stake then
running down the meanders of said island in Tennessee
River and around so as to include the entry of good
land.

                       Samuel B. Mead

Received for
the State
$1.00   Fees of office paid $1.00
Certified Copy Isued

                       Cornelius Milliken
                       Entry taker for Hamilton
                       County By his Deputy
                       John Mitchell

PAGE 127

No. 104
Henry Braden
640 Acres
General
Entry   :   State of Tennessee Henry Braden Enters 640 Acres of
                               land in said County on Wallens Ridg
                Hamilton County on the waters of chickamoga in the
                           Big Horse Shoe near William Gants
Entry Begining a hickory tree Running thence westward 320 poles then Northward 320 poles then North-
Location Re-
ceived and
this entry
mad this
22 Aprile
1828   ward 320 poles then Eastward 320 poles to the Beginning.

                       Henry Braden

Fees for the Stat $6.40
fees office $1.00

Received for
the Stat $6.40   Cornelious Milliken, Entry taker
                       for Hamilton County by his Deputy
                       John Mitchell

PAGE 128 :

No. 105 : State of Tennessee| Henry Braden Enters 300 Acres
Henry Braden : | of Land in said County on Wal-
300 Acres : Hamilton County | lens Ridg on the waters of Chick-
Gen. Entry : amaga inCluding mullinses Improv-
: ment Begining on a hite oak tree Runing thence west
: ward 160 poles thence Southward 320 poles thence
Location : Eastward 160 poles then to Beginning.
Received :
and this : Henry Braden
Entry :
mad : fees of office $1.00
this 22 April : fees for the State $3.00
1828 :
: Corneleous Millikin
Received for : Entry taker for Hamilton
the Stat : County by his Deputy
$3.00 : John Mitchell
:

PAGE 128 :

No. 106 : William Clift and Robert C. McRee Enters 200 Acres
Wm. Clift : of land in Hamilton County on Wallens Ridg and on
& : the waters of Santy Creek Begining on a Black oak
Rob. McGee : near a creek called little Oven Rockhouse creek
: or Board camp fork of Santy thence West 150 to a
: stak thence East 150 to a Stak thence to the Begining.
Location :
Received and : William Clift
this Entry : &
mad this : Robert McGee
20th May : Fees for the State $2.00
1828 :
: Cornelious Millikin
: Entry taker for Hamilton
: County by his Deputy
Received for : John Mitchell
the State $2.00 :
:

PAGE 129 :

No. 107 : State of Tennessee| William Hickman and William Hick-
William Hickman : | man Enters two Hundred acres of
& : Hamilton County | Land Lying on Waldens Ridge on t
William Hickman : the west side of a creak known
200 acres : By the name of brush Creek and a fork of Sail Creek
General Entry : begining on a white oak and sweet gum corner to a
: hundred acre survey that belongs to said Hickman and
: on the West side of said Hickmans Hundred acre Sur-
Location Re- : vey thence north two hundred poles to a stake thence
ceived and : west one hundred and sixty poles to a stake thence
this Entry :
made July the :
24 Day 1828 :
:

Recd. for
the State
$2.00

: south two Hundred poles to a stake then a straight
: line to the Beginning.

William Hickman
&
William Hickman

Due Cornelius
Milliken
$0.45

PAGE 130

No. 108
Isaac Clark
100 Acres
General Entry

: State of Tennessee} Isaac Clark Enters 100 Acres of
: } land in said County between the
: Hamilton County } main Valley Road and mountain Cr
: Creek Begining on a Black oak and
post oak marked M Begining corner to an eighty acre
entry mad by Benjamin Cherry of N 5 dated 10th
Aprile 1826 and reversing the lines of said Entry
to the top of Mountain Creek Ridg thence NorthEast
wardly along the top of said Ridg to the due west
line from the mouth of North Chickamoga Creek
thence East with Said line so as to in Clude 100
Acres by runing paralel with the line on the Ridg
to the above named Entry.

Location Re-
ceived and
this Entry
made this
9th September
1828

Received
for the
State
$1.00

Isaa Clark
Entryer

Cornelius Milliken
Entry taker for Hamilton
County By his Deputy
John Mitchell

PAGE 131

No. 109
Martha Richmond
200 Acres
genneral
Entry

: State of Tennessee} Martha Richmond Enters 200 Acres
: } of land on the Mountain in said C
: Hamilton County } County and on the waters of Rock
: Creek Begining on a hickory and
Mapel on a Branch of Said creek and Runing South
wardly 254 poles to a stak thence westwardly 126 to
STAKE THENCE Northwardly 254 poles to a Stake thence
a direct line to the Begining.

Location
Received and
this Entry
mad this

Martha Richmond

11th September
1828
Received for
the State
$2.00

fees of office $1.00 paid
fees for the State $2.00 paid

Cornelius Millikin, Entry taker
for Hamilton County by his Deputy
John Mitchell

PAGE 131

No. 110
Samuel R. Russel
$43\frac{3}{4}$ Acres
gennaral
entry

Location Received this 11th September 1828

Received for the State \$0.$43\frac{3}{4}$

State of Tennessee } Hamilton County } Samuel R. Russel Enters $43\frac{3}{4}$ acres of land on the waters of Sail Creek and on the side of the Mountain in said County Begining in the due west line from the mouth of Highwasse at the foot of the mountain on the N. W. side of a Branch of said creek and Runing Eastwardly with the meanders of the Branch 120 poles thence Northwardly up to the side of the mountain 60 poles thence according to law to the B$_{e}$gining.

Samuel R. Russel
Enterer

fees of office \$1.00 paid
fees for the State \$0.$43\frac{3}{4}$
Copy Issued

Cornelious Millikin
Entry taker for Hamilton
County by his Deputy
John Mitchell

PAGE 132

No. 111
Samuel R. Russel
$43\frac{3}{4}$ Acres
Gennaral
Entry

Location Received and this Entry mad this 11th September 1828

Received for the State \$0--$43\frac{3}{4}$

State of Tennessee } Hamilton County } Samuel Rl Russel Enters $43\frac{3}{4}$ acres of Land in said clunty adjoining Fields reservation Beginning on a black oak and Post oak S.E. corner of said Reservation and running N. to the corner of James Smiths 54 acre Survey Then E. to W. H. Stringers 25 acre Survey Then S. 30 W--to the corner of the same Then S. 20 W--100 poles Then W-to a line of James Smiths 50 acre Entry Then N. to said Reservation Then E. to the beginning.

Samuel Russell
Enterer

fees of office \$1.00 paid
fees for the State $43\frac{3}{4}$ ¢ paid
Copy Issued

Cornelious Millikin
Entry taker for Hamilton
County by his Deputy
John Mitchell

PAGE 132

No. 111
Samuel R.
Russel
43¾ Acres
Genneral
Entry

Location
Received
and this
Entry mad
this 11th
September

Received
for the
State
$0-43¾

State of Tennessee | Samuel R. Russel Enters 43¾
                   | Acres of Land in said county
Hamilton County | adjoining Fields reservation
                     Beginning on a black oak and
Post oak S.E. corner of said Reservation and running
N. to the corner of James Smiths 54 acre Survey Then
E. to W.H. Stringers 25 acre Survey Then S. 30 W to
the corner of the same Then S. 20 W-100 poles Then
W- to a line of James Smiths 50 acre Entry Then N.
to said Reservation Then E. to the beginning.

                    Samuel Russell
                    Enterer

fees of office $1.00 paid
fees for the State 43¾ paid
Copy Issued

                    Cornelious Millikin
                    Entry taker for Hamilton
                    County by his Deputy
                    John Mitchell

PAGE 132

No. 112
Wm. Hickman, Sr.
      &
Wm. Hickman, Jr.
50 acres
Gen. Entry

Location
Received and
this Entry
made this
18th
October
1828

Received for
the State
$0-50

State of Tennessee | Wm. Hickman Senior and Wm. Hick-
                   | man, Junior Enters 50 acres of
Hamilton County |
                     Land in said county and on the
East Side of Wallens Ridg Beginning on a pine and
and Hickory on or near Patrick Martains & Edward
Grays line on the left side of the trace known by
the name of Qawles trace and on the North side of
the Roraing Fork of Sail Creek thence Northward by
crossing Qawals trace 80 poles to a Stak thence
westwardly 100 poles to a stak thence southward 80
poles then to the Beginning so as to include 50
acres.

                    Wm. Hickman Senior
                         &
                    Wm. Hickman Junior

Fees for the Stat $.50 paid
fees of office $.00 paid
Copy Issued

                    Cornelious Millikn
                    Entry taker for Hamilton
                    County by his Deputy
                    John Mitchell

PAGE 133

No. 113	:	State of Tennessee	John W. Richey Enters 100 Acres
John W. Richey	:		of Land in Said County on Wal-
100 Acres	:	Hamilton County	lens Ridg on the head waters of
General	:		Chickamoga Creek or otherwise
Entry	:	Caine Creek Begining at a larg Bluff on a Black oak

marked W Thence Eastwardly 100 poles thence Northwardly 50 poles then westwardly 40 poles then Northwardly so far as to in Clud 100 Acres and Round to

Location :
Received : the Begining.
and this :
Entry mad : John W. Richey
this 21st :
October : fees of office $1.00 paid
1828 : fees for the State $1.00 paid
: Copy Issued
:
Received : Cornelious Milliken
from the : Entry taker for Hamilton
State : County by his Deputy
$1-00 : John Mitchell

PAGE 133

No. 114	:	State of Tennessee	John Lovelady Ro-enters twenty
John Lovelady	:		five acres of Land in said C
25 Acres	:	Hamilton County	County Beginning on a post oak
General	:		marked thus X from thence Run-
Entry	:	ning northwardly 85 poles thence westwardly forty

two and a half poles thence southwardly Eighty five
poles to a stake thence Eastwardly to the Beginning
Location : so as to In Clude the place where Shephard F. foster
Received : now lives and to Include the 25 acres he heretofore
and this : Enterd
Entry :
made this : John Lovelady
24th : Locator
Oct. 1828 :
:
: Oct. the 24th 1828
heretofore : Certified Copy Issued and
Recd. for : Delivered to the Enterer
State--25¢ : (No signature)

PAGE 134

No. 115	:	State of Tennessee	Benjamin Cherry Enters 100 Acres
Benjamin Cherry	:		of land in said County and on
100 Acres	:	Hamilton County	Wallens Ridg and on a Creek
Gen. Entry	:		Called Big falling watter creek

Beginning on a Chestnut marked B stand on the North

Location
Received and
this Entry
mad this
27th November
1828

: Bank of said Creek oposit the mouth of a hollow Run-
: ing thence westward up said Creek 100 poles to a stak
: thence Southward Crosing said Creek 160 poles to a
: stak thence Eastwardly 100 poles to a stak thence
: southward Crosing said Creek 160 poles to a stak
: thence Eastwardly 100 poles to a stak then to the
: Beginning.

Received for
the State
$1-00

:   Benjamin Cherry

: fees of office $1.00 paid
: fees for the State $1.00 paid

:   Cornelious Millikin
:   Entry taker for Hamilton
:   County by his Deputy
:   John Mitchell

PAGE 134

No. 116
James Haney
100 Acres
Gen. Entry

: State of Tennessee│ James Haney Enters 100 Acres of
:   │ land in said County on Wallens
: Hamilton County   │ Ridg and on the North East Side
:   │ of Bomans Nob on the Waters of
: Santy Begining on a Black oak tree Runing thence East-
: wardly then Northwardly then westwardly then to the
: Beginning so as to in Clud 100 Acres and a Spring

Location
Received and
this Entry
mad this
4th December
1828

:   James Haney

: fees of office $1.00 paid
: fees for the state $1.00 paid
: Certified Copy Issued.

Received
for the
State $1.00

:   Cornelious Millikin
:   Entry taker for Hamilton
:   County by his Deputy
:   John Mitchell

: "Settled with the State
: from the Back."

PAGE 135

No. 117
Samuel R.
Russel
50 Acres
Gen. Entry

: State of Tennessee│ Samuel R. Russel Enters 50 Acres
:   │ of land in Said County including
: Hamilton County   │ his former Entry of 43½ Acres of
:   │ N. 110 Begining on a black oak
: and post oak S.E. corner to Fields Reservation on
: Mill Creek and runing N. 56 poles to a Spanish oak
: in a line of Said Reservation marked J.S. corner
: to James Smiths 54 Acre Survey thence East with a

Location Received and this Entry made this 6th January 1829	: line of the same 54 poles to Stringers 25 Acre Entry : thence South 30-W with a line of the same 10 poles : thence S. 60-E with another line of the same 30 : poles thence W-to a line of a 50 acre Entry made : by James Smith thence with a line of the same No. : to a line of said Reservation thence with Said line : East 40 poles to the Begining.

Samuel R. Russel

Received for the State 80-6½	: fees of office $1.00 paid : fees for the State 80-6½ : Cirtifiyed Copy Isued

Corneleous Milliken
Entry taker for Hamilt on County
by his Deputy   John Mitchell

<u>PAGE 136</u>

No. 118 Jacob Hartman Gen. Entry of 640 Acres	State of Tennessee] Hamilton County	Jacob Hartman Enters 640 acres of land in said county on Wallens Ridge of Cumberland mountain on the hed of the Herican fork of

suck Creek a branch of Tennessee River and lying on
booth sides of a trace leading from Mountain Creek
to seequechee known by the name of Keenies Trace Beginning at a black ock and Hickory marked J.H. on
top of the South bluff of said Herican fork of said
Suck Creek thence southwardly 60 poles to a stak on
the south side of a hill thence Westwardly 500 poles
Crossing said Keenies trace and falling water creek
thence Northwardly 343 poles thence westwardly 500
poles crossing a branch of said falling water creek
and said Keenies trace to the Beginning so as to include 640 acres.

(Location: Received and Entry made 7th Jany. 1829)

(Received for the State $6.40)

Jacob Hartman

Fees of Office $1.00
Fees for state $6.40

(Received fees of office $1.00)

(Coppy Isd. 9 July 1831)

Cornelius Milliken
Entry taker for Hamilton
County By John Mitchell,
Deputy

<u>PAGE 137</u>

No. 119 Thomas Jackson 100 Acres	State of Tennessee] Hamilton County	Thomas Jackson Enters 100 acres of land in said County on Wal- lons Ridg of Cumberland Moun-

Gen. Ent.	tain and on Coopers Creek on the South East Side of a Nob Beginning at white oak on the South West Side of Said Creek Runing thence Westwardly 160
Location Received and this Entry made this 3th February 1829	poles to a Stak thence Southwardly 160 poles to a Stak thence Southwardly 80 poles thence Eastwardly 160 poles thence westwardly 80 poles to the Beginning

Thomas Jackson

fees of office $1.00
fees for the State $1.00

Cornelious Milliken
Entry taker for Hamilton
County by his Deputy
John Mitchell

PAGE 137

No. 120 Major A. Jackson 100 Acres	State of Tennessee Major A. Jackson 100 acres of Land in Said County on Wallens Hamilton County Ridg and on the Hed waters of Chickmaga or on Hicksons Champ(?) Branch Begining on a Black oak tree on the North side of Said Branch runing thence Southwardly then East-
Location Recd. and this Entry made this the 3rd February 1829	wardly then to the Beginning including boathe Sulfer Spring and Rickets(or Pickets) Cabin.

Major A. Jackson

fees of office $1.00 paid
fees for the State $1.00 paid

Received for the State $-00	Corneleous Milliken Entry taker for Hamilton County by his Deputy John Mitchell

PAGE 188

No. 121 James Cunning- ham 25 acres General Entry	State of Tennessee James Cunningham Enters twenty five acres of land lying on both Hamilton County sides of the Mountain Creek Road Beginning on the South Side of said Road at a Black Jack Corner to a 25 acre Grant of the State of Tennessee to John Keeny Running thence southwardly to a Blackoak as a North-
Location Received and this Entry	east Corner of Stringers and Johnsons 50 acre Entry thence with their Line westwardly in the whole from the Beginning. Eighty poles Thence Northwardly fifty

made this 24th day August 1829	poles Westwardly Eighty poles thence to the Beginning. August 24th 1829
	James Cunningham Locator
Received for the State $-25	fees of office Paid $1-60 Certify Copy Issued
	(No signature)

PAGE 138
No. 122
John Brown
Ten Acres
General
Entry

John Brown Enters Ten Acres of Land in Hamilton County In a small Valley between Tennessee Valley and Mountain Creek and near to Mill Creek beginning on a Black oak Corner To James Smith and Running with his Line fifty Seven poles to a white oak thence Northwardly fifteen poles to a line of A sixty two acre and a half Entry made by Benjamin Cherry & John Cummings

Location
Received and
this Entry
made this
21st of
November
1829

thence along said Line fiftyseven poles to a stake thence to the Beginning.

John Brown
Locator

November 21st 1829
Certified Copy Issued

Received for
the State$--25

(No signature)

PAGE 139

(Blank)

PAGE 140

Entries made under the provisions of an Act of the General Assembly of the State of Tennessee Entitled "An Act to Authorize the entering and Obtaining Grants for any quantity of land under five thousand Acres and for other purposes passed at Nashville the 9th day of January, 1830

PAGE 140

No. 1
Jesse Sutton
&
Uriah Gann
25 Acres

State of Tennessee Jesse Sutton & Uriah Gann Enters twenty five acres of land in said Hamilton County County on the South side of Wallens ridge on the Waters of falling Water & north of the main Creek Beginning on two White Oaks Thence north eastwardly to a Stake Thence Southwardly to a Stake. Thence Westwardly to a Stake

Location received &
this entry made 15 March 1830

Fees of Office Received & Copy issued

State of Tennessee | Jesse Sutton & Uriah Gann Enters
| twenty five acres of land in said
Hamilton County | County on the South side of Wal-
| lins ridge on the Waters of fal-
ling Water & north of the main Creek Beginning on
two White Oaks Thence north eastwardly to a Stake
Thence Southwardly to a Stake. Thence Westwardly to
a Stake Thence a direct line to the beginning so as
to include the James Agee improvement and to include
twenty five acres March the 3rd day, 1830

Jesse Sutton
&   Locators
Uriah Gann

PAGE 141

No. 2.
Anderson Skillern
&
Joseph G. Smith
5000 Acres
General
Entry

Location
Received
&this
Entry
made
2nd April
1830

Received
Entry Takers
fee .25¢

State of Tennessee | Anderson Skillern, Joseph G. Smith
| of Bledsoe County Enters five thou-
Hamilton County | sand acres of land in Hamilton
| County on Wallens Ridge of Cumber-
land Mountain on the Waters of Sale Creek Beginning
at a Dogwood, white oak and Pine trees standing on
a point on the east side of a rivulet known by the name
of the lick branch about one and a half miles near a
west bearing from John Russell Esquire's Runing thence
South Westwardly. Thence South Eastwardly. Thence
north eastwardly & NorthWestwardly to the point of
beginning to include Sale Creek as near the Centre of
the Survey as practicable the Survey to be made in an
oblong form the length to be down Sale Creek and to
be double the width.

Anderson Skillern
&   Locators
Joseph G. Smith

1st April 1830

PAGE 141

No. 3
John Skillern
&
Henry Miller
5000 acres
General Entry

Location Re-
ceived &
this Entry

State of Tennessee | John Skillern & Henry Miller of
| Bledsoe County enters five thou-
Hamilton County | sand acres of land in said County
| of Hamilton on Wallens Ridge of
Cumberland on the Waters of Sale Creek Beginning at
the 3rd Corner of a 5000 acre entry made this day in
entry takers Office of the County in the name of Anderson Skillern & Joseph G. Smith which corner stands
on the south west side of sale Creek Runing thence
Southeastwardly northeastwardly and north westwardly
to the 4th Corner of said 5000 acre entry and thence

made 2nd April
1830

Received
Entry Takers
fee 25 cents

Certified
Copy issued
the same
day of
Entry

with the same South westwardly to the point of beginning to include Sale Creek as near the Centre of
the survey as practicable and the Survey to be an
oblong Square twice as long as wide the length way
down the Creek

John Skillern}
&   } Locators
Henry Miller()}
1st April 1830

PAGE 142

No. 4
Wm. James
100 acres
General
Entry

Location Re-
ceived & this
Entry made
April the 20th
1830

Certified Copy
issued and sent
to Locator by
James Brock
7 June, 1830

State of Tennessee} William James this Day Enters one
                   } hundred Acres of Land in Said County
Hamilton County   } on Roaring fork of Sale Creek on
                    foot of Waldens Ridge Beginning on
two Hickory the fourth Corner of John Witt, Shelton
and Cambles Entry Thence Northwardly with Said line to
the third Corner of Said Entry Thence with Said Line
to the Second Corner thence So as to Include One hundred Acres

Wm. James, Locator

Entry fees paid $-25

PAGE 142

No. 5
John Russell
and Others
200 Acres
General Entry

Location Recd.
and this
Entry made
this 21st Day
of April 1830

Certified
Copy Issued

State of Tennessee} John Russell George Reed James
                   } Jones & Henry L. Smith Enters two
Hamilton County   } Hundred acres of Land in said
                    County Beginning on a double Sy-
camore Markt with the Letters R.B. on the South west
Side of Ooltewah Island in the Tennessee River near
Low water Mark Running Down Said River to Lower point
of Said Island thence with the meanders of the River
to the upper point of Said Island thence Down the meanders of the River to the Beginning So as to include
the Ooltewah Island.

John Russell, George Reed
James Jones, H. L. Smith
Locators

PAGE 143

No. 6.   : State of Tennessee| Entry Takers Office 29th April
Jeremiah Jones   :   (1830
150 Acres   : Hamilton County | Jeremiah Jones Enters one hundred
General   :   and fifty acres of land on the
Entry   : side of Wallons ridge in sd. County of Hamilton Be-
                     : ginning on a Maple marked J.J. on the bank of Soddy
Location Re-   : Creek & Running north Eastwardly with the various
ceived and   : meanders of the sd. Wallons Ridge 300 poles to a
this Entry   : Stake at the foot of said Ridge to include an improve-
made here   : ment made by said Jones & now occupied by Andrew Mitch-
29th April   : ell. Thence Westwardly eighty poles to a stake thence
1830   : Southwardly 300 poles to the bank of said Soddy Creek
                     : Thence down the various meanders of said Creek to the
Received Entry   : beginning.
Takers fee   :
Seventy five   :   J.H. Jones, Locator
cents   : A Copy of the Original Location.
                     :
Certified   :
Copy issued   :
& delivered   :
to Locator   :
same day of   :
Entry   :
                     :
PAGE 143   :
                     :
No. 7   : State of Tennessee| Entry Takers Office Dallas., 11th
Thomas A. Moore   : | May 1830 Thomas A. Moore Enters
En. 300 acres   : Hamilton County |0   three hundred acres of land in
General Entry   :   said County Beginning at a Black
                     : Oak Tree in the most northwardly line of John Browns
Location Re-   : Reservation tract of land marked with the letter M
ceived & this   : and supposed to br corner to Robert Cozby's 100 acre
Entry made   : Entry of No. 13. Running thence East along said
the 11th May   : Reservation line — poles to the Corner of Richard
1830   : G. Waterhouses 52 acre Entry No. 34 Thence North
                     : with the line thereof to another or others of water-
Received Entry   : houses Entries to the north west Corner of Entry No.
Takers fee   : 26 whereon Thomas James now lives. Thence North-
Seventy five   : westwardly to Entry No. 3 of 160 acres Whereon William
Cents   : H. Stringer now lives Thence Southwestwardly with
                     : said Stringer to Henry R. Simmermans & Robert Coz-
Certified Copy   : by's lines to the beginning.
issued and   :
delivered to   :   Signed
Locator the same: Thomas A. Moon
day of Entry   :   Locator
                     :
PAGE 144   :
No. 8   : State of Tennessee| Hardy Hagle. His Location made
Hardy Hagle   : |25 May 1830 and enters one hun-
Enters 100 Acres: Hamilton County |dred acres of land beginning on

General Entry

Location Received and this Entry made the 25 May 1830

Received Entry takers fee Seventy five cents

Certified Copy

PAGE 145

No. 9
John B. Russel
William Rogers
&
Henry L. Rogers
240 ----
General Entry

Entry made
25 May
1830

fees of office
paid
fees 75¢
& Coppy Isd.

PAGE 146

No. 10
Elisha Rogers
&
Henry L. Smith
Enters 480
Acres
General Entry

Location re-
turned this
Entry made
29 May 1830

Received
Entry Taker

---

a chestnut Corner of McSpadans Line near the foot of Wallans ridge runing Northward Sixty poles to a Stake thence Westward along the South Side of Said ridge to Terry Riddles Corner on a white oak thence along said line to the west fork of opossom Creek thence down Said Creek to the said McSpadans Line thence along sd. McSpadans Line to the beginning.

Hardy Hagle
Locator

A copy for the original.

State of Tennessee) John Russell, James B. Russel
William Rogers & Henry L. Smith
Hamilton County   enters Two Hundred & forty acres
of land in Said County on the
Side of Walens Ridge Begining on a Chestnutt on the South Side of McGills Creek thence South 10 East 140 poles to a double Chestnut thence South 60 East 200 poles to James B. Russell Line thence with said line North 70 poles to a Blackoak & Two post oaks thence North 30 west 28 poles to three Populars thence North 60 west 220 poles, to the Beginning so as to Include Two Hundred & forty acres.

John Russel
James B. Russel
William Rogers
Henry L. Smith
Locators

State of Tennessee) Elisha Rogers and Henry L. Smith
Enters fore Hundred & Eighty
Hamilton County   acres of Land in Said County on
the Side of Wallens Ridge Begin-
ing on a white oak Near James Keenys Brick House thence North East fore Hounndred & Eighty poles with the various Couses of James Keenys Line To a Stake thence west one Hundred & Sixty poles to a stake thence South west four Hundred & Eighty poles to a State thence according to Law to the Geginning so as to in Clude 480 acres 28 May, 1830.

fees 75¢   Elisha Rogers
Coppy Isd.   H.L. Smith
                  Locators

PAGE 147

No. 11
Elisha Rogers
&
Henry L. Smith
640 Acres
General Entry

Location Returned:
this Entry made
29 May 1830

Received Entry
takers fees 75

Copy Isd.

State of Tennessee   Elisha Rogers & Henry L. Smith
                       this Day enters 640 acres of
Hamilton County   Land in Said County Beginning
                       on the Side of Wallens Ridge
on a Hickory and Red Ellum thence North East with
the general Couses of Wallens Ridge 320 poles to
a stake thence Northwest thre Hundred & Seventy
poles to a Stake on the side of the afforesaid
Ridge thence South west 320 poles to a stake thence
according to Law to the Beginning including the
House whate John Hopper now Lives also the place
where James Agee lives and the place whare Isaak
Barnes lives and the mill so as to include the six
Hundred & forty acres.
May 27, 1830

                       Elisha Rogers
                       H.L. Smith
                       Locators

PAGE 148

No. 12
Enters 80
Acres of
Land
General
Entry

Location
returned and
Entry
made
1 June
1830

State of Tennessee   Entry Takers
                     Dallas
Hamilton County   1 June 1830
                     Elisha Rogers enters eighty acres
of Land on the waters of Mountain Creak begining at
a white oak and Black oak marked with the Letter B.
Standing near the Line between Robert Lauderdil &
Elisha Rogers at the foot of Wallens Ridge & runing
thence north Eastwardly with the various meandors
of the foot of wallens Ridge to a Lane between Said
Rogers & James Keeny Thence North westerly up the
said Ridge forty poles. Thence Southwesterly to a
point on Wellans Ridge for whitch an East line will
strike the point of beginning at 40 poles thence
East 40 poles to the begining.

                       Elisha Rogers
                       Locators

PAGE 149
No. 13
Asahel Rawlings
100 acres
of land
General
Entry

Location
received
and this
Entry

State of Tennessee   Entry takers Office
                     Dallas,
Hamilton County   1st June 1830
                     Asahel Rawlings Enters one hun-
dred acres of land on Wallins Ridge on the waters of
Rocky Creek. Beginning at a Chestnut Oak Tree standing on the top bluff of Rocks a few poles north of
the Fields old trace on the Ridge west of the first
hollow from where said trace goes up the mountain
and runing thence northwardly along said bluff or
top brink of said Ridge 30 poles.
Thence northwestwardly one hundred poles. Thence
Southwestwardly to the bluff of Rocky Creek---thence
down with the meanders of the Clift bluff of said

made 1st June
1830

Creek to the brink of the said ridge or hill thence
up with the meanders of the top bluff & brink of the
Ridge to the beginning to include a Calebiate or
other mineral spring of water issueing from the south
edge of said Fields old trace Running across said
Ridge

(Signed) Asahel Rawlingsl,Locator

PAGE 150

No. 14
James Keny
General Entry
125 acres

Location re
turned this
entry made
2 Day June 1830

rsceived entry
takers fee
Coppy Isd.

State of Tennessee   James Keny enters one hundred
                      and twenty five acres of Land
Hamilton County   in Hamilton County on the Side
                      of Wallens ridge, Begining on a
Walnut and poplar marked B on the west bank of Mountain Creek Runing up said Creek Northward two hundred poles to a Stake thence westwardly one hundred
poles to a Stake thence Southwardly two hundred poles
to a stake thence Eastwardly with the division Line
between James Keeny and William Lauderdale one hundred
poles to the Beginning to include one hundred and
Twenty five acres of Land

James Keney
Locator, 2 June 1830

PAGE 151

No. 15
James Brock
100 acres
Prefference or
Occupant
Entry

Location Re-
ceived and this
Entry made
7th June 1830

Received
Entry Takers
fee
75¢

State of Tennessee   Entry Takers Office 7th June 1830
                      James Brock enters one hundred
Hamilton County   acres of land in said County on
                      the south side of Wallins Ridge
on the Waters of Sale Creek Beginning at a pine and
chestnut Trees Standing on the Spur of said Ridge
that divides the Waters of Russulls and Rogers Branches Runing thence northwardly one hundred and eighty
poles along the sout side of the Ridge to a stake.
Thence Eastwardly ninety poles to a stake near Russells branch at the foot of Wallens Ridge. Thence
South westwardly along with the various meanders of
the foot of Wallens Ridge one hundred and eighty
poles to a stake. Thence Westwardly to the beginning.

(Signed) James Brock
Locator
Certified Copy of this location issued and delivered
to Locator on the day od Entry

PAGE 151

No. 16
Elisha Rogers

State of Tennessee   Elisha Rogers enters three hun-
                      dred and fifty acres of land
Hamilton County   in Said County on Mountain
                      Creek Begin-

General Entry

ing at a black oak at the foot of Wallens Ridge Corner to William and Robert Lauderdells tracts of land

Location received:
and this entry
8 JUNE 1830

& Runing thence Eastwardly with the line between the said tracts of Robert Lauderdell & the track laid off for William Lauderdle & whitch is n w owned & possessed by Elisha Rogers to the back line thereof about 250 poles thence North Eastwardly with the line of said Survey to a Chestnut tree Corner to James Keeneys line thence north Westwardly to the foot of Wallens Ridge thence Down with the various meanders of the foot of Wallens Ridge to the begining.

Copy Isd.
14 March
1831

Elisha Rogers
Locator, 8 June, 1830

PAGE 152

No. 17
James Keeney
Enters
400 acres
General
Entry

State of Tennessee| James Keeney Enters four hundred
                  | acres of land in Said County on
Hamilton County | Mountain Creek Begining at a
                  | Post Oak & two black oaks on a
spur of Wallens Ridge marked as a Corner of William Lauderdils & James Keeneys tracts of land & Runing thence South 63 West 246 poles to a Chestnut another Corner to Said Survey thence north 20 East three hundred poles thence north westwardly to a white oak at the foot of Wallens Ridge marked as a Corner to Said Keeneys Servey 339 acres made by Samuel R. Russell thence Down with the various meanders of the foot of Said Ridge to the point of Begining.

This Location
and this
Entry made
8 June 1830

received
Entry takers
fees 75¢

James Keeney, Locator
8th June 1830

Certified Copy Issued this
13th April 1831

Cornelius Milliken
E. T. H. C.

PAGES 153 & 154
(Blank)

PAGE 155
No. 18
Terry Riddle
&
Elisha Rogers
1600 General
Entry

State of Tennessee| Terry Riddle & Elisha Rogers
                  | Enters Sixteen hundred acres
Hamilton County | of Land on Mountain Creak in
                  | said County Begining at a white
oak Tree Standing on a Spur of Wallons Ridge marked as a Corner to James Keeneys Land Runing thence north Eastwardly along Said Keeneys line of the 2000 acre Grant of North Carlina to Stokeley Donelson of No. 283 dated 20 July 1795 thence North Sixty three Degrees East along the line of said

Location returned:
8 June 1830
this entry made
the same day

GRANT nine hundred poles thence northwardly to Wallens Ridge thence a direct Course to the Begining.

Entry takers
fees paid 75¢

Terry Riddel
Elisha Rogers
Locators

Copy Isd.
14 March
1831

PAGE 156

No. 19
John Lovelady
25 acres
General Entry

State of Tennessee) John Lovelady Enters twenty five acres of land in said County Between John Browns Reservation and Hamilton County) David Fields Reservation Begining on a post oak on Waterhouses line thence Runing with said line Sixty four poles Southwardly to a Stake on or near Robert Cozbys Line then Sixty four poles to a stake then Northwardly Sixty four poles to a stake then to the Beginning So as to Include 25 acres June the 15th Day 1830

Location Received and
this
Entry
15th June
1830

John Lovelady
Locator

Certified Copy Issued this 18(?) of April 1831

Cornelius Milliken
E. T. H. C.

PAGE 156

No. 20
George Birdwell
100 acres of
land
Wallens Ridge

State of Tennessee() George Birdwell enters one hundred and seventy acres of land Hamilton County () on the side and top of Wallens Ridge of Cumberland Mountain. Beginning on a small Poplar Marked B & hickory standing on the south east side of said Ridge about 10 or 12 poles eastwardly from a calebiate spring issuing from the side of said Ridge. Runing thence northwestwardly about one hundred and eighty poles to the second Corner of an Entry of 100 acres made on said Ridge by Asahel Pawlings of No. 13 dated 1st June 1830. Thence with a line of said Pawlings' Entry Northwestwardly along the bluff & Cliff of a hill one hundred and fifty poles thence Eastwardly about one hundred and eighty poles & thence a direct line along the side of the Mountain or Ridge to the beginning to include said Calibeate spring.

Location Received &
this
Entry
made
15th June 1830

Entry Takers
EEE 75¢
Received

George Birdwell, Locator
15th June, 1830

PAGE 157

No. 21
John Ritchmond
Enters 75 Acres
of Land on
Wallens Ridge

Location Returned
and this entry
made 1 July 1830

Fees paid 75¢
Copy Isd.
21 December 1830

State of Tennessee |
Hamilton County (

John Ritchmon Enters Seventy
five acres of Land in said
County on the Top of Wallens
Ridge on the South Side of
waters of opossum Creek Begining on a Vhestnut red
oak on the East end of Andrew Mitchells Entry of
fifty acres thence Southwardly 140 thence Eastwardly thence Northwardly thence westwardly to the beginning so as to include seventy five acres of
land 1 July 1830

John Ritchmon
Locator

PAGE 157

No. 22
William C. Henly
enters 500 acres
of Land on
Wallens Ridge

Location returned
and this entry
made 19 July 1830

fees of office
paid 75

State of Tennessee |
Hamilton County (

William C. Henley enters five
hundred acres of land in Said
County on the top of Wallens
Ridge on the waters of Rockky
Creek Beginning on a pine tree thence Northwardly
thence Westwardly thence Southwardly thence Eastwardly to the beginning so as to include the improvement James Singleton(?) improved and also to include
five Hundred acres of land.

William C. Henly
Locator

July 19, 1830

No. 23
PAGE 158
ElishaRogers
Terry Riddle
&
Henry L. Smith
Enters 35 acres
of land

this Location
returned and this
Entry made
21 July 1830

fees of office
paid 75 cents

State of Tennessee |
Hamilton County (

Elisha Rogers, Terry Riddle &
Henry L. Smith Enters Thirty
five acres of land in Said
County begining on a black
oak the Corner of Elisha Rogers three Hundred &
fifty acres thence East Eighty poles to a stake t e
thence South 63 west one Hundred poles to John
Keeneys line thence with Sd. Keeneys line Sixty
poles to post thence Straight Line to the Beginning so as to in Clude Thirty five acres.
July 21, 1830

Elisha Rogers
Terry Riddel
H. S. Smith
Locators

PAGE 158
No. 24

State of Tennessee |
Hamilton County (

Terry Riddel Elisha Rogers
Henry L. Smith Benjamin Cherry
and John Cummings Enters one

Terry Riddle
and others
1000 acres of
land

This Location
returned
and this
Entry made
21 July 1830

fees of office
paid
75¢

thousand acres of land in Sd. County Beginning on a
black oak on the North Side of the Main Mountain
Creek Road on the East side of Elisha Rogers track
of land where he now lives Runing thence North Sixty
Three east Six hundred poles to a stake at the by
Ridge on the Side of the Brown's ferry Roads thence
along the Said of said Ridge Seven hundred poles to
a stak thence North two hundred to a stake thence a
direct line to the begining.
21 July 1830

Terry Riddel
Elisha Rogers
Henry L. Smith
Benjm. Cherry
John Cummings

PAGE 159

No. 25
John Keeney
enters
60 acres
of land on
Mountain Creek

This Location
returned and
this Entry made
24 July 1830

fees of office
paid 75 cents

Certified Copy
Issued this
18th Aprile 1831

STATE of TENNESSEE   John Keeney enters sixty acres
                      of Land in Hamilton County Be-
HAMILTON COUNTY   gining on a west line Runing
                      from the mouth of North Chicka-
mogga to the foot of wallens Ridge Begining on a
pine on said west line and at the foot of Said Ridge
marked J.K.B. Runing thence North Sixty three degrees
West one hundred and fifty poles to a stake on a line
botween Robert Lauderdill and William Lauderdill thence
westwardly with Said line to the foot of Waldens Ridge
to a Stake thence to the Beginning so as to include
Sixty acres this 23 July 1830.

John Keeney
Locator

PAGE 160

No. 26

(This space
blank)

Andrew Jackson McLemore and Archabal Overton Lyon
and Christopher H. Stump By Virtue of And Act of
Assembly passed at Nashville on the 9th day Jany
1830 Enters five thousand Acres of land in Hamole-
ton County and to Begin on the North Bank of Tennessee River and at the Mouth of Suck Creek thence
Northwardly with the East Boundery of Marion County to t
to the top of Waldens Ridge and thence East.
July 31, 1830

John Stump
Locator

PAGE 160

No. 27

(blank)

Andrew Jackson Mclemore and Acrhable Overton Lyon
and Christopher H. Stump by virtue of and act of assembly passed at Nashville on the Ninth Day Jany.
1830 enters five thousand acres of land in Hamilton
County and on the waters of Chickamogga Creek and
on the Spurs of Walddens Ridge and to begin at
North East Corner of a track of land this day Entered in the Name of Andrew Jackson Mclemore and
Archabel Overton Lyon and Christopher H. Stump to
Rund North and East
July 31, 1830

                              Jno. Stump
                              Locater

PAGE 161

No. 28

(Blank)

Charles Walker & Fredrick H. Stump By Virtue of and
act of assembley passed at Nashville on the Ninth
Day of Jany. 1830 Enters five thousand acres of land
in Hamilton County and on the waters of Sandy Creek
and on the Gap and Spurs of Waldens Ridge to begin
on the North East Corner of a frack of land this
Entered in the Names of Andrew Jackson Mclemore
and Christopher H. Stump and to Run North & East
July 31, 1830

                              Jno. Stump
                              Locator

PAGE 162
No. 29
(Blank)

State of Tennessee | William James and James Brock
                   | this Day Enters one hundred &
Hamilton County | Sixty acres of land in said
                     County on Wallens Ridge waters
of Sale Creek Beginning on a Red Oak and Black Gum
on Tiptons line thence Southwardly one hundred &
Sixty poles to a stake thence Eastwardly one hundred
and Sixty pole to a stake. Thence northwardly one
hundred and Sixty poles to a stake thence westware-
ly one hundred and sixty poles to the Beginning.

                              William James
                              James Brock
                              Locators
Oct. the — 1830

Certified Copy Issued this 24th of May 1831
                    (No signature)

PAGE 162

No. 30

(Blank)

State of Tennessee| William James and James Brock
this Day Enters Two hundred
Hamilton County | acres of Land on Waldens Ridge
waters of Sale Creek on both
Sides of Witts Turnpike Road Beginning on a Sassafras and Dogwood thence Southwardly three hundred
& twenty poles to a stake thence Westwardly one
hundred poles to a stake thence Northwardly three
Hundred and twenty poles to a Stake thence Eastwardly one hundred poles to the Beginning.
October the 18th 1830

William James
&
James Brock
Locators
Certified Copy Issued this 24th of May 1831

(Entry taker's name omitted)

PAGE 163

No. 31
Arnel Moss
Enters 100
acres of ——

This Location
received
9 September
1830
This entry
made the
same day

fees of
office
paid 75

State of Tennessee| Arnol Moss enters one hundred
acres of Land Lying and being in
Hamilton County | Hamilton County aforesaid at the
foot of Waldens Ridge near the
Tennessee River Begining on a white oak near the h ead
of a spring inCluded in a preceding entry made by
Thomas Hopkins on the place whare said Moss now lives
Thence Running Southwardly Northwestwardly & westwardly and thence to the begining so as to include
one hundred acres
9th Sept. 1830

Arnold Moss
Locator
Coppy Isd. 6 June 1831 and returned(?).

(No signature)

PAGE 163

No. 32

(Blank)

State of Tennessee| Entry Takers office Dallas
18th Sept. 1830
Hamilton County | Laran Smith enters three Hun-
dred acres of Land on Waldens
Ridge of Cumberland Mountain begining at a Chestnut
Tree Standing on the East Side of McIntufs fork of
Chickamaga Creek & Runing thence North Eastwardly
to Middle Creek thence up with the manders of mid-

del Creek to a Stake thence westwardly to said Mcintufs Creek thence Down said Creek with the manders
thereof to the beginning.

Layton Smith
Locator

PAGE 164

No. 33

(Blank)

State of Tennessee) Solomon Baker two Hundred acres
                     of Land in said County Beginning
Hamilton County   on a Spanish oak Standing on a
                     Clift of a branch of Oposom Creek
                     on the south side of said Creek
Running westwardly 127 poles to a Stake Southwardly
254 poles to a Stake thence Eastwardly 127 poles to
a Stake thence to the Beginning so as to Include 200
acres. October the 19th Day

Solomon Baker
Locator

Certifyd Copy Issued 1830 same Date.

PAGE 164

No. 34
John Ritchmon
Enters Eighty
acres of
Land

General Entry

fees of office
paid 75¢

Coppy Isd.
10 March
1831

State of Tenesee) John Ritchmon enters Eighty acres
                     of Land lying in Said County on
Hamilton County   the deviding Ridge between the
                     waters of Rocky and oposom Creek
at the foot of Waldens Ridge in Cluding the month of
a Cave between said Creeks Beginning on a white oak
tree Standing near the foot of Said Waldens Ridge
and near a Small branch whith runs into oposom first
after it comes out of the mountain Runing Northwardly
160 poles then Eastwardly thence Southwardly and westwardly and westwardly to the beginning including the
Spring at the side of said Waldens Ridge
December 1830

John Ritchmond
Locator

PAGE 165

No. 35
John Talaferro
250 acres

General Entry

State of Tennessee) John Talaferro Enters 250 acres
                     of Land in hamilton County on
Hamilton County   the North bank of Tennessee Riv-
                     er Beginning on a Sycamore tree
at or near the Tumbling Shoals Running Eastward up
said Tennessee River to George Williams Corner thence

Location Recd. : along Said Williams line to Freeman line thence North-
and this : ward thence westwardly thence southwardly to the Be-
entry : ginning so as to inClude 250 acres of Land.
made this : 30th December 1830
30th :
December 1830 :
: John Talaferro
: Locator
Copy Isd. :
13 September 1831: Fees of -- paid $.75
:
:

PAGE 165 :
:
No. 36 : State of Tennessee| George Williams and Cornelius
George Williams : | Milliken Enters 2 acres of Land
& : Hamilton County | in Sd. County Lying on Each of
Cornelius Mil- : | Middle Creek Beginning on a Dog-
liken 2 acres : wood on the East side of Sd. Creek Supposed to be on
: or near James Qualls line of fifteen acre tract and
: near Kellys turnpike Road Running North 20 poles to
General Entry : A stake at the foot of a Clift thence west 16 P to a
: stake thence 20 p. Down said Creek to a Stake to the
: Beginning so as to InClude two acres of land
Location : January the 10th 1831
Recd. and :
this :
Entry : George Williams
made : &
January : Cornelius Milliken
the 10th : Locators
1831 :
: Certifyd Copy Issd. this 10th of January 1831
:
: Cornelius Milliken
: Entry taker for
: H. County
:
:
:
:

PAGE 166 :
:
No. 37 : State of Tennessee| George Williams and Cornelius Mil-
G. Williams : | liken Enters Twenty five acres of
& : Hamilton County | Land in Said County and on the
Cornelius Mil- : | North Side of Kelly's turnpike
liken : Road beginning on a white oak Corner to Arnold Mosses
25 acres : Entry Running thence northwardly fortytwo & ½ P thence
: westwardly 85 P thence Southwardly 42½ P thence East-
: wardly 85 P to the Beginning So as to Include 25 acres
General : of Land.
Entry : January the 10th 1831
:
: George Williams
: &
: Cornelius Milliken

Location | fees of office paid $.75
Received and | Certified Copy Issued this
this Entry | 10th January 1831
made the
10th Day of | Cornelius Milliken
June, 1831 | En. taker for
| H. County

PAGE 166

No. 38 | State of Tennessee | George Williams & Cornelius Mil-
G. Williams | | liken Enters 50 acres of Land
& | Hamilton County | in said County Beginning on a
C. Milliken | | Dogwood Just below Qualles Mill
50 acres | and on the line of a 15 acre tract of Land whereon
| James qualls now lives and Running with Sd. line 140
| p to a stake on or near McVeys line thence with Sd.
General | line 70 P. westwardly to a stake thence northwardly
Entry | 140 p So as to Include a small field to a Stake thence
| a Straight line to the Beginning So as to Include 50
| acres of Land.

Location | George Williams
Recd. and | &
this Entry | Cornelius Milliken
made this | Locators
10th
of January | January the 10th 1831
1831 | Fees of office paid $.75
| Certified Copy Issued this 10
| of January 1831

| Cornelius Milliken
| Entry taker for H. County

PAGE 167

No. 39 | State of Tennessee | James Moss enters twelve & a half
James Moss | | acres of land in said County. Be-
12½ acres of | Hamilton County | ginning on a sycamore tree on the
land by | | north bank of Tennessee River
| thence runing northwardly to Milliken and Williams line
| Thence westwardly with their line to Tallafero's line
General Entry | to the River. Thence up the River with the meanders
| thereof to the beginning so as to include twelve and a
| half acres of land.
Location re- | 19th Jan. 1831.
ceived & this
entry made this | James Moss
19th day of Jan.
1831. Office
recd. & Copy isd.

PAGE 167

No. 40
Alexander
Freeman
50 acres
of land by
General
Entry

Location
received &
Entry made
24 Jan. 1831

Office fee received Certified
Copy Issued this
13th Day of
April 1831

State of Tennessee Alexander Freeman Enters fifty
acres of land in said County. Beginning on a white Oak corner of
an entry made by Joshua Johnson

Hamilton County

and William H. Stringer for fifty eight acres. Southwardly with George W. Williams line to David Fields
reservation line Thence Eastwardly along said Reservation line Corner of an Entry made by Hugh Cunningham
for twenty five acres thence northwardly along the
said Cunningham's line to two post oaks corner to the
same Thence Eastwardly along the said Cunninghams line
thence northwardly along Sciveleys line so as to intersect a corner of an Entry made by Johnson and Stringer,
Thence Westwardly along Johnson and Stringers line to
the beginning. This 34th day of January 1831

Alexander Freeman
Locator

PAGE 168

No. 41
John Frederick
5000 acres
of land by
General Entry

Location Received and this
Entry made 3d.
day of February
1831

State of Tennessee John Fredrick enters 5000 acres
of land in said County in Tennessee State lying and being in
Hamilton County on the Top of

Hamilton County

Wallens Ridge beginning on a double White Oak marked
H.B. at the northwest corner of Bradens 640 acre
survey. Thence runing north Westwardly nine hundred
and sixty poles thence a north eastwardly Course
crossing some headwaters of North Chickamaga Creek
Thence round South Eastwardly & South westwardly to
the beginning for complement.
Exclusive of all old Entries.

John Frederick
Locator

3 February 1831
I assign and transfer and convey the above entry with
all of it appurtenances to Laton K. Smith this 20th
Day of January 1838

John Frederick (sel[?)

PAGE 168

No. 42
Asahel Rawlings
Junior 100 acres
of land by

State of Tennessee Asahel Rawlings Junior enters
one hundred acres of land in
said County on Wallens Ridge
of Cumberland Mountain on the

Hamilton County

General Entry

Location
Received
& this
entry made
3 February
1831

most westwardly draughts of Soddy Creek. Beginning
at a Post Oak tree about 50 poles South of Suttons
Cabbin on the trace crossing said ridge between
Hastin Poe's and Alexander Kellys running thence
West 80 poles thence North 100 thence east 160 poles
thence South 100 poles thence West 80 poles to the
beginning to include said Cabbin near the Center of
said survey.

> Asahel Rawlings
> Locator
> 3 February 1831

PAGE 169

No. 43
David Beck
1500 Acres

General Entry

Location
recd. and
this Entry
made this
14th of
February
1831

State of Tennessee |
Hamilton County |

David Beck Enters fifteen Hundred acres of land in said County on the north Side of Tennessee River Beginning on a Post oak Corner to Elisha Parkers and the said David Becks Entry Running westwardly along Parkers line to Waterhouses line thence along the said line to a fifty acre Entry made by Thomas James Senr. thence along his line to his Corner northwestwardly thence to the head of a hollow Eastwardly thence to waterhouses ash Corner on the River thence to the Beginning so as to Include 1500 acres.
February the 14th Day 1831

> David Beck
> Locator

Certifyd Copy issued

PAGE 169

No. 44
James Brimer
100 acres
General
Entry

Location
Received and
this Entry
made
15 Feb.
1831

Copy Issued
10th March
1839

State of Tennessee |
Hamilton County |

James Brimer Enters one hundred acres of land in said County Begining on a black oak Corner of Mager A. Jacksons one hundred Acre Entry runing Northwardly thence Eastwardly thence Southwardly thence various Corses to the begining so as to include one hundred of land.
15 Februry 1831

> his
> James X Brimer
> mark

Attest.
Thomas Windham

PAGE 170

No. 45
James Brock
125 Acres

General Entry

Location
Recd. and
this
Entry
made this
28th Day
of February
1831

State of Tennessee | James Brock Enters one Hundred
                   | and Twenty five acres of Land
Hamilton County | in said County on the South
                   | Side of Wallens Ridge on the
watters of Sale Creek on whats Called McGills Creek
Beginning on a Sycamore and Poplar trees Standing
on the north side of said Creek Running thence Southwardly along the South Side of said Ridge one Hundred
and Sixty poles thence Eastwardly one Hundred and
Twenty-five poles to a stake thence northwardly one
Hundred and Sixty poles to a stake thence westwardly
according to Law to the Beginning.

James Brock
Locator

Certifyd Copy Issued the 28th Day of February 1831

PAGE 171

No. 46
George W. Wil-
liams
Alford Rogers
3000 acres

General Entry
made 14 March
1831

Fees of
Office paid
75¢

Coppy Isd.
14 March
1831

State of Tennessee | George W. Williams and Alford M.
                   | Rogers enters three thousand
Hamilton County | acres of land in Hamilton County
                   | on the waters of Chickamaga
Creak Beginning on a Hickry and Red Ellum on the side
of Wallens Ridge thence Southwestwardly meanding said
Ridge thre hundred and twenty poles to a stake thence
Southwardly to the Northwest Line of the twenty thousand acre track belonging to McClung & Cozby thence
with said line North Eastwardly so as to inClude three
thousand acres thence Northwestwardly to the foot of
said Ridge thence with the meanders of the Said Ridge
to the Begining.
14th March 1831

Geo. W. Williams
&
Alflord M. Rogers
Locators

PAGE 172

No. 47
James Bunch

General
Entry
made 25 March
1831

State of Tennessee | James Bunch Enters three hundred
                   | acres of land on the Waters of
Hamilton County | Coopers Creek a branch of Chick-
                   | amaga Creek on Wallens Ridge of
Cumberland Mountain. Beginning at a marked White Oak
And persimmon trees Standing on the south side of an
Eastern branch of said Coopers Creek and runing thence
North eastwardly 40 poles Thence southwardly thence
Westwardly. Thence northwardly for complement to the

PAGE 172

No. 49
Merrideth
Webb
&
Thomas Webb
Enters
March
25th
1831

State of Tennessee] Merrideth Webb & Thomas Webb enters two hundred acres of land in
Hamilton County | said County on Coopers Creek a branch of Chickamaga Creek on Wallens Ridge Beginning on a marked black Oak tree standing on the north bank of said Coopers Creek Runing thence northeastwardly thence northwestwardly thence Southwestwardly & southeastwardly for Compliment to the beginning to include two small improvements made by the Webbs.
25th March 1831

fees of
office
paid

Copy issued the
day of Entry

his
William X Bunch
mark

PAGE 173

No. 49
Henry Simmerman
Enters
75 acres

State of Tennessee] Henery R. Simmerman Enters Seventy five acres of Land in Said
Hamilton County | County Beginning on the North Corner of an Entry made of fifty one acres made by Henery R. Simerman No. 18 Dated 5 July 1824(?) thence runing along a Line of an Entry made by William H. Stringer to Samuel R. Russels Entry of 43¾ No. 111 Dated 11 September 1828. Thence runing with Said Lines to Fieldes Reservation then Southwestwardly with Said Line to an Entry made by James Smith near Heckbeth Tabors thence Southwardly with said Entry to an Entry made by John Lovelady of twenty five acres thence South east to a Line of of fifty one acres Entry by Henry R. Simerman No. 17 Dated 5 July 1824(?) thence running Northwardly to a Corner of said fifty one acres thence Southwardly with Said Line of 51 acres to a corner tree near the top of a Ridge near Rode Ledding to Rosses ferry thence Northwardly to a corner of fifty one acres before stated and the same being No. 18 thence Northwardly with Said Line to a corner of Said fifty one acres thence with Said Line to the Beginning this 26 March 1831

General Entry

Fees of office
paid 75¢

This Entry
received
this Entry made
26 March
1831

Coppy Isd.
December
1831

Coppy Isd.
19 April 1833

Henry R. Simmerman
Locator

PAGE 174
No. 50
Henery R. Simmer-
man

State of Tennessee] Henry R. Simmerman Enters in Said County Seventy five acres of Land
Hamilton County | beginning on a black oak on a

Enters 75 acres	Line of a preference Entry made by Ritchard G. Water- house and being the Same william H. Stringer at pres- ent resides and being on the South Side of Said Entry
	thence Southwardly with Said Line to an Entry of Twen-
General Entry	ty acres entered by william H. Stringer thence South- wardly with Said Line to an entry made by Henry R. Sim- merman and No. 18 dated 5 July 1824 thence Southwardly with Said Line 128 poles to a corner of said Entry
This Location received andthis Entry made 26 March 1831	thence South 60 East to an Entry made by Ritchard water- house thence with said Line Northwardly to an Entry made by Thomas James Esquire thence Northwardly with said Line to a corner of Said Entry thence Northwardly to the beginning 26 March 1831

Henry R. Simmerman
Locator

fees of -- paid 75¢	Coppy Isd. 19 April, 1833

PAGE 175

No. 51 Thomas Shirley & John Cummings 434 acres	State of Tennessee} Thomas Shirley and John Cummings Hamilton County } Entere four Hundred and thirty four acres of Land in said County Beginning on the South Side of Wallens Ridge and on the north Side of tennessee River
General Entry	Beginning on a post oak and three pine trees about a half a mile above the tumbling Shoals in Said River Running thence South two Hundred and forty poles to a Hackberry and Box Elder Markt T.S. crossing a slew of Tennessee River to an Island the first above the
Location Recd. and this Entry made this 18th Day of April 1831	Suck in said River thence with the meandering said River North fortyeight west Twenty one poles to two ashes thence South Eleven Degrees East fifty four poles to a hackberry thence South nine East fifty poles to an ash thence South Six East thirty six poles to an ash thence south two west forty two poles to an ash thence South two west forty two poles to an ash thence South Eleven East thirty Eight poles to an ash thenceSouth fifteen East fifty four poles to a hack- berry thence South Ten East forty poles to Box Elder thence South two East twenty Six poles to a maple thence
Certifyd Copy Issued this 19th of April 1831 Cornelius Milliken E.T.H.C.	South fifteen East thirty poles to a sassafras thence South Twenty Seven East twenty Eight poles to a box elder thence South twenty four East Twentyeight poles to a box Elder thence south thirty Seven East Twenty four poles to a locust thence South fifty three East thirty poles to a Hackberry thence South Sixty one East thirty four poles to a Maple thence South Sixty two East twenty poles to a Cherry tree thence south Seventy five East twenty poles to a Black Locust thence South

<table>
<tr><td>

fees
of
office
paid
$00.75

</td><td>

Eighty six East thirty poles to a Black Locust at
the upper End of said Island thence North fifty three
West, Twenty poles to a Black Walnut thence North
Seven West Sixty two poles to an ash, thence North
twenty-four west 8 poles toa Black oak, thence North
six west fifty four poles to a mulberry thence north
6 East twenty two poles to two poplars, thence North
Seven East twelve poles to a forked Mulberry thence
North twenty four poles to a black Locust thence N
North Seven East twenty poles to a black Locust thence
north twenty poles to a poplar thence North Seven west
twenty poles to a Sassafras thence North twenty four
west fifty two poles to a sassafras thence North forty
four west thirty Eight poles to two mulberrys thence
north fifty west thirty Eight poles to a poplar thence
north forty eight west Eighty Eight poles to a Mulberry
thence thirty sect twenty Eight poles to an ash, thence
North fortyeight west twan four poles to a Box Elder
thence a straight line to the Beginning so as to in-
clude an Island called Browns Island the first above
the Suck in Tennessee River.

Thomas Shirley
&
John Cummings
Locators

</td></tr>
</table>

PAGE 176

<table>
<tr><td>

No. 52
Josiah Gent
300 acres

General Entry

Location
Received
and this
Entry made
this 20th
Day of
April
1831

</td><td>

State of Tennessee| Josiah Gent Enters three hundred
                   | acres of Land lying on Wallens
Hamilton County | Ridge in hamilton County afore-
                       Said Beginning on a Double white
oak near a Sulphur Spring Running thence westwardly
across Chickamauga Creek to McGrews Creek thence
south wardly Eastwardly and northwardly to the Begin-
ning so as to include a house and orchard on said Moun-
tain and the Complement of Law aforesaid 19th Aprile
1831

Cornelius Milliken
Entry Taker for
said County

</td></tr>
</table>

PAGE 176

<table>
<tr><td>

No. 53
Thomas A. More

General Entry

</td><td>

State of Tennessee| Thomas A. More enters twelve hun-
                  | dred acres of land begining on the
Hamilton County | top of a ridge between Tenasee Riv-
                       er and the Vally rode leeding
from Washington to Ricksons ferry at the head of a hol-
low leading up from near whare Middleton Smith now

</td></tr>
</table>

1200 acres

fees
of
office
paid
75¢

lives on a black oak and two blackjacks marked T
Thence East to a grant climed by John Cornet whereon
James Smith and others lives thence North Eastwardly
to the Due West Line of the twenty thousand acre
Survey Claimed by McClung thence west to an Entry
or entrys where Wm. Archer(?) and David Cunningham
Lives thence with a line or lines of the same southwardly to a track of Land Whereon Thomas Roilston
lives thence southwardly with a line of the same to
the North(?) East corner of the same thence East to
the Beginning this 6 May 1831

Thomas A. More
Locator

PAGE 177

No. 54
George W. Williams
Enters
600 acres
of Land

Locqtion
Received
and this
Entry
made
6 June
1831

fees of office
paid 75¢

State of Tennessee | George W. Williams Enters Six
Hundred acres of Land in Said
Hamilton County | County on the Side of Waldens
Ridge Beginning on a white oak
on the North Bank of Tensee River near an old Camp
that James Arnel occupied Runing Northwardly thence
westwardly thence southwardly to Tenesee River thence
Eastwardly meandering said River to the Begining so
as to include the number of acres above named of
vecant land.
June 6, 1831

George W. Williams
Locator
Coppy Isd.

PAGE 177

No. 55
General Entry
John Cummings
Enters
300 acres

Location re-
ceived and
this Entry
made
July 9, 1831

State of Tennessee | John Cummings Enters three Hun-
dred acres of Land in Said Coun-
Hamilton County | ty on Wallins Ridge and on Coop-
ers Creek a branch of Chickamaga
creek and ajoining a sixty fore acre Entry made by
William Bunch and an other Entry made by James Bunch
on which the said Bunches now live Beginning on a
white oak and persimmon trees corner to said Bunches
Entrys standing on the south side of an Eastern Branch
of said Coopers Creek and Running thence north 23 degrees East 40 poles to another corner of James Bunches Entry thence northwardly thence Westwardly thence
Southwardly thence Eastwardly so as to include three
Hundred acres together with several springs in said

fees of office paid 75 cents : creek July 9, 1831

John Cummings
Locator

Coppy Isd.
July 9
1831

PAGE 178

No. 56
George B. Rogers
Enters 200
acres
of Land

State of Tennessee | George B. Roberts Enters two Hundred acres of Land on Waldens

Hamilton County | Ridge on Coops Creek begining on a pine and white oak Standing in a Drain Runing thence Northwardly to the fork of said branch to a stake thence westwardly thence southwardly thence Eastwardly for Complement to the begining.

George B. Roberts
Locator

Location
Received
and
this entry
made
6 August
1831

Coppy Isd.
6 August 1831

fees of office
paid 75¢

PAGE 178

No. 57

State of Tennessee | S. B. Hawkins Enters five thousand acres of Land in Said County

Hamilton County | and on Wallens Ridge of Cumberland mountain beginning on a Black oak marked thus S.B. near the falls of Suck Creek off of the mountain thence Eastwardly along the top of the mountain one thousand and fifty poles to a stake thence northwardly five hundred and twenty five poles to a stake thence westwardly one thousand and fifty poles to a stake thence a Straight line to the Beginning so as to Include five thousand acres of Land.   August the 16th day 1831

S. B. Hawkins
Locators

Page 179

No. 58
John Russell
and others

State of Tennessee | George Reed, John Russell and B.B. Cannon and James Jones Enters a

Hamilton County | Certain piece of Land Containing two hundred acres Begining on an

Enters	Elm on or near Asahel Rolings line on thenorth side
200 acres	of Tenesse River thence aCross the Sluice to the North
of land	west bank Ooltewah Island thence down the Sluce with
in Said	its meanders to the Lower end of Said Island thence
County	up the River with its meanders to the upper end of
	Said Island thence a direct line to the begining so as
	to include said Island
this Location	23 August 1831
received	
and this	John Russell
Entry	and others
made	Locators
23 August	
1831	Certified Coppy
	Isd.
fees of office	
paid 75¢	

PAGE 180

No. 59	State of Tennessee	John Taleafarro Enters one Hundred
John Tallefaro		acres of land in Said County on
General Entry	Hamilton County	the Side of Waldens Ridge Begin-
100 acres of		ning on an Elum thence North 29
land	E. up Waldens Ridge to a stake thence Northwardly to
	a stake Corner to George Williams & Millikens 50 acre
this Location	Entry then with a line thereof Southwardly to a dog-
received and	wood on a line of Tallefarros fifteen acre Survey then
this Entry made	with the meanders of the same Survey to the beginning.
15 Sept.	
1831	John Tallcaffaro
	Locator
fees of	
office	Copy Isd.
paid 75¢	Sept. 15th, 1831

PAGE 180

No. 60	State of Tennessee	George W. Williams Enters two hun-
George Williams		dred Acres of land in said county
Enters 200 acres	Hamilton County	on the side of Waldons Ridge be-
of land		ginning on a Postoke corner to
General Entry	George Williamses Tract of land whitch he perched of
	R. Waterhous then with the line of a fifty acre Entry
this Location	made by Stringer & Johnson---Eastwardly to a line of
received and	an Entry made by Jas. Cunningham then Northwardly
this Entry made	then southwardly to the beginning so as to include
15 Sept. 1831	two hundred Acres.
	Septr. 15th 1831
fees of office	
paid 75¢	Coppy Isd. George W. Williams
	25 October 1831 Locator

PAGE 181

No. 61
Charles Coleman
Enters
640 acres
of Land in
said County

this location
received and
this Entry made
20th Sept. 1831

Fees
of office
paid 75¢

State of Tennessee | Charles Coleman enters Six hundred and forty acres of land lying and being in Said County aforeSaid on Waldens Ridge Beginning on James Bunches South Corner of the place where he now Lives Running North of East with Daid Bunches Line to Cany Branch thence Down Cany branch and Round for Complement to the Beginning so as to include to the afore Said six hundred and forty acres 20th September 1831

Hamilton County

Charles Coleman
Locator

the Coppe Isd.

PAGE 181

No. 62
James Roberts
150 acres
Hamilton Cty.
made
10th Oct.
1831

Entry fees
75
Paid

State of Tennessee | James Roberts enters One hundred and fifty acres of land situate lying and being in the County aforesaid On the top of Waldens Ridge On the waters of Chickamauga Creek Beginning on a black oak tree near said creek thence south east and round for complement(so as to include one hundred and fifty acres) to the beginning 10 Oct. 1831

Hamilton County

Jas. Roberts
Loct.

PAGE 182

No. 63
Geo. B. Roberts
200 acres
Hamilton
County
made 10 Oct.
1831

Entry fee
75
paid

State of Tennessee | George B. Roberts enters two hundred acres of land in said county on Wallens Ridge On the Waters of Coops Creek Beginning at a whitw oak near a place known by the name of the "Rock House." Running thence North east across the said Creek and around for complement to the begining so as to include the aforesaid two hundred acres of land Oct. 10, 1831

Hamilton County

George B. Roberts
Loct.

PAGE 182
No. 64

State of Tennessee | Absolom Scively Enters on hundred acres Land in said County in a small valley between Ten-

Hamilton County

nessee River and the where Creek William H. Stringer
now lives and adjoining and Entry made by John Lovelady on which he now lives and another made by James
Smith and another made by Henry R. Simmerman Beginning on a post Oak Corner to Lovelady Entry then East
with a line there of to Simmermans Line then northwardly to an Entry made by Russell then westwardly to
Smiths line and the same to the Corner than to the
beginning for Complement Oct. 17th 1831

Abeslam Scively
Locator

PAGE 183

No. 65
Nathan N. Tygart:
Enters 500
Acres of land
in said Cy.
General Entry

Location received
and the Entry
mad the20
October 1831

fees of office
paid 75¢

State of Tennessee| Nathan N. Tygart Enters five
| Hundred acres of land in said
Hamilton County | County on Wallens Ridge Begining
on the West side of Cain Creek
and on a red oak runing Southwardly thence Southwardly thence to the Begining So as to include five Hundred acres of land and the improvement whare said
Tygart now lives this 20 October 1831

Nathan N. Tygret
Locator

the Coppy Isd.
and received

PAGE 183

No. 65
Nathan N. Tygart:
Enters 500 acres:
of land in
said Cy.
General Entry

Location re-
ceived and the
Entry mad the
20 October 1831

fees
of office
paid 75¢

State of Tennessee| Nathan N. Tygart Enters five
| Hundred acres of land in said
Hamilton County | County on Wallens Ridge Begin-
ning on the West side of Cain
Creak and on a red oak runing Southwardly thence
South Eastwardly thence North Eastwardly thence to
the Begining So as to include five Hundred acres
of land and the improvement whare said Tygart now
lives this 20 October, 1831

Nathan N. Tygret
Locator

the Coppy Isd.
and received

PAGE 183

No. 66
William Hixen
Enters

William Hixen Enters one hundred acres of land on
Waldens Ridge of said County the waters of Bord
Camp Break on north side of said Crek Hamilton
County and State of Tenessee begining on a pine run-

100 acres
of land

ING Southwardly then westwardly then Northwardly then
Eastwardly then to the begining for Complement the
28 October 1831

this location
received
and this
Entry made
28 October 1831

William Hixen
Locater

Copy Isd.
19 Aprail
1833

fees of office
pd. 75¢

PAGE 184

No. 67
Isack and
Stephen Clement
Enters 200 acres
of Land in said
County

State of Tennessee Isack Clement and Stephen Clement
of said county enters hundred
Hamilton County acres of Land Lying in the fork of
possam Creak on Waldens Ridge
part of Cumberland mountain Said Survey begining on a
black oak Corner then Runing South of west 160 poles
then Runing East of south 200 poles then Runing East

this location
received and
the Entry
made
1 November 1831

of south 200 poles whtn Runing Eastwardly 160 poles
then Runing up the North fork of Said posom onthe
west side of Said Crek to begining Corner Gint Entry
these from under our hands and Seals

fees of office
paid
75¢

Isack Clement
Stiphen Clement
Locators

Coppy Isd.

PAGE 184

No. 68
William and
James Clement
Enters
320 acres of
land in said
County

State of Tenesee, Hamilton County William Clement and
James Clement Enters thres hundred and twenty acres
of land Lying on the South fork of Rock Creek on
Waldens Ridge being part of Cumberland mountain Situated as follows Begining on the ridge between
said Creek and posom Creak Corner Black oak thence
Runing Eastwardly three hundred and twenty Poles then
west of north then westwardly then to the begining

This Location
received and
this Entry
made
November 5
1831

acording to law making three hundred and twenty
acres of land Conluding the Entry that Terry Riddel
made where John Clement now lives by Consent of said
Riddel these from under our hands and seals
By the Byonr—

fees of
paid 75¢

John Clement
William Clement
James Clement

Coppy Isd.

PAGE 185

No. 69
Thomas Cummings
Enters
25 acres of
land in
said
Hamilton County

this location
received and
this Entry
made this
5 December 1831

fees
of
office
paid
75¢

State of Tenessee | Thomas Cummings Enters 25 acres
of Land in said County on the East
Hamilton County | side of mountain Creek Begining on
a hickory Corner to James Mitchels
90 acre Entry on whitch Thomas Cummings now lives
then with a line of the same North 18 poles to a dogwood on the same line on Corner to an Eight acre
Entry made by Thomas Cummings then a Line of the
same North 34 East 53 poles to A spanish oaks Corner
to the same and on a sest line Runing from the mouth
of North Chickamaugy to Waldens Ridge then with the
same East 48 poles to Chestnut oaks Corner to Cornelius Millikens Entry then South 33 degrees west 102
poles to a stake thence North 45 west 30 poles to the
Begining.

Thomas Cumings
Locator

Coppy Isd. 5 December 1831

PAGE 186

No. 70
James Brimer
Enters 300
of land

this location
received and
this Entry
11 January
1832

FEES
of office
paid
75¢

State of Tennessee | James Brimer Enters three hun-
dred acres of Land on Waldens
Hamilton County | Ridge beginning on a Lorrel on
the west bank of Standifer
Creak a branch of Chickamaga between whare Hoppers
trace and Hamilton County Line Crosses said Creak
thence westwardly thence Northwardly then Eastwardly then southwardly to the begining including a
marked Black oak and Chesnut whare Hamilton County
Line Crosses said Hoppers trace so as to include
three hundred acres as aforesaid
11th January 1832

James Brimer
his successor
Locator

PAGE 186

No. 71
Henry R. Sim-
merman
Enters
three Hundred
acres of
land

State of Tennessee | Entry Takers office
Dallas 6 day of February
Hamilton County | 1832
Henry R. Simmerman Enters three
hundred acres of land in said County on the top of
Wallans Ridge lying on the North side of a trace
cauled Gosses Trace and on the waters of fallen
Water begining on a black oak not far from the Clift
of said fallen water and the same whats some person

in said
County

has built a house and Runing southwardly thence Eastwardly according to law to best advantage so as to
include three hundred acres to the begining.

fee
paid
75¢

Henry R. Simmerman
Locator

Coppy 19 Aprail, 1833

PAGE 187

No. 72
Henry R. Sim-
merman

General Entry

Enters 250
Acres of land
in said
County
6 Febry.
1832

fees
of
office
paid
75¢

State of Tenesee] Entry Takers office
Dallas
Hamilton County | 6 day of Febry. 1832.

Henry R. Simmerman Enters two Hun-
dred and fifty acres of land in said County on the
Top of Waldens Ridge lying on the south side of a
trace Called Gesses trace and on the waters of suck
Creek and lying on the North west side of and Entry
of six hundred and forty acres Entered by Jacob Hartman beginning forks of two branches on a white oak
and Running Northwardly and thence Westwardly according to law so as to include two hundred and fifty
acres to the begining.

Henry R. Simmerman
Locator

Coppy 19 Aprail 1833

PAGE 187

No. 73

(Blank)

State of Tennessee] Woodford R. Hanna enters one hundred acres of land in said County
Hamilton County | on the south East side of Waldens
Ridge Begining on a pine on a
Bench of said Mountain Below Little Sandy Creek mark
W.H. thence southwardly thence Eastwardly thence Northwardly thence westwardly to the Beginning so as to include one Hundred acres of land as afors said Febury
25 Day 1832

Woodford R. Hanna
Locator

PAGE 188

No. 74
James Lea
350 acres

State of Tennessee] February the 25th 1832 James Lea
Enters three Hundred and fifty
Hamilton County | acres of land in said County ly-
ing on the top of Wallens Ridge

General Entry

Location
Received
and this
Entry
made this
27th Feb.
1832

fees
of office
Paid $00.75

and known by the name of William Holemans improvement
and being the same where William Hoalman Resided
on said Wallens Ridge and situaded on a Creek called
Middle Creek Beginning on a black oak on the north
side of said Middle Creek and below where the said
Wm. Hoalman Cleared a small field thence running
westwardly thence running northwardly thence southwardly Crossing said Middle Creek so as to in Clude
a Cabbin built By a Mr. Owen thence to the best advantage to the beginning.

Certified Copy   James Lea
Issued and Delivered Locator
to the Enteror
25th Feb. 1832

PAGE 188

No. 75
Jesse Walker
Enters
640 acres

General Entry

Location
Received
and rhis
Entry
made this
7 May
1832

fees
of office
paid 75¢

State of Tennessee]   Jesse Walker to Poy Enters 640
                         acres of land in said Hamilton
Hamilton County   County Beginning on the side
                         of Waldens Ridge on a Hickory
and Red ellum thence North East with the General Corses of Waldins Ridge to Chickemaga Creak thence North
West thence South West thence according to law to
the Begining including the house whare John Hopper
now lives also the place whare James Ages Did live
and the mill whare the said Walker now lives so as
to include the six hundred and forty acres of land
this 7 May 1832

                    Jesse Walker
                    Locator

Coppy Isd.
31 October 1832

PAGE 189

No. 76
John Moyers(?)
Enters
50 acres
of land
6 August

the Location
Received 6 August
& this Entry
made 6 Aug. 1832

fees of office
paid 75¢

State of Tanessee]   Entry takers office Monday 6 Aug-
                      ust 1832 John Moyers Enters fifty
Hamilton County   acres of land in the Gulf of Sandy
                      Creak begining on Jerimiah Jones
Corner where sd. Creek brakes thrugh the mountain
on Waldens Ridge and Runing up said Creak on the
south side and down sd. Creak on the North Side with
the verious meanders of the mountain oppesite said
Jones Corner so as to include fifty acres.

                    John Moyers
                    Locator

Coppy Isd.

PAGE 189 :
:
:
No. 77 : State of Tenesse. Entry takers office
John Myers : John Moyers Enters two hundred
Enters : acres of land on the top of Wal-
200 acres : dens Ridge or mountain Begining
: on a Chestnut oak on or near the bluff of big Sandy
: Creak and Runing Round the various meanders of the
this location : top of the mountain to Little Sandy Creak thence
received and : along the bluff of Said Creek and a Cross to the
this Entry : Begining for Compliment
made :
9 August : John Myers
1832 : Enterer
:
feew of office : Coppy Isd.
paid 75¢ :
:
:
:
PAGE 190 :
:
No. 78 : State of Tenesee David W. Lawhorn Enters two hun-
David W. Lawhorn: dred and fifty acres of land insaid
Enters : Hamilton County Hamilton County Begining on a black
250 acres : Oak on the South side of Rockey
of land : Creak Runing Northwardly thence Westwardly thence
: southwardly thence Eastwardly to the Begining so as
this Entry : to include two hundred and fifty acres of land this
Received and : 3 September 1832
this Entry made :
this 3 September: Coppy Isd. David W. Lawhorn
1832 : 3 September 1832 Locator
:
:
:
PAGE 190 :
:
No. 79 : State of Tenesee William C. Taylor Enters Three
William C. Tayler : Hundred acres of land Situated
Enters : Lying etc. in the County aforesaid
300 acres : Hamilton County on the waters of Rogers Creek at the
of land : the foot & on the side of Waldens
: Ridge Begining on a large Chestnut tree near the said
this Location : Creak thence Runing Northwardly Westwardly and South-
Received and : wardly thence a sirect line to the begining so as to
this Entry : include three Hundred acres of land this 20th Septem-
made this : ber 1832
20 September1832:
fees of office : William C. Tayler
paid 75¢ : Locator
:
PAGE 191 : State of Tenesee Alford N. Paterson Enters 800 acres
No. 80 : of land in Hamilton County on Rock-
Alford N. Paterson Hamilton County O y Creek Begining on a pine and two

Enters
800 acres
of land
in said
County

This Entry
received
and the
Entry
made
this 1st Oct.
1832

fees of office
paid 75¢

Chesnuts on the highest part of the first spir of
the mountain that puts into the Creek on the South
west side thence North 25 East Crosing said Creek
330 poles to a stak thence North 65 W. 400 poles
to a pine thence S. 25 W. 300 poles to a stake in
the S. W. bank of said creek thence meandering the
S.W. bank and bluff of said creek 300 poles when
reduced to a straight line to a stake thence — 65
E 100 poles to the Begining
this 28 Sept. 1832

        Alford N. Paterson
        Locater

Certy fyed Copy Isd.
1 Sept.

PAGE 191

No. 81
John Brown
Enters
400 acres
of land

This Location
received and
this Entry
made
3 Oct. 1832

fees of office
paid 75¢

State of Tennessee John Brown Enters four hundred
             acres of land in said County
Hamilton County on Sandy Creeks Beginning on
            a mapel on the East Side of Littel
Sandy Creek Running Eastwardly thence Northwardly to
big Sandy Creek thence Westwardly meandering the Bluff
up said Creek whtnce Southwardly to the Begining so as
to in Clude fore hundred acres of land this the 3 Oct.
1832

        John Brown
        Locator

Coppy Isd 3 October 1832

PAGE 192

No. 83
300 acres
D.W. Lawhorn

Location Recd.
& this Entry
made this
26th Day of
November
1832

fees of
office
Paid
$00.75

State of Tennessee David W. Lawhorn Enters three
             hundred acres of Land in Said
Hamilton County County on Rocky Creek begin-
            ning on a pine on the north East
Side of Said Creek and Running Westwardly to said Creek
so as to Include the saltpeter Caves on the north Side
of sd. Creek thence up said Creek and to the Best advantage agreeable to Law for Compliment, this the 21st
Day of November 1832

        David W. Lawhorn
        Locator

Certifyd Copy Issued & Delivered to Enterer 26th Day of
November 1832 ---Isd. 17 January 1835 and delivered

PAGE 192

No. 83
Jesse Walker
Enters four
hundred acres

General Entry

Location
Received and
this Entry
made
15 December
1832

fees
of
office
paid
$00.75

State of Tennesee | Jesse Walker Enters four hundred
acres of land in said County on Wal-
Hamilton County | dens Ridge of Cumberland Mountain
Begining on a white oak and two Black
oaks on James Browns reservation
line Thence south 51 West along a spur of said Ridge
three hundred and forty eight poles to a Black Walnut
on a point a few Rods south of mountain spring thence
North 39 West to a line of said Walkers six hundred
and forty acre Entry thence North Eastwardly and North W
Westwardly with said lines to two Chestnut oaks and
a black oak thence Northwestwardly thence south Eastwardly to said Reservation line thence with said line
to the Beginning so as to include four hundred acres
As near as natural Bounderies and others lines will
permit 15 December 1832

                    Jesse Walker
                    Locater

PAGE 193

NO.84
B. B. Cannon
Enters two
hundred acres
of land in
said County

General Entry

This Entry
received and
this Entry
made 15 Decem-
ber 1832
fees of office
paid $00.75¢

State of Tennessee | B.B. Cannon Enters two hundred
acres of land on Waldens Ridge of
Hamilton County | Cumberland Mountain Begining on a
Laurel on the bluff of North Chicka-
maga Creak a few rods below whare a mineral spring branch
FALLS INTO SAID creak Runing thence Northwardly thence
North Eastwardly thence South Eastwardly thence Westwardly to the Beginning so as to include said mineral
Spring & an old encampment in a square or oblong December 15, 1832

                    B.B. Cannon
                    Locator

Copy Isd.

PAGE 193

No. 85
Jesse Walker
Enters 160 acres
of land in said
County

General Entry

State of Tennessee | Jesse Walker Enters one hundred
and Sixty acres of land on Wal-
Hamilton County | dens Ridge of Cumberland Moun-
tain Beginning on a black Gum
marked with the letter W. Running thence South Eastwardly fifteen poles to the foot of said Ridge thence
North Eastwardly thence Northwestwardly thence South
westwardly to the Beginning so as to in Clude said

this Location
Received and
this Entry made
15 December 1832;

one hundred and Sixty acres in a square or oblong
15 Desember 1832

Jesse Walker
Locator

fees of office
paid $00.75

Coppy Isd.
15 Desember 1832

PAGE 194

No. 86
Jesse Walker
Enters 200
acres of Land
on Waldens Rig.

Location received
and this entry
made 22 Dec.
1832

State of Tenesee | Jesse Walker Enters two hundred
acres of land in said County on
Hamilton County | Waldens Ridge of Cumberland Mountain Begining on a white oak on
the southeast side of said ridge Runing thence south
Eastwardly to H. Poes Line thence northeastwardly
with said line thence Northwestwardly thence South
west wardly thence South Eastwardly to the begining so
as to include two hundred acres in a square or oblong
if the lines of others and natural boundreys will parmit
22 Desember 1832

fees
of office
paid 75¢

Jesse Walker
Locator

PAGE 194

No. 87
Seth Waddel
Enters 400
acres of Land
on Waldens Rig.

Location Received and
this Entry
made
14 February
1833

State of Tenesee | Seth L. Waddel Enters four Hundred
acres of Land on the Side of Waldens
Hamilton County | Ridge of Cumberland mountain beginning on a red Ellum and Hickry the
begining of Six Hundred and forty acre entry made by
Jesse Walker dated 7 May 1832 Runing thence Southwestwardly with the foot of the said Ridge thence North
westwardly thence NorthEastwardly thence to the Begining so as to Include for Hundred acres in a square or
oblong 14 Febry 1833

Seth Waddel
Locator

Copy Isd 13 Feb. 1834

PAGE 195

No. 88
George Burket
Enters
100 acres

State of Tennessee | George Burkhart enters one hundred acres of land in said County
Hamilton County | lying on the side of Wallens ridge
Begining at a Black Gum tree marked
with the letter W---- Corner to Jesse Walker 160 acre

this location
Received
and this entry
made
11 April
1833

| | Entry No. 85 made 15 Dec. 1832 Runing thence with the line of said Walkers entry up to the mountain 70 poles poles along the side of the Ridge or mountain south wardly 100 poles thence down the mountain to a branch at the foot of the Ridge or mountain thence up the Branch and Round to the Begining for Complement 11 April 1833 |

his
George X Burket
mark
Locator

Coppy Isd. 16 May 1833

fees of
office
paid
75¢

PAGE 195

No. 89
S. B. Hawkins
5000
acres

General Entry

State of Tennessee
Hamilton County

Samuel B. Hawkins Enters five thousand acres of Land in said County and on Wallens Ridge Beginning on a black oak merkt S.B.H. on the Top of the north East Boundary of said Hawkins Entry No. 57 thence along the meanders of said mountain Eastwardly so far as to Include five Thousand acres of Land March the 15th Day 1833

Location
Recd.
and
this
Entry
made
15 Aprile
1833

S. B. Hawkins
Locator

fees of office paid $—75
Certifyd Coppy Issued and Delivered to the Enterer this Day of April 1833

Cornelius Milliken
Entry taker for Hamilton County

PAGE 196

No. 90
William Burwick
20 Acres

General Entry

State of Tennessee
Hamilton County

William Burwick Enters two hundred Acres of land in the County & state afforesaid on the west side of the Roaring fork of Sale Creek begining on a chestnut near the bluff & a short distance above a small sulphur spring on Waldens Ridge runing thence Westwardly then southwardly then Eastwardly then northwardly to the begining according to law so as to include two hundred acres Aprile 15th 1833

Location Recd.
and this Entry
made 15 Aprile
1833

fees of office
Paid 75¢

William Burwick
John Witt
by Locator

PAGE 196

No. 91
Paschel Simpson
Enters
350 Acres

Location Received
and this
Entry made
29 April 1833

fees
paid 75¢

State of Tennessee | Paschel Simpson Enters three
| hundred and fifty acres of land
Hamilton County | on Wallens Ridge of Cumberland
| Mountain Begining on a Chestnut
Marked P.S. runing Northwardly to the bluff of Rocky
Creek thence Northwardly with said bluff thence South
wardly thence Eastwardly to a point opesit the Begining thence to thebegining so as to inClude saidthree
hundred and fifty acres as near as Natural boundres
will parmit 29 Day of Aprail 1833
                    Paschel Simpson
                    Locator

PAGE 197

No. 92
S. B. Hawkins
5000 acres
General Entry

Location Recd.
and this Entry
this 27th
May
1833

State of Tennessee | S. B. Hawkins Enters fivethousand
| acres of land in said County Be-
Hamilton County | ginning on a black oak Markt S.B.H
| and Corner to his former Entry of
No. 89 thence Running Eastwardly along the Break of the
mountain thence Northwestwardly on line his former Entry thence along the lines of said Entry to the begining so as to Include 5000 acres May the 11th Day 1833
                    S. B. Hawkins
Certifyd Issd.   Locator

PAGE 197
No. 93
S. B. Hawkins
5000 acres
By General Entry

Location Recd.
and this
Entry
made
this 27th May
1833

State of Tennessee | S. B. Hawkins Enters five Thou-
| sand acres of land in said County
Hamilton County | Begining on the West Side of Mid-
| dle Creek near the Break of the
Mountain on a black oak Runing Southwardly Down the
mountain to John Talliaferros line thence along said
line to Lewis Montgomery's line thence along his line
to the next appropriated line and along such lines so
appropriated so far as to Include 5000 acres and Join
his former Entry on the Break of the Mountain
                    May the 11th Day 1833
                    S. B. Hawkins
Certified Issd.   Locator

PAGE 198
No. 94
John Talliaferro
50 acres

General Entry
Location Recd.
and this Entry
made this the
28th May 1833

State of Tennessee | John Talliaferro Enters Fifty acres
| of Land in said County and on the
Hamilton County | waters of Middle Creek thus so Run-
| ing Eastwardly then northwardly
begining on a Chestnut Oak Markt T then westwardly
then southwardly then to the Begining so as to Include
a Supplur or Kalebrate Spring and also to Include fifty acres of Land May the 27 day 1833
                    John Talliaferro
Certifyd Issd.   Locator

PAGE 198

No. 95
George Burkhart

State of Tennessee, Hamilton County Hasten Pos enters
100 acres of land on Waldens Ridge of Cumberland Moun.sd.

100 Acres

General Entry

Location
Recd and
this Entry
made
this 29th May
1833

County Beginning on the West Corner of his Hundred
Acre Entry of No. 88 on the East Side of Wallens Ridge
Running thence southwardly then Eastwardly then north-
wardly then to the beginning so as to Include one Hun-
dred acres
May the 29th Day 1833

        George Burkhart
        Locator

Certifyd Issd.

PAGE 199

No. 96
Hastan Poe
Enters
100 Acres

General Entry

THIS location
Received and
this Entry
made
26 June
1833

fees of
office
paid 75¢

State of Tennessee | Hasten Poe enters one hundred acres
of land on Waldens Ridge of Cumber-
Hamilton County | land mountain in said County Be-
ginning on a doubel Hickory marked
P on the firtt Bench of said Ridge about six poles South
west of the rode leading from said Poes acrows said
Ridge and on the southeast face of said ridge thence
Northeastwardly along the Bench of said ridge Crossing
the afore said rode onw hundred and sixty poles thence
Northwestwardly one hundred poles thence southwestwardly one hundred and sixty poles thence to the Begining so
as to in Clude a small spring on the North E. side of
the afore mentioned Road including one hundred acres
24 June 1833

        Hasten Poe
        Locater

PAGE 199

No. 97
B.B. Cannon
Enters
200 acres

General Entry

this location
Received &
this Entry
made
17 July
1833

fees of office
paid 75

State of Tennessee | Benjamin B. Cannon enters two hun-
dred acres of land on Wallens ridge
Hamilton County | of Cumberland Mountain in said Coun-
ty on the waters of Opossom Creek
adjoining a fifty acre entry made by andrew Mitchell
No. 56 Beginning on a Spanish Oak Thence westwardly
thence southwardly Thence Eastwardly thence to the Beginning including as entry westwardly from the aforesaid entry No. 56 and so as to include two hundred acres
in a square or oblong
this 17th day of July 1833

        B.B. Connor
        Locator

Certified Copy issued

PAGE 200

No. 98
James H.
Reynolds
and
B.B. Cannon
Enters
200 acres
of land

General Entry

this Entry Re-
ceived and this
Entry made
25 July 1833

fees of office
paid 75¢

State of Tennessee | James H. Reynolds and Benjamin
                   | B. Cannon enters two hundred
Hamilton County | acres of land on Waldens Ridge in
                   | said County Begining on a Black
oak on a bluff of north Chickamooga a ful Rods south
East of a branch whare it falls off they bluff thence
Northeastwardly thence Northwestwardley thence South
westwardly thence to the begining so as to include
an allum Cave and two hundred acres of land in a
square or oblong this 25 day July 1833

                              James H. Reynolds and
                              Benjamin Cannon
                              Locaters

Coppy Isd

PAGE 200

No. 99
Ephraimm Hughes
Enters
500 acres of
land

General Entry

THIS LOCATION
Received and
this Entry made
3 Day Aug. 1833
fees of office
pd. 75¢

State of Tennessee | Ephraim Hughes enters five Hun-
                   | dred acres of land on Wallens
Hamilton County | Ridge of Cumberland mountain on
                   | the Waters of Santy Creek on the
South side of Oven Rock house Creek a branch of Santy Creek aforesaid Begining in said County on a
black Oak Running thence Northwestward thence southwestward thence Southeastwardly thence North Eastwardly to the Beginning so as to include two hundred
acres in a Square or Oblong this the 3 day of August
1833

                              Ephriam Hughes
                              Locator

PAGE 201

No. 100
Jacob Reynals
Enters 100 acres
of Land

General Entry

this Location
received and
this Entry made
26 August 1833

State of Tennessee | Jacob Reynolds Enters one hundred
                   | acres of land on Walkens Ridge
Hamilton County | of Cumberland mountain between
                   | Faling Water and Chickmoggy Creaks
Beginning on a blackoak thence Northwardly thence
Southwestwardly thence Southeastwardly thence to the
Begining so as to include a coprcus Cave and one hun-
dred acres of land in a square or oblong 26 August
1833

Coppy Isd   Jacob Reynolds
30 September 1833   Locater

PAGE 201

No. 101
Jacob Reynolds
Enters
200 acres
of Land

General Entry

this Entry
Received and
this Entry made
26 August
1833

State of Tennessee)   Jacob Reynolds Enters two hun-
              dred acres of land on Waldens
Hamilton County   Ridge of Cumberland mountain
              in said County on the North Side
of Poes road on the head Waters of Littel Sanda Begining on a double mapel thence Eastwardly thence
Northwestwardly thence to the begining so as to include two hundred acres of land in a square or oblong
26th August 1833

                  Jacob Reynolds
                  Locater

Coppy Isd. 30 Sept. 1833

PAGE 202
No. 102
S.B.Hawkins
5000 acres

General Entry

Location
Received and
this Entry
made
this 27th
Day of August
1833

State of Tennessee)   S. B. Hawkins Enters five Thou-
              sand acres of Land in Said Coun-
Hamilton County   ty and on Waldens Ridge Beginning
              a black oak Corner to a former
Entry made by said Hawkins of No. 92 Running thence
Eastwardly thence northwardly thence westwardly and
then to the beginning so as to inClude 5000 acres
31st Day of May 1833

fees of office   S. B. Hawkins
paid 75
Certified Copy Issd. and Delivered to the Enteror
this 27th Day August 1833

PAGE 202

No. 103
William C. Henley
Enters two
hundred
acres of Land

General Entry

this Location
Received and this
Entry made 27
Aug. 1833
fees of office
paid
75¢

State of Tennessee)   William C. Henley Enters two
              hundred acres of Land in said
Hamilton County   County Beginning on a doubel
              Mapel on Littel Sandy Creek
thence Eastwardly thence Northwardly thence Westwardly thence Southwardly to the Begining so as to include two hundred acres of land in a square or oblong
this 27 August 1833

                    his
             William X Henley
                 mark

Coppy Isd. to the Enterer the
27th of Augst 1833

PAGE 203

No. 104 James More and Robert Jack Enters 100 acres	State of Tennessee Hamilton County	James More and Robert Jack enters 110 acres of land in Said County on Waldens Ridge of Cumberland Mountain on one of the Branches

of Sail Creek Begining on a Burch Spruce pine and pop-
ler on the south Bank of Said Creek runing westwardly
thence Northwardly thence Eastwardly thence southward-

General Entry ly to the Begining so as to include a bank of Stone

Coal and one hundred acres of land in a square or ob-

this Location long this 7th September 1833
Received and
this Entry
made
7th September
1833

Robert Jack
Locater

Copry Isd. 7 September 1833

PAGE 203

No. 105 Jacob Reynels Enters two hundred acres of Land	State of Tenesee Hamilton County	Jacob Reynels Enters two hundred acres of land on Waldens Ridge in said County begining on a black oak on the North Side of Poes and

Rawlings Road on the west side of a branch that runs
into Deep Creek on the South Side of said Creek thence

General Entry Westwardly thence Southwardly thence Eastwardly thence

to the Begining so as to include two hundred acres of

this Location Land in a square or ob Long this the 20Day of Sept. 1833
Received and
this Entry
made this
30 September
1833

Jacob Reynels
Locater

Coppy Isd. 30 Sept. 1833

PAGE 204

No. 106 Location Hastan Poe 100 acres	State of Tennessee Hamilton County	Hasten Poe Enters one hundred acres of Land on Waldens Ridge of Cumberland Mountain on Each side of the Turnpike Road Led-

ding across said Ridge from said Poe to Hensons in

General Entry Sequachey Valley and including a Spring the head

sutherun drafts of Sandy Creek near whitch spring

this Location Stands a Dogwood tre marked with Sa--letters Begin-
Received ing at a stake & Red Oak points Corner to a 90 acre
and this Entry made by Elisha Rogers in the Entry takers of-
Entry fice of this County of No. 16 dated 5 July 1824 and
made Buning thence with the back line of said Entry North-
20 October 1833 westwardly 180 poles thence southwestwardly ninety
poles thence Southeastwardly 180 poles thence a di-

fees of office rect line to the Begining to include one hundred

fees paid 75¢
Coppy the 11 April 1834

acres in oblong square

Haston Poe
Locator
1 Day October 1834

PAGE 204

No. 107
Hezekiah
Hughs
Enters
640 acres
of land

State of Tenesee]
Hamilton County |

Hezekiah Hughs Enters six hundred and forty acres of land on Waldens Ridge in Hamilton County Begining on a black oak Begining Corner to a five hundred acre Entry made by Ephraim Hughs and number 99 thence south Eastwardly thence south westwardly thence Northwestwardly thence North Eastwardly to the Begining to include six hundred and forty acres as near natural boundrays will purmit this 4th Day Nov. 1833

Location
Received and
this
Entry
made
4 November
1833

Hezekiah Hughs
Locator

Coppy Isd.

PAGE 205

No. 108
Henry R.
Simmerman
Enters
2000 acres

State of Tennessee]
Hamilton County |

Henry R. Simmerman Enters two thousand acres of Land on Wallens Ridge of Cumberland Mountain in said County Begining on Jacob Hartmans South East Corner of a Six hundred and forty acre Entry of No. 118 thence North Eastwardly to Falling Water Creek thence South Eastwardly with the meanders of said Creek Thence South westwardly thence to the Beginning so as to Include two thousand acres this 28th Day of December 1833

General Entry

Location Recd.
and this Entry
made this
28th Day of
December 1833

Henry R. Simmerman
Locator

Fees of office paid $00.75

PAGE 205

No. 109
E. Hughs
enters 150
acres

State of Tennessee]
Hamilton County |

Valldiah Hughs Enters one hundred and fifty acres of Land in said County on the side of Waldens Ridge of Cumberland Mountain Begining at George T.(?) Gelaspy North Corner of the track of land Sold to John Hughs

Location filed 8th Febry. 1834	Running thence Southwardly along said line thence Westwardly thence Northwardly thence Eastwardly to the Begining so as to include one hundred and fifty acres of land
Entry made same day	this 8th Febury 1834
fee 75¢	Ezekiah Hughs Locater

PAGE 206

No. 110
J. Smith
enters
25 acres

State of Tennessee}
Hamilton County

Jesse Smith Enters 25 acres of land in said County on the north side of the Valley Road Leading from Washington to Hixsons Ferry on Tennessee River and on the waters Chickamauga Creek on the south side of the mountain Beginning on a post oak marked J.S. on or near the north East line of Thomas Gillespies Survey Running thence northwardly forty five poles to a Stake thence westwardly eighty nine poles to a Stake thence southwardly forty-five poles to a Stake thence Eastwardly Eighty nine poles to the Beginning so as to Include Twenty-five acres of Land this Feb. 8th Day 1834

Location filed
8 Febry.
1834
Entry made same day

fees
75¢

Jesse Smith
Locater

PAGE 206

No. 111
J. Smith
enters
31¼ acres

State of Tennessee}
Hamilton County

Jesse Smith Enters thirty one and a fourth acres of land in said County on the South side of the Vally Road Leading from washington To Hixons Ferry on Tennessee River formerly Browns Ferry beginning on a post oak Corner to a 50 acre Entry made by Stringer and Johnson Runing northwestwardly with Stringer and Johnsons line Fifty poles to a Stake thence Eastwardly one hundred poles to a stake thence southwardly Fifty poles to a stake thence a Direct line to the Beginning so as to Include thirty one and a quarter acres of land this December the 10th Day 1835

Location filed

fees
75¢

Jesse Smith
Locater

PAGE 207
No. 112

State of Tennessee}
Hamilton County

William Smith Enters one hundred acres of land on Wallens Ridge in said County on the north side

(Blank)

: of Poss Road and on the waters of Little Sotts ad-
: joining a two hundred acre Entry of Jacob Reynolds
: on the East Side of Said Entry beginning on the East
: Side of Said Entry beginning on theEast Corner of Rey-
: nolds Entry thence Eastwardly thence northwardly thence
: westwardly hence to the Beginning so as to Include
: one hundred acres in a square of oblong this 10th Feb-
: ruary 1834

                          William Smith
                          Locator

PAGE 207

No. 113
Woodford R.
Hanna
Enters
100 acres
of land

Loaction re-
ceived and
this entry
mad this 5
March 1834

fees of office
paid 75¢

State of Tennessee
)
Hamilton County

Woodford R. Hanna Enters one Hundred acres of land in said County
on the south East side of Waldens
Ridge Begining on a pine on a Bench
of said mountin below Little Sandy Creek marked W.H.
thence southwardly thence Eastwardly thence Northwardly thence Westwardly to the begining so as to include
one hundred acres of land as afore said
5 March 1834

                          Woodard R. Hanna
                          Locater

Coppy Isd.
1 March 1834

PAGE 208

No. 114
George R.
Cannon
Enters
five thousand
acres of
land

this Location
Received
and the
Entry mad
this 26 March
1834

State of Tenesee
Hamilton County

George R. Cannon Enters five thousand acres of land in Hamilton County Beginning on a whitw oak on the
line that devids Hamilton and Mhey
Countyes and Running with said County line South sixty two degrees East sixty poles to Donnelsons now
McCllungs(?) 20,000 acre survey thence with his line
southwestwardly as far as to include five thousand
acres of inapproated lands if Natural boundrys and
appropated lines purmit. Entered this 26 March 1834.

                          George R. Cannon
                          Locater

Coppy Isd. 26 March 1834

PAGE 208

No. 115

State of Tennessee
Hamilton County

Jacob Reynolds Enters one hundred and Fifty acres of land
in said County and on the South

(Blank)   side of Wallens Ridge Beginning on or near Hannas(?) 1000 acre Corner on a Chesnut thence South Eastwardly along Hannas(?) line to the line of the $20,000 acre Survey thence northeastwardly with said line Two hundred and Twenty poles to a stake thence north westwardly one hundred and ten poles to a stake thence south westwardly Two Hundred and Twenty poles thence to the Beginning so as to Include one hundred and Fifty acres of Land March 11th(?) Day 1834

      Jacob Reynolds
      Locator

PAGE 209

No. 116

  State of Tennessee   Jacob Reynolds Enters one hundred
          acres of land in said County and
  Hamilton County   on the south side of the Valley
          Road leading from Washington to

(Blank)

Hixson's Ferry on Tennessee River Beginning on a Black Oak near the South Corner of a Twentyfive acre Entry made by Jesse Smith thence Running with a line of said Entry westwardly one hundred poles to a line of said Entry westwardly one hundred poles to a stake then Southwardly 160 poles to a stake thence Eastwardly one hundred poles thence northwardly to the Beginning so as to Include one hundred acres March 10th or 18th(?) 1834

      Jacob Reynolds
      Locator

PAGE 209

No. 117
R.C. McRee
& John Brown
enters 2000
acres of land
the 24th Decr.
1834

  State of Tenessee   Robert C. McRee & John Brown Sen.
          Enters two thousand acres of land
  Hamilton County   in Hamilton County afore said on
          the waters of Littel Sandy Creek
Begining on a mountain Burch on the North Bank of said Creek thence down the meanders of the Creek to McLung & Cozby's line of the 20,000 acre Grant thence with said line North Eastwardly thence North westwardly to

Location re-
ceive and
filed the
date
above

the Extreme top of the Bluff of Waldens Ridge thence with the Extreme top of said Bluff as a natural Boundry Southwestwardly to the Beginning to include 2000 acres as aforesaid December the 24th 1834

Fees of
office
paid
75¢

     R.C. McRee
      and
     John Brown
  Certified Copy   Locators
  Isd.

PAGE 210

No. 118
Entry
William Brown
122 acres
Chickamaga
Creek
Ham. Cty.

Entered 31st
Oct. 1834

fees of office
75¢ paid

State of Tennessee

Hamilton , Dec. 31 1834

William Brown Enters One Hundred and twenty two acres of land in Hamilton County in a small cove of Wallins Ridge on Chickamauga Creek Beginning on a Black Oak Marked T.G.Corner of Thomas Gillespee Survey running north fifty degrees east crossing said creek below Smith's Mill To a spur of the Mountain Thens with they various courses of the Ridge to the Beginning—

Coppy issued
17 Nov. 1834

William Brown
Locator

PAGE 210

No. 119
Entry
M. Varner
John Moyers, Jr.
Danl. Jones
John Hughs, Jr.
Soddy Creek
1860 acres
9 Jany. 1835

fees of
office
75
Paid

Copy
Isd.
5 Jany.
1835

State of Tennessee

Hamilton County

Madison Varner John Moyers, Jr. Daniel Jones & John Hughs Jr. Enters One thousand eight hundred & sixty acres of land lying and being in said County. Beginning on a stake in a line of the 20,000 acre Grant on the So.-East Bank of Soddy Creek thence No. Eastwardly along the line of said Grant at the foot of the mountain, One Thousand eight Hundred and Sixty poles to a white Oak corner to John Hughs, Sr. Thence Northwardly One Hundred & Sixty poles to a stake at the foot of the Bluff of Rocks at the top of the Mountain, Thence So. Westwardly along the Bluff of the mountain a natural Boundry parallel with the first line to Soddy Creek thence with said Creek along its various meanders to the Beginning.

9th July 1835

Madison Varner
John Moyers, Jr.
Danl. Jones
John Hughs
Locators

PAGE 211

No. 120
William W.
Rogers Enters
100 acres of
Land

LOCATION Received and

State of Tennessee

Hamilton County

Entry takers office 14th January 1835 William W. Rogers Enters one Hundred acres of Land in said County on Waldens Ridge on the head waters of Chickamoga Creek nearly opposite John Hoppers in Tenesee Valley Beginning on a Post Oak Beginning Corner of Henory Bradens(?) one Hundred acre entry thence North Eastwardly thence Northwestly thence southwestwardly

and Entry
made this
14 January 1835
fees of office
paid 75¢

and around to the Begining so as to inClude one Hundred acres of land

> William W. Rogers
> Locater

PAGE 211

No. 121
James Pafford
Enters 300
acres
of Land

this Location
Received and
this Entry
made the
19 January
1835

fees of office
paid 75¢

State of Tennessee
Hamilton County

James Pafford Enters three Hundred acres of land on Waldens Ridge Begining on a post oak on the west of Chicamogga thence east near or on a line of Jacob Runnels entry of 200 acres or near a branch that empties in to deep Creak thence Eastwardly thence Northwardly to deep Creak thence up deep Creek as a Natural boundry Westwardly thence southwardly to the Begining so as to include three hundred acres in a square or oblong as near natral Coundried and others Lines will permit 19 January 1835

> James Pafford
> Locater

PAGE 212

No. 122
Clift
&
McRae
Enters
50 acres
of land in
said Conty

this Location
Received
and this Entry
made this
21 Day January
1835

fees of office
paid 75¢

State of Tennessee
Hamilton County

Clift & McCree Enters fifty acres of land luing and being in Hamilton County on Waldens Ridge and bounded as follows Beginning on a maple on the Northeast Bank of Big Sanda Creak marked C.M. thence up said Creek with the verious meanders ther of 200 poles to a stake thence North 30 East 100 poles to a Stake thence East 250 poles to a stake thence a short line to the Beginning to be Run so as -- include a Bank of stone Coal on the North East Bank of Big Sandy Creak known of by John Brown Madeson Varner & others done in the Entry takers office in the town of Dallis this 21 Day of January 1835

> Clift & McRae

Certified Copy Issued

PAGE 212

No. 123
John Brown jr.
Madison Varner

State of Tennessee
Hamilton County

Entry Takers office No. 123— Entry John Brown Jr. and Madison Varner enters one Hundred acres of land in said county

100 acres
of land
Hamilton Cty.

Location Recd.
Entry made
28 Jany 1835

fees office
Paid 75¢

Copy Issd.
28 Jany 1835

on the waters of a small creek known by the name of
board Camp Beginning on a spruce pine Marked with
the letter B. On the south side of said Creek Thence
running Eastwardly thence Northwardly thence westwardly thence around agreeable to law for Complement
so as to include a Bank of stone Coal—on the North
Bank of said Creek a little distance above the mouth
of a small branch and also an old cabbin Entered this
28th day of January 1835

                    John Brown &
                    Madison Varner
                    Locators

PAGE 213

No. 124
James Finly
&
John Sullivan
Enters 100
Acres of land

this location
Received and
this Entry
made
this
30 January
1835

State of Tennessee ⎰ James Finley Enters one hundred
                   ⎱ acres of land in said County on
Hamilton County   ⎰ the watters of oposom Creek at the
                   ⎱ foot of Waldens Ridge or near it
Begining on a poplar on the North side of said Creek
on the top of a Bluff Runing Northwardly along said
Bluff or Ridge thence Westwardly thence southwardly
thence around for Compliment to the Begining so as
to include a coal bank at the foot of said Bluff in the
aforesaid one hundred acres of land located 30 January 1835

                    James Finley &
                    John Sullivan
                    Locators

fees of
office
paid 75¢

A certified Copy Issued the 3rd day of Feby. 1837
                    S. T. Igo
                    Deputy E.T.

(Note) (Pages 213-217 inclusive are missing from original book. The following entries—No's 125-132 are
copied from the transcript to complete Book 1)
(No. 125 would be on page 214 in original)

PAGE 215

No. 125

(Blank)

State of Tennessee ⎰ Jacob Reynolds Enters three Hun-
                   ⎱ dred Acres of Land in said County
Hamilton County   ⎰ and between the Valley Road and
                   ⎱ Tennessee River Beginning on the
west corner of a hundred acre Entry made by said Reynolds running thence westwardly to E. Parkers Line,
thence along said line to a black oak, thence N. East-
wardly-thence N. Westwardly-to the Beginning so as to

include three Hundred acres of Land. February the
23rd day, 1835

Jacob Reynolds
Locator

PAGE 215

No. 126

State of Tennessee| John Taliaferro & Wm. H. String-
er enters five hundred Acres of
Hamilton County   ◊ land in Hamilton County aforesaid, Beginning on a Black oak
corner to Henry R. Simmermans 75 acre entry No. 50
thence Northwardly. Thence Eastwardly thence South-
wardly-thence Westwardly to said Simmerman's line of
the entry No. 50 Thence with the lines of said entry
to the beginning so as to include 500 acres of appropriated lines permit made 16th March 1835

John Taliaferro
Wm. H. Stringger
Locators

PAGE 216

No. 127
Thomas Coulter
and
Robert Jack
Enter 1000 acres
of land

this Location
Received &
the Entry
made the
22d of
April
1835

fees 75¢

State of Tennessee| Thomas Coulter and Robert Jack
enters One Thousand Acres of land
Hamilton County ◊ on Wallens Ridge of Cumberland
Mountain Beginning on three Pines
on a point between the forks of rock Creek thence
North wardly with and meandering the Cliffs of said
Creek the main branch thereof for enough to include
the number of acres aforesaid, thence across to the
other branch of said Creek and to the Cliffs thereof
thence with and meandering said Cliffs to a point opposite the Begining thence to the Beginning to include the Pound where James Singleton formerly lived
and both branches of said Creek far enough to include
One thousand Acres this 22rd day of April 1835

Thomas Coulter
&
Robert Jack
Locators
(This is the last of the few pages copied from the
transcript, pages which are missing from the orig-
inal)

PAGE 216
No. 128

Richard Waterhouse, William H. Stringer and John Talliaferro enters Two Thousand Acres of land in Hamilton County on Tennessee River:- Beginning at the

Richard Water-
house &
William H.
Stringer &
John Talliaferro:
Enter 2000
acres

mouth of North Chiccamogga and running West to the foot
of Walden's ridge and with the foot of Waldens Ridge
to Tennessee River and with the river as it meanders
to the Beginning so as to include all the vacant land
in said Boundary.
25th May 1835

Richard Waterhouse
William H. Stringer
John Talliaferro
Locators

Location filed
25th May 1835
fees of
office 75¢

Certified Copy
issued 25 May 1835

PAGE 217

No. 129
B.B. Cannon &
H.R. Simmerman
Enters
1000 acres

State of Tennessee} B.B. Cannon & H.R. Simmerman enters One thousand acres of land
Hamilton County ON THE FACE OF Wallens ridge in
said County. Beginning on Jesse
Walkers Corner on James Smiths Reservation line. Thence
with said reservation line North & East to McClung &
Cozby line at the foot of the Mountain thence along
McClung & Cozbys & other appropriated lines to N. Chiccamogga Creek thence up said Creek to a point opposite
the extreme S. E. top of said Mountain thence up said
Mountain & along the sd. extreme top as a natural boundary to a point opposite the Beginning, thence to the
beginning to include 1000 acres 24th August 1835

Location filed
24th August
1835

Entry
made
same date

B.B. Cannon &
H.B. Simmerman
Locators

fees 75¢

PAGE 217

No. 130
Peter Dunn
enters
5000 Acres

State of Tennessee} Peter Drum enters five thousand acres of land on Wallens
Hamilton County Ridge of Cumberland Mountain
Beginning where the back line
of George R. Cannons entry No. 114 crosses big Soddy
Creek. Thence North eastwardly with said back line
Thence North eastwardly with said back line. Thence
Southwardly thence Southeastwardly to said back line
thence Northeastwardly to the beginning so as to include said five thousand acres of unappropriated
land with big Soddy Creek as near the middle as practicable and in a square or oblong
21st Sept. 1835

Location recd.
and entry
made the
21st Sept. 1835

Certified Copy
issued
same
day

Peter Drum
Locator

fees 75¢

PAGE 218

No. 131
John Moyers
enters
2000 acres

Location Recd.
recd. &
filed
23rd Sept.
1835

entry made
same day
fees 75¢ paid

Certified Copy
issued 23rd.
Sept. 1835

State of Tennessee} John Moyers enters two Thousand
Acres of land lying on Wallins
Hamilton County } ridge Beginning on the line of
the 19000 Acre Survey when the
same crosses little Soddy thence up the same with
Clift & McRee's line to the west corner of the same
thence with the back line and the back line of my 200
acre survey across to big Soddy thence with the waters and various courses of the creek up to the Mouth
of Deep Creek thence up the waters of said Creek including the waters of the same with the various courses of the said deep Creek to a point above Suttons
Cabbins thence Southwestwardly to Chiccamogga Creek
so as to include said Suttons Cabbins on Poes Road
thence down the waters of Chiccamogga including said
Water-course to the said 19000 acre line, thence with
said line to the Begining.

John Moyers
Locator

PAGE 218

No. 132
W. Clift &
R.C. McRee
enter
5000 acres

Location re-
ceived & filed
25th Sept. 1835

Entry made
same
day

fees
75¢ paid

Certified
copy issued
26 Sept. 1835

State of Tennessee} William Clift & Robert C. McRee
enters five thousand acres of
Hamilton County } land lying and being in Hamilton
County and bounded as follows:
Beginning on a rock on the South west bank of Cppos-
umcreek at the foot of Wallens ridge thence down the
mountain one hundred and fifty poles thence up said
Creek including the highest bluffs of the mountain
with the various courses of the Creek to the head
waters thereof thence up the mountain one thousand
poles including the head waters of the several branches of said creek to a stake, Thence eastwardly to the
mountain, thence along the foot of the mountain to the
Beginning so as to include 5000 acres of unappropriated land done in the Entry taker's office in the Town
of Dallas this 26th day of September 1835

William Clift
Robert C. McRee
Locators

PAGE 219
No. 133
R.C. McRee
&
B.B. Cannon

State of Tennessee} Robert C. McRee and Benjamin B.
Cannon enter five thousand acres
Hamilton County } of unappropriated land in Hamil-
ton & Marion Counties beginning

Enter
5000 acres

Location recd.
and entry
made
the 10th Oct.
1835

Certified Copy
Issued
same day

fees
75¢
paid

(PAGE 220
is blank)

PAGE 221

PAGE 222

in Hamilton County on a Black Oak marked for S.D.
Hawkins corner of entry No. 93 Thence Northeastwardly across Middle creek to the top of the Bluff of
the Mountain Thence with the top of said bluffs as
a natural boundary up the said creek two miles
thence across said creek westwardly and across suck
creek to the extreme top of the Southwest bluff of
the Southwest bluff of said last mentioned creek
Thence Thence along the top of the said bluff as a
natural boundary to a stake in the——
Turnpike road thence with said road to a stake in
the bank of Middle creek below Taliaferro's sawmill
thence a direct line to the beginning to include the
gulfs of Middle and suck creeks two miles up each
and five thousand acres of unappropriated land
Made the 10th Oct. 1835

                    Robert C. McRee
                    B.B.Cannon
                    Locators

State of Tennessee Know all men by these presents
                    that we George W. Rider and Judge
Hamilton County   Trewitt of the State of Tennessee
                    and County of Hamilton are held
and firmly bound unto Andrew Johnson Governor of the
State of Tennessee and his successors in office in
the penal sum of Five Thousand Dollars good and lawful money of the United States for the payment of
which sum we bind ourselves our heirs executors and
assigns forever firmly by these presents in witness
whereof we have here unto set our hands and affixed
our seals this Eleventh day of December 1864 and of
American Independence the 88th year.

The conditions of the above obligation is such that
whereas the said George Rider and Judge Trewitt have
this day bought of the State of Tennessee a certain
tract of parcel of land lying and being in the County
of Hamilton and State of Tennessee near the town of
Chattanooga. (Not signed)

State of Tennessee Know all men by these presents
                    that we W.C. Norman & Co. of the
Hamilton County   State and County aforesaid are
                    held and firmly bound to John
C. Brown Governor of said State and his Successors
in office in the sum of Ten Thousand Dollars good
and lawful mony of the Unighted States for payment
of which Sum we bind ourselves our heirs Executors
Administrators and assigns forever. (Not signed)

PAGE 223

: This day personally appeared before me Cornelius Mil-
: liken one of the acting Justices of the peace for
: Hamilton County George Russell Surveyor for said Coun-
: ty and made oaths that the land cove---d by General
: Entry No. 3 date 5th July 1824 Entered in the name
: of William Rogers is taken by an older Entry.
: Sworn to and subscribed this 28 February 1825.
:
:   George Russel
:   Attest. Cornelius Milliken
:   J. P.
:
: Coppy of Vandikes Deposition at
: Pikeville for Thos. W. Spicer.
:
:
: C hattanooga
: Tennessee
: December Eleventh 1864
: Twelve months after date I promise to pay to the order
: of John L. C. Danner one thousand Dollars value recd.
: (Note: This is on the last page of the book.)
:
::
:   (End of "Original Book".)

(Beginning of transcript book)

PAGE 225   : State of Tennessee⟧ Benjamin B. Cannon and John
                        :   ⟧ Taleaferro enter five hun-
No. 134   : Hamilton County   ⟧ dred acres of land on the face
B. B. Cannon   :   of Wallens Ridge beginning on
    &   : a black oak marked S. B. H. Beginning corner of
John Taleaferro   : a five thousand acre entry made by Robert C. Mc-
                        : Ree and Benjamin B. Cannon No. 133. Thence with
                        : a line of said entry Northeastwardly crossing mid-
Entry   : dle Creek to the top of the Bluff of the Mountain
MADE   : Thence along the top of said Bluff Northeastwardly
17 Oct.   : to where Shoal Creek falls of of Mountain and a-
1835   : cross to the top of the Bluff of the Mountain north-
Location   : east of said Shoal Creek. Thence Southeastwardly
filed   : including the Gulf's of Shoal Creek to George W.
same day   : Williams line thence Southwestwardly with appropriat-
                        : ed lines to the Beginning to include five hundred
                        : acres of unappropriated land made this
Fees 75¢   : 17th day of October, 1835
paid by   :
B. B. Cannon   : Copy issued same day & date.

PAGE 225   :

No. 135   : State of Tennessee⟧ Robert C. McRee and Benjamin
R. C. McRee   :   ⟧ B. Cannon enter five thou-
    &   : Hamilton County   ⟧ sand acres of land on Wallens
B. B. Cannon   :   Ridge in said County Beginning
Enters   : on a Spruce pine and large stone on the bank of
5000   : McGills Creek thence Northeastwardly up the Moun-
acres   : tain to the main bluff of the Mountain. Thence
                        : still Northeastwardly along the main bluff when
                        : reduced to a straight line one mile from the said
Location   : Creek, thence Northwestwardly four miles. Thence
filed   : Southwestwardly crossing said Creek two miles,
24 October   : Thence Southeastwardly to the main bluff of the
1835   : Mountain. Thence along the main bluff and down the
Entry   : Mountain to the Beginning so as to include said Mc-
made   : Gills Creek as nearly running through the center as
same   : practicable and five thousand acres of land.
day   :
                        :   Robert C. McRee
                        :   &
fees   :   B. B. Cannon
75 ¢   :   Locators
paid by   :
B. B. Cannon   : Copy issued the date above.
                        :

PAGE 226

No. 136 Thos. Parks enters 5000 acres	State of Tennessee Thomas Parkes enters five thous- and acres of land on Wallens Ridge Hamilton County of Cumberland Mountain and in said County of Hamilton beginning on

the SouthEast corner of a five thousand Acre Entry made
by Robert C. McRee and Benjamin B. Cannon No. 135.

Location filed : Thence Southwestwardly along the main bluff of the moun-
and entry : tain crossing rocky creek to William Clift and Robert C.
7th Nov. 1835 : McRees entry No. 132. Thence with their line Northwest-
: wardly, Thence NorthEastwardly to Robert C. McRees and
: Benjamin B. Cannon's entry No. 135, thence with a line

office fees : of their entry to the Beginning so as to include five
75 : thousand acres of unappropriated land with Rocky Creek
: running as nearly through the middle as practicable.
: 7th November, 1835

Certified copy :
issued same : Thos. Parkes
day & date : Locator

PAGE 226

No. 137 : William Parks enters five Thousand acres of unappropriated
Wm. Parkes : land on Wallens ridge of Cumberland Mountain in said Coun-
enters : ty --- Beginning on the SouthEast corner of Clift & Mc-
5000 acres : Rees entry No. 132. Thence Southwestwardly along the main
: bluff of the Mountain to North Chiccamogga. Thence up the
: Creek to a stake. Thence NorthEastwardly to Clift & Mc-
Location filed : Rees Line of entry No. 132 aforesaid. Thence with said
and entry made : line to the Beginning so as to include five thousand
7th Nov. 1835 : acres of unappropriated land.
: 7th Nov. 1835

office fees : Thomas Parker
paid 75c : Locator

Certified Copy :
issued same :
day and date :

PAGE 227

No. 138 : Thomas B. Eastland enters five thousand acres of land
T. B. Eastland : in Hamilton County, Beginning at a point in the line
enters : which divides Hamilton County and Marion County at eight
5000 acres : hundred poles Northwardly from the foot of the Moun-
: tain nearest the Tennessee river, on the South side of
: said river and running thence east so far that a line
Locationfiled : South to the foot of the Mountain and with the same bor-
and entry made : dering on prior claims to the line of Marion County,

the 26th March 1836	and with the same to the Beginning -- excluding all prior claims, will include the quantity. Located the 23th March 1836 by No. 138.
fees of Office 75c	Thos. Eastland & J. A. Lane <u>Loctrs</u>
	Certified Copy issued the day & date above.
	B. B. Cannon Depty. E. T.

PAGE 227

No. 139 Thos. Eastland enters 5000 acres	Thomas Eastland enters five thousand acres of land in the County of Hamilton. Beginning at the North East corner of an entry in the name of Thomas B. Eastland for five thousand acres of land and running thence South to the South East corner of said Entry thence
Location filed entry made 28th March 1836	with the foot of the Mountain in eastwardly, border- ing on prior entries so far that a line Northwardly bordering on prior claims, to a point due east of the Beginning -- excluding all prior claims, and includ- ing the quantity. Located the 28th March 1836 by No. 139
fees of Office paid 75c	Thomas Eastland & J. A. Lane Locators
	Certified Copy issued the day and date above.
	B. B. Cannon Depty. E. T.

PAGE 228

No. 140 J. A. Lane enters 5000 acres	Jacob A. Lane enters five thousand Acres of land in the C County of Hamilton, Beginning at the Beginning corner of an entry in the name of Thomas B. Eastland, for five thousand acres, running thence east Twelve hundred and sixty poles, thence north so far that a line west to the
Location filed and entry made 28th March, 1836	line of Marion County, and with the same to the Begin- ning will include the quantity--excluding all prior claims. Located 28th March, 1836 by No. 140.
	Thos. Eastland & J. A. Lane, Locators
Fees office paid 75c	Certified Copy issued the day and date above B. B. Cannon Dept. E. T.

PAGE 228

No. 141
N. Oldham
enters
5000 acres

Location filed
and entry made
28th March
1836

Fees of Office
paid 75c

Nicholas Oldham enters five thousand acres of land in Hamilton County, Beginning at the Northwest corner of an entry in the name of Jacob A. Lane, for five thousand Acres in the line of Marion County, and running thence East twelve hundred and sixty poles, thence North so far that a line West, to Marion County line and with the same to the same to the Beginning, excluding all prior claims will include the Quantity. Located 28th March 1836 by No. 141.

Thos. Eastland &
J. A. Lane,
Locators

Certified Copy issued the day and date above

B. B. Cannon
Depty. E. T.

PAGE 229

No. 142
S. V. Carrick
enters
5000 acres

Location filed
and entry
made 28th March
1836

Fees of office
pale 75c

Samuel V. Carrick enters five thousand acres of land in Hamilton County, Beginning in the line of Marion County at the north west corner of an entry in the name of Nicholas Oldham for five thousand acres, and running thence east twelve hundred and sixty poles, thence North so far that a line west to the line of Marion County, and with the same to the Beginning excluding all prior claims will include the quantity. Located 28th March, 1836 by No. 142.

Thos. Eastland
J. A. Lane,
Locators

Certified Copy issued the day and date above

B. B. Cannon
Depty. E. T.

PAGE 229

No. 143
M. M. Carrick
enters
5000 acres

Moses M. Carrick enters five thousand acres of land in Hamilton County, Beginning at the North west corner of an entry in the name of Samuel V. Carrick, for five thousand acres, and running thence East twelve hundred and sixty poles thence North so far that a line West to the line of Marion County and with the same to the be-

PAGE 229(cont'd.): ginning excluding all prior claims will include the
                   quantity.
Location filed & : Located 28th March 1836 by No. 143.
entry made
28th March   :   Thos. Eastland &
1836   :   J. A. Lane
                   :   Locators

Fees of Office   : Certified Copy issued the day and date above.
paid 75c   :
                   :   B. B. Cannon
                   :   Depty. E. T.

PAGE 230   :

No. 144   : James M. Carrick enters five thousand acres of land
J. M. Carrick   : in Hamilton County. Beginning at the North West cor-
enters   : ner on the line of Marion County of an entry in the
5000 acres   : name of Moses M. Carrick for five thousand acres and
                   : running thence East twelve hundred and sixty poles,
                   : thence North so far that a line west to the line of
Location filed   : Marion County and with the same to the Beginning, ex-
and entry made   : cluding all prior claims will include the quantity.
28th March   : Located 28th March 1836 by No. 144,
1836   :
                   :   Thos. Eastland &
                   :   J. A. Lane,
                   :   Locators
Fees of office   :
paid 75c   : A Certified copy issued the day and date above.
                   :
                   :   B. E. Cannon,
                   :   Depty E. T.

PAGE 230   :

No. 145   : John Warren enters five thousand acres of land in Ham-
John Warren   : ilton County Beginning at the North west corner of an
enters   : Entry in the name of James M. Carrick, for five thous-
5000 acres   : and acres of land on the line of Marion County and
                   : running thence East twelve hundred and sixty poles,
                   : thence North so far that a line North and west to the
Location filed   : line of Marion County and with the same to the Begin-
and entry made   : ning, excluding all prior claims will include the
28th March   : quantity.
1836   : Located 28th March 1836 by No. 145
                   :
                   :   Thos. Eastland &
Fees of office   :   J. A. Lane
paid 75c   :   Locators
                   : A certified Copy issued the day and date above.
                   :   B. B. Cannon
                   :   Depty. E. T.

PAGE 231

No. 146
Wm. Bruster
enters
5000 acres

Location filed
and entry
made 28th March
1836

Fees of office
paid 75c

William Bruster enters five thousand acres of land in Hamilton County at the Northwest corner of an entry in the name of John Warren and running thence East twelve hundred and sixty poles thence North so far that a line, went to the line of Marion County and with the same to the Beginning excluding all prior claims will include the quantity.
Located 28th March 1836 by No. 146.

Thos. Eastland &
J. A. Lane
Loctrs

A Certified copy issued the date above.

D. B. Cannon
Depty. E. T.

PAGE 231

No. 147
R. M. Eastland
enters
5000 acres

Location filed
and Entry made
28th March
1836

Fees of office
paid 75c

Robert M. Eastland enters five thousand acres of land in Hamilton County Beginning at the South East corner of an entry for five thousand acres in the name of Jacob A. Lane and running thence East twelve hundred and Sixty poles, thence North for compliment bordering on priorclaims west & c and excluding all prior claims and excluding the quantity.
Located 28th March 1836 by No. 147.

Thos. Eastland &
J. A. Lane
Loctrs

A certified copy issued the day and date above.

B. B. Cannon
Depty. E. T.

PAGE 232

No. 148
Wm. Glenn
enters
5000 acres

Location
filed &
entry made
28th March
1836

William Glenn enters five thousand acres Beginning at the North west corner of a tract of land in the name of Robert M. Eastland for five thousand acres of land and running thence East twelve hundred and sixty poles, thence Northwardly for Compliment west & c excluding prior claims and including the quantity. Located 28th March 1836 by No. 148.

Thos. Eastland &
J. A. Lane
Locaters

(Cont'd)

PAGE 232 (Cont'd)   A Certified copy issued the day & date above.

Office fees
paid
75c

               B. B. Cannon
               Depty. E. T.

PAGE 232

No. 149
J. A. Carrick
enters
5000 acres

Location
fi ed and
entry
made 28th
March 1836

John A. Carrick enters five thousand acres of land in Hamilton County, Beginning at the North West corner of an entry in the name of William Glenn for five thousand acres and running thence East twelve hundred and sixty poles, thence Northwardly with the foot of the Mountain, so far that a line west, etc. to the Beginning bordering on former entries, and excluding prior claims will exclude the quantity.   Located 28th March 1836 by No. 149.

               Thos. Eastland &
               J. A. Lane
                 Loctrs

Office fees
paid 75c

A certified copy issued the day and date above.

               B. B. Cannon
               Depty. E. T.

PAGE 233

No. 150
S. L. Carrick
enters
5000 acres

Location filed
and entry
made March 28th
1836

Seth L. Carrick enters five thousand acres of land in the County of Hamilton Beginning at the North west corner of an entry in the name of John A. Carrick for five thousand acres of land, and running thence East twelve hundred and sixty poles, thence Northwardly with the foot of the Mountain for compliment, west & c bordering on former entries, excluding all prior claims and including the quantity. Located 28th March by No. 150.

               Thos. Eastland &
               J. A. Lane
               Locators

Office fees
paid 75c

A certified copy issued the day and date above.

               B. B. Cannon
               Depty. E. T.

PAGE 233

No. 151
H. L. Carrick
enters
5000 acres

Hugh L. Carrick enters five thousand acres of land in the County of Hamilton Beginning at the North west corner of an entry for five thousand acres of land in the name of Seth L. Carrick and running thence East twelve hundred and sixty poles, thence Northwardly with the foot of the Mountain so far that a line west

Location filed and entry made 28th March 1836

& c. bordering all prior claims will include the quantity.
Located 28th March 1836 by No. 151.

Thos. Eastland
J. A. Lane
Locators

OFFICE fees paid 75¢

A certified copy issued the day & date above.

B. B. Cannon
Depty. E. T.

PAGE 234

No. 152
D. L. Mitchell
enters
5000 acres

David L. Mitchell enters five thousand acres of land in Hamilton County. Beginning at the North west corner of an entry for five thousand acres of land in the name of Hugh L. Carrick and running thence East twelve hundred and sixty poles thence Northwardly with the foot of the Mountain so far that a line

Location filed and entry made 28th March 1836

west & c. bordering on former entries excluding all prior claims and including the quantity.
Located 28th March 1836 by No. 152.

Thos. Eastland &
J. A. Lane
Loctrs

Office fees paid 75¢

A certified copy issued the day and date above.

B. B. Cannon
Dept. E. T.

PAGE 234

No. 153
W. P. White
enters
5000 acres

Woodson P. White enters 5000 acres of land in the County of Hamilton Beginning at the Northwest corner of an entry for five thousand acres in the name of David L. Mitchell and running thence East twelve hundred and Sixty poles, thence Northwardly with the foot of the Mountain so far that a line west & c

Location filed and entry made 28th March 1836	bordering on former entries will include the quantity, excluding all prior claims. Located 28th March 1836 by No. 153.

Thos. Eastland &
J. A. Lane
Loctrs

Office fees paid 75c

A certified Copy issued the day and date above.

B. B. Cannon
Depty. E. T.

PAGE 235

No. 154
D. Snodgrass enters 5000 acres

David Snodgrass enters five thousand acres of land in Hamilton County. Beginning at the North West corner of an entry in the line of Marion County in the name of William Bruster, for five thousand acres of land and running thence East twelve hundred and sixty poles, thence North so far that a line west to the line of Marion County and with a line of the same to the Beginning — excluding all prior claims, will include the quantity.
Located 28th March 1836 by No. 154.

Location filed & entry made 28th March 1836

Thos. Eastland &
J. A. Lane
Loctrs

Office fees paid 75c

A certified copy issued the day and date above.

B. B. Cannon
Depty. E. T.

PAGE 235

No. 155
J. Snodgrass enters 5000 acres

James Snodgrass enters five thousand acres of land in Hamilton County, Beginning on the North west corner of an entry for five thousand acres of land in the name of Woodson P. White and running thence East Twelve hundred and sixty poles, thence Northwardly with the foot of the mountain, so far that a line west &c. bordering on former entries and excluding all prior claims, will include the quantity.
Located 28th March 1836 by No. 155

Location filed entry made 28 March 1836

Thos. Eastland
J. A. Lane
Loctrs

(Cont'd)

Office fees paid 75c	A certified copy issued the day and date above.
	B. B. Cannon Dept. E. T.

PAGE 236

No. 156 T. Lane Ser. enters 5000 acres	Turner Lane Sen. enters five thousand Acres of land in Hamilton County, Beginning on the line which divides the Counties of Marion and Hamilton at the South west corner of an entry for five thousand acres of land in the name of Thomas B. Eastland and running thence with said County line Southwardly eight hundred and ninety poles, thence East for compliment North and with the lines of former entries to the Beginning excluding all prior claims, and including the quantity.
Location filed & entry made 28th March 1836	Located 28 March 1836 by No. 156.
made void J. A. Lane Loc	Thos. Eastland & J. A. Lane Loctrs
Office fees paid 75c	A certified Copy issued the day and date above.
	B. B. Cannon Depty. E. T.

PAGE 236

No. 157 T. Lane, Jr. enters 5000 acres	Turner Lane Jr. enters five thousand acres of land in Hamilton County, Beginning at the North East corner of an entry for five thousand acres in the name of Turner Lane senr. and running thence South eight hundred and ninety poles, thence East for Compliment North and West with former entries to the Beginning including the quantity excluding all former entries.
Location filed & entry made 28 March 1836 made void J. A. Lane Loctr.	Located 28th March 1836 by No. 157.
	Thos. Eastland & J. A. Lane Loctrs
	A certified copy issued the day and date above.
Office fees paid 75c	B. B. Cannon Dept. E. T.

PAGE 237

No. 158
D. Schoolfield
&
J. C. Smith
100 acres

David Schoolfield & Joseph G. Smith enters One hundred acres of Land in Hamilton County near the town of Dallas, Beginning at the most Northern point of an Island oposite to Dallas on the South Est. Bank of a Sluice of Tennessee River and running Southward with said Sluice as a natural boundary to the main River thence Northward with said River as a natural boundary to the beginning for Compliment.

Location filed
& entry made
16th May

Located 16 May 1836 by No. 158.

David Schoolfield &
J. G. Smith

Office fees
paid 75c

A Certified copy issued the day and date above.

Samuel Igou
E. T.

PAGE 237

No. 159
G. W. Williams
hath this day
entered
250 acres

G. W. Williams hath this day entered Two hundred & fifty acres of Land lying on the side of Walding Ridge beginning on a white oak near Shoal Creek-- Running Northwardly meandering said Creek to the Bluff, thence Eastwardly meandering said Bluff rocks thence Southwardly. thence Southwardly back to the Beginning so as to include Two hundred & fifty acres of vacant Land this 6 June 1836

Location
filed and
entry made
16th June
1836

G. W. Williams

A certified copy issued the day and date above written.

Office fees
paid
75c

Saml Igou
E. T.

PAGE 238

No. 160
Thomas Cornwall
Enters
5000 acres

Thomas Cornwell Enters 5000 acres of land in Hamilton County Beginning at a point in the line which divides Hamilton County and Marion County at eight hundred poles Northwardly from the foot of the Mountain near- est the Tennessee River on the South side of said river running thence East so far that a line South to the foot of the Mountain & with the same bordering

Location filed

and entry made 25 Nov. 1836	on prior claims to the line of Marion County & with the same to the Beginning for Compliment excluding all prior claims. Location made 25th Nov. 1836. Tennessee By No. 160.
Fees of office paid 75c	Hezekiah Smith Locator A certified Copy issued the day and date above. Saml T. Igou Depty. E. T.

PAGE 258

No. 161 J. Freeman enters 5000 acres	Joseph Freeman Enters 5000 acres of land in Hamilton Beginning at the North East corner of an Entry in the name of Thomas Cornwell for 5000 acres of land and running thence South to the South East corner of said Entry thence with the foot of the Mountain eastwardly bordering on prior entry so far that a line Northwardly bordering on prior claims to a point dew east of this, Beginning excluding all prior Claims and including the quantity.
Location Filed and entry made 25th Nov. 1836	
Fees of office paid 75c	Hezekiah Smith Locator Tennessee November 25, 1836 A certified Copy issued the day and date above. Saml. T. Igou Depty. E. T.

PAGE 259

No. 162 Chas. Roberts enters 5000 acres	Charles Roberts enters 5000 acres of land in Hamilton County. Beginning at the North west corner of an Entry in the name of Joseph Freeman for five thousand acres of land in the line of Marion County and running thence East 1260 poles thence North so far that a line west to Marion County line and with the same to the Beginning excluding all prior claims will include the quantity, Tennessee, Nov. 25th 1836
Location filed and entry made 25th Nov. 1836	
Fees of office paid 75c	Hezekiah Smith Locator A certified Copy issued the day and date above. Samuel T. Igou Depty. E. T.

PAGE 239

No. 163 : Charles Lombert enters 5000 acres of land in Hamilton
Charles Lombert : County, Beginning at the Beginning corner of an En-
Enters 5000 : try made in the name Charles Freeman for 5000 acres
acres : of land running thence East Twelve hundred and Six-
: ty poles, thence North so far ahat a line west to
: the line of Marion County and with the same to the
Location filed : Beginning for Compliment excluding al prior Claims--
and Entry made : Tennessee Nov. 25th 1836
25th Nov.
1836 :

: Hezekiah Smith
: Locator

fees of : A certified Copy Issued the day and date above.
office paid
75c :

: Saml. T. Igou
: Depty. E. T.

PAGE 240

No. 164 : Lewis S. Caryell enters 5000 acres of land in Hamilton
Lewis S. Caryell : County. Beginning in the line of Marion County at
enters 5000 : the North East corner of an Entry made in the name of
acres : Charles Roberts for 5000 acres of land & running
: thence East twelve hundred & Sixty poles thence North
: so far that a line west of the ine of Marion Coun-
Location filed : ty & with said line to the Beginning fore Compliment
& entry : excluding all prior claims Tenn. Nov. 25th, 1836
made 25th Nov.
1836 :

: Hezekiah Smith
: Locator

Office fees : A certified Copy issued the day and date above.
paid 75c

: Saml. T. Igou, Depty
: E. T.

PAGE 240

No. 165 : Joseph Reaves Enters 5000 acres of land in Hamilton
Joseph Reaves : County, Beginning at the North west corner of an En-
Enters : try in the name of Lewis S. Conyell for five thous-
5000 acres : and acres, and running thence East 1260 poles, thence
: North so far that a line west to the line Marion County
: and with the same to the Beginning excluding all claims
Location filed : will include the quantity. Tennessee Nov. 25th 1836.
Entry made : Hezekiah Smith
25th Nov. 1836 : Locator

: A certified Copy issued the day and date above.
Office fees
paid 75c : S. T. Igou, Depty.
: E. T.

PAGE 241

No. 165 Isaac Reaves enters 5000 acres	: Isaac Reaves enters 5000 acres of land in Hamilton County. Beginning at the North West corner on the line of Marion County of an Entry in the name of Joseph Reaves for 5000 acres and running thence East twelve hundred & Sixty poles, thence North so far

Isaac Reaves enters 5000 acres of land in Hamilton County. Beginning at the North West corner on the line of Marion County of an Entry in the name of Joseph Reaves for 5000 acres and running thence East twelve hundred & Sixty poles, thence North so far that a line West to the line of Marion County and with the same to the Beginning for Compliament--- Excluding all prior Claims.
Tenn^se Nov. 25th 1836

Location filed & entry made 25th Nov. 1836

Hez^a Smith
Locator

office fees paid 75c

A certified Copy issued the day and date above.

S. T. Igou, Depty.
E. T.

PAGE 241

No. 167
George McCallen
Enters
5000 acres

George McCallen Enters 5000 acres of land in Hamilton County Beginning at the North West corner of an entry in the name of Isaac Reaves for five thousand acres of land on the line of Marion County and running thence East 1260 poles, thence North so far that a line North and West to the line of Marion County and with the same to the Beginning excluding all prior claims will include the quantity.
Tennessee Nov. 25th 1836

Location filed & entry made 25th Nov. 1836

Heze. Smith
Locator

Office fees paid 75c

A certified Copy issued the day and date above.

Samuel T. Igou
E. T.

PAGE 242

No. 168
Samuel McCallen
Enters
5000 acres

Samuel CmCallen Enters 5000 acres of land in Hamilton County, Beginning on the Line of Marion County at the North West Corner of an Entry in the name George Mc-Callen for 5000 acres & running thence East twelve hundred & Sixty poles thence North so far that a line to the line Marion Comty & North the same to the Beginning for Complaiment, excluding all older claims
Tenn^se Nov. 25th 1836

Location filed Entre made 25th Nov. 1836

Hezekiah Smith
Locator

(Cont'd)

Office fees paid 75c : A certified Copy issued the day and date above

Samuel T. Igou
Depty. E. T.

PAGE 242

No. 169
Jennet Painter
Enters
5000 acres
: Jennet Painter Enters 5000 acres of land in Hamilton County Beginning at the South East corner of an Entry for five thousand acres in the name of Charles Roberts, running thence East 1260 poles bordering on prior claims west and excluding all prior claims and including the quantity. Tennessee

Hezekiah Smith
Locator

Location
filed and
Entry made
25th Nov.
1836
: Nov. 25, 1836
A certified Copy issued the day and date above.

fees of Office
paid 75c
: Samuel T. Igou
Depty E. T.

PAGE 243

Ashley Green
Enters
5000 acres
: Ashley Green Enters 5000 acres of Land in Hamilton County. Beginning at the North west corner of a tract of Land in the name of Janet Paointer for 5000 acres running thence East twelve hundrd & Sixty poles, thence Northwardly for compleament west excluding all prior Claims.
Tennessee
Nov. 25th 1836

Location
filed and
Entry
made
25th Nov.
1836
: Hezekiah Smith
Locator

A Certified Copy issued the day and date above.

fees of Office
paid 75c
: Samuel T. Igou
Depty. E. T.

PAGE 243

No. 171
William Badger
Enters 5000
acres
: William Badger Enters 5000 acres of land in Hamilton County, Beginning at the North west corner of an Entry in the name of Ashley Green for five thousand acres and running thence East 1260 poles thence Northwardly with the foot of the Mountain so far that a line west and to the Beginning on former entries

FEES OF office paid 75¢	and exc uding prior claims will include the quantity.
	<div align="center">Hezekiah Smith Locator</div>
	Tennessee Nov. 25, 1836
	A certified Copy issued the day and date above.
	<div align="center">Samuel T. Igou Depty. E. T.</div>

PAGE 244

No. 172 Samuel Badger Enters 5000 acres	Samuel Badger enters 5000 acres of Land in Hamilton County Beginning at a North West corner of an Entry in the name of Wm. Badger for 5000 acres of Land & running thence East twelve hundred and Sixty poles, thence Northwardly to the foot of the Mountain for Complaiment &c bordering on former Entries excluding
Location filed and Entry made 25th Nov. 1836	all prior claims for quantity.
	<div align="center">Hezekiah Smith Locator</div>
	Tennee. Nov. 25, 1836
fees of office paid 75¢	A certified Copy issued the day and date above.
	<div align="center">Samuel T. Igou Depty E. T.</div>

PAGE 244

No. 173 Anthony Newbold Enters 5000 acres	Anthony Newbold enters 5000 acres of land in Hamilton County, Beginning at the Northwest coner of an Entry for five thousand acres of land in the name of Samuel Badger and running thence East 1260 poles, thence Northward with the foot of the Mountain so far that a line west and Bordering on former entries, excluding all prior claims will include the quantity.
Location filed and entry made 25th Nov. 1836	Tennessee Nov. 25th 1836
	<div align="center">Hezekiah Smith Locator</div>
fees of office paid 75¢	A certified Copy issued the day and date above.
	<div align="center">Saml. T. Igou Depty. E. T.</div>

PAGE 245

No. 174
Joseph Warner
Enters
5000 acres

Joseph Warner Jun. Enters 5000 acres of land in Hamilton County Beginning at the North west corner of an Entry in the line of Marion County in name of Samuel McCallen for 5000 acres of land and running thence East twelve hundred & Sixty thence North so fare that a line west to the line of Marion County & with a line of the same to the Beginning for Complainent excluding all other claims.

Location filed and Entry made 25th Nov. 1836

Tennee Nov. 25th 1836

Hezekiah Smith
Locator

fees of office paid 75c

A certified Copy issued the day and date above.

Saml. T. Igou
Depty. E. T.

PAGE 245

No. 175
Joseph Philips
Enters
5000 acres

John Philips enters 5000 acres of land in Hamilton County. Beginning at the North west corner of an Entry for five thousand acres of land in the name of Anthoney Newbold and running thence East 1260 poles, thence Northwardly with the foot of the Mountain so far that a line west and Bordering on former Entries, excluding all prior claims and including the quantity.

Location filed and Entry made 25th Nov. 1836

Tennessee Nov. 25th 1836

Hezekiah Smith
Locator

fees of offce Paid 75c

A certified Copy issued the day and date above.

Samuel T. Igou
Depty. E. T.

PAGE 246

No. 176
Joeph Crozier
Enters
5000 acres

Joseph Crozier Enters 5000 acres of land in Hamilton County, Beginning on the North west corner of an Entry for 5000 acres land in the name of Joseph Warner and running thence East 1260 poles thence Northwardly with foot of the Mountain so far that a line west and Bordering on former Entries and excluding all prior claims will include the quantity.

Location filed and Entry made 25th Nov. 1836

Tennessee Nov. 25th 1836

Hezekiah Smith
Locator

fees of
office
Paid
75c

A certified Copy issued the day and date above.

Saml. T. Igou
Depty. E. T.

PAGE 246

No. 177
Samuel McCracken
Enters
5000 acres

Location filed
and Entry made
26th Nov.
1836

Samuel McCracken Enters 5000 acres of land in Hamilton County. Beginning on the line which divides the Countes of Marion and Hamilton at the South west corner of an Entry in the name of Thomas Cornwell for 5000 acres running thence with said County line Southwardly Eight hundred & Ninty poles thence East for Compliment North and with the line of former Entres to the Beginning excluding all prior claims including quantity.

Hezekiah Smith
Tennee   Locator
Nov. 25th 1836

fees of
office Paid
75c

A certified Copy issued the day and date above.

Saml. T. Igou
Depty. E. T.

PAGE 247

No. 178
Henry I. Kinsmon
Enters
5000 acres

Location filed
and Entry
made 26th Nov.
1836

Henry I. Kinsman Enters 5000 acres of Land in Hamilton County. Beginning at the North East Corner of an Entry for five thousand acres in the name of Samuel McCracken and running thence South 890 poles thence East for Compleament North and west with former Entries to the Beginning including the quantity excluding all former Entreis.

Hezekiah Smith
Tennessee   Locator
Nov. 26th 1836
A certified Copy issued the day and date above.

fees of
office 75c

Saml. T. Igou
Depty. E. T.

PAGE 247

No. 179
Joanna Painter
Enters
100 acres

Location filed
and Entry
made 26 Nov. 836

Joanna Painter Enters 100 acres of land in Hamilton County near the town of Dallas, Beginning at the most Northern point of an island oposite to Dallas on the South East Bank of a Slou of Tennessee River & running Southward with said Slouice as a natural Boundary to the Main River thence northward with said River as a Natural Boundary to the Beginning for Complaiment.

Hezekiah Smith, Locator

fees of Office paid 75c	Tenn.⁰⁰ Nov. 26th 1836.
	
	A certified Copy issued the day and date above.
	
	        Saml. T. Igou
	        Depty. E. T.

PAGE 248

No. 180 M. Todd Enters 5000 acres Location filed and Entry made 26 Jany. 1837	Mary Ann Todd enters five thousand acres of land in Hamilton County where the line between said County and the County of Marion leaves Suck Creek running North Eastwardly and with the line which divides Hamilton & Marion Counties, thence Northwardly, three hundred poles, thence so far East that a line South &c. and to the County line and with the same to the Begin Beginning excluding all prior claims will include the quantity. Located 26 January 1837 by No. 180 Jacob A. Lane, loct

Office Paid 75c	A certified Copy issued the 24 day of June.
	
	       S. T. Igou,
	       D. E. T.

PAGE 248

No. 181
A. Collins
enters
5000 acres
 	
Location
filed and
Entry made
26 Janry
1837
	Ann Collins Enters five thousand acres of land in the County of Hamilton Beginning at the North East corner of an Entry of five thousand acres of land in the name of Mary Ann Todd, thence East eight hundred and Ninty-four poles, thence South for Complement excluding all prior claims west &c. to the Beginning including the quantity. Located 26 January 1837 by No. 181
	
	       Jacob A. Lane
	       Loct.
	
	A certified Copy issued the 24th June, 1837.
	
	       Saml. T. Ogou
	       D. E. T.

Office fees paid 75c	

PAGE 249

No. 182 A. Eagland Enters 5000 acres Location	Ayelsy Eagland enters five thousand acres of land in Hamilton County Beginning at the North west corner of an entry in the name of Mary Ann Todd for five thousand acres of land and running thence Northwardly with the line of Hamilton & Marion Counties One thousand poles, thence East for complement, excluding prior claims &c. and South & west to the Beginning will in-

filed and
Entry made
26 Jany.
1837

clude the quantity. Located 26 January 1837 by No.182

Jacob A. Lane
Locator

A certified Copy issued the 25th Jan. 1837.

Saml. T. Igou
Depty. E. T.

PAGE 249

S. Adair
Enters
5000 acres

Stephen Adair enters five thousand acres of land in
Hamilton County Beginning at the North west corner
of an Entry for five thousand acres of land in the
name of Ayelsy Eagland and running thence with the
western Boundary line of Hamilton County Northward-

Location
filed and
Entry made
26 Jany.
1837

ly One thousand poles thence East for Compliment excluding all prior clames South and west to the Beginning including the quantity. Located 26th Jan.
1837 by No. 183.

J. A. Lane,Loct.

Office fee
75¢

A certified Copy issued the 26th June 1837.

Saml. T. Igou
Depty. E. T.

PAGE 250

No. 184
J. Largent
Enters
5000 acres

John Sargent enters five thousand acres of land in
Hamilton County Beginning at the North west corner
of an entry of five thousand acres of land in the
name of Stephen Adair, standing in the west boundary line of said County and running thence Northwardly with the line between said County and the County

Location
filed and
Entry made
26 Jany. 1837

of Marion one thousand poles, thence East for Compliment excluding prior claims, thence South and west
to the Beginning including the quantity.
Located 26th January 1837 by No. 184

Jacob A. Lane
Locator

fees of
Office
75¢

PAGE 250

No. 185
J. M. Smallmen
Enters

James M. Smallmen Enters five thousand Acres of land
in Hamilton County Beginning at the North west corner
of an entry of five thousand of land in the name of John
Sargent and running thence with said County line North-

5000 acres : wardly one thousand poles to a stake in said line
: thence East for compliment-- excluding prior claims
: thence South West &c including the quantity.
Location filed : Located 26th January 1837 by No. 185
and Entry
made 26th Jany. :   Jacob A. Lane
1837 :   Locator

Office fees :
Paid 75c :

PAGE 251 :

No. 186 : Daniel Kelly enters five thousand acres of land in
Daniel Kelley : Hamilton County Beginning at the North West Corner
Enters : of an Entry of five thousand acres of land in the
5000 acres : name of James M. Smallman and running thence with
: said County line Northwardly One thousand poles
: thence East for Compliment excluding prior claims
Location : thence South, thence west to the Beginning including
filed and entry : the quantity.
made 26th Jan. : Located 26 January 1837 by No. 186
1837 :
:   Jacob A. Lane
:   Locator
fees of :
office :
paid 75c :

: Q
PAGE 251 : :

No. 187 : Hiram Knowles enters five thousand acres of land in
Hiram Knowles : Hamilton County Beginning on the North West corner
enters : of an entry for five thousand acres of land in the
5000 acres : name of Daniel Kelly and running thence Northwardly
: with the Western boundary line of said County one
: thousand poles to a stake in said line thence East
Location filed : for compliment excluding prior claimes thence South
and entry made : & west to the Beginning including the quantity.
: Located 26 January 1837 By No. 187
:
:   Jacob A. Lane
:   Locator

PAGE 252 :

No. 188 : John Rotan enters five thousand acres of land in Ham-
John Rotan : ilton County Beginning in the west boundary line of
enters : said County at the North west Corner of an entry for
5000 acres : five thousand acres of land in the name of Hiram
: Knowles and running thence with said County line

Location filed and entry made 26 Jany 1837	Northwardly one thousand poles thence East for compliment -- excluding all prior claims thence South and west to the Beginning including the quantity. Located 26th January 1837 by No. 188
Location filed and entry made 26 Jany, 1837	J. A. Lane Loct.
fees of office 75c	

PAGE 252

No. 189 J. Elens enters 5000 acres	Jonathan Elens enters five thousand acres of land in Hamilton County Beginning at the North west corner of an entry for five thousand acres of land in the name of John Rotan and in the western boundary line of said County and running thence with said line Northwardly one thousand poles, thence East for Complement -- ex-
Location filed and Entry made 26 Janry. 1837	cluding all prior Claimes thence South and west to the Beginning including the quantity. Located 26th January 1837 by No. 189.
fees of office paid 75c	J. A. Lane Loct.

PAGE 253

No. 190 J. Johnston enters 5000 acres	Joseph Johnston enters five thousand acres of land in Hamilton County. Beginning in the western boundary line of said County at the Northwest corner of an en- try for five thousand acres of land in the name of Jonathan Elens and running thence Northwardly with said line one thousand poles thence East for Compli-
Location filed and Entry made 26th Janry.1837	ment -- excluding prior claimes --thence South and west to the Beginning, including the quantity. Located 26 January 1837 by No. 190
fees of office paid 75c	Jacob A. Lane Loct.

PAGE 253

D. Clark enters 5000 acres	Davids Clark enters five thousand acres of land in the County of Hamilton Beginning at the South East corner of an Entry for five thousand acres of land

Location filed : in said County in the name of Ayelsy England and
and entry made : running thence East Nine hundred poles, thence North
26 Janry. 1837 : for Compliment excluding prior Claims than west &c.
: including the quantity.
: Located 26th January 1837 by No. 191

fees of office :
paid 75c :   Jacob A. Lane
:   Locator
:
:
:
PAGE 254 :
:
No. 192 : Hannah Dilton enters five thousand acres of land in
Hannah Dilton : Hamilton County Beginning at the North West corner
enters : of an entry for five thousand acres of land in said
5000 acres : county made in the name of Darias Clark thence East
: Nine hundred poles thence North for Comp ement ex-
: cluding prior Claimes west &c. including the quantity.
Location filed : Located 26 January 1837 by No. 192.
and entry made :
January 26, 1837: Jacob A. Lane
:   Locator
:
:
:
PAGE 254 :
:
No. 193 : William Sparkman enters five thousand acres of land in
William Sparkman: Hamilton County Beginning at the North west corner of
enters : an entry for five thousand acres of land in said County
5000 acres : in the name of Hannah Dilton running thence East nine
: hundred poles, thence North for Compliment excluding
: prior claims west &c. including the quantity.
Location filed : Located 26 January 1837 by No. 193
and entry made :
26 Jany. 1837 : Jacob A. Lane
:   Locators
:
Office fees :
paid 75c :
:
:
PAGE 255 :
:
No. 194 : Arnold Moss enters five thousand acres of land in
A. Moss : Hamilton County Beginning at the North west corner
enters : of an entry in said County for five thousand acres
5000 acres : of land in the name of William Sparkman and running
: thence East Nine hundred poles, thence North for
: compliment excluding all prior claimes west &c.
Location filed : including the quantity.
and entry made : Located 26 January 1837. By No. 194
26 January 1837 :
fees of office : Jacob A. Lane
paid 75c :   Loct.

PAGE 255

No. 195
A. Moss
enters
5000 acres

Location filed
& entry made
26 January 1837

fees of office
paid 75c

Pleasant Massa enters five thousand acres of land in Hamilton County, Beginning at the North West corner of an Entry in said County for five thousand acres of land in the name of Arnold Moss thence East Nine hundred poles, thence North for Compliment excluding prior claims, thence west &c including the quantity located 26th January 1837 by No. 195.

Jacob A. Lane
Locatr

PAGE 256

No. 196
George Cline
Enters
5000 acres

Location filed
& entry made
26 Jany. 1837

fees of Office
paid 75c

George Cline enters five thousand of land in Hamilton County Beginning at the Northwest corner of an entry in said County for five thousand acres of land in the name of Pleasant Massa and running thence East nine hundred poles, thence North for Compliment including prior claims, thence west & c. including the quantity. Located 26th January 1837 by No. 196

J. A. Lane
Locator

PAGE 256

No. 197
J. Cline
enters
5000 acres

Location filed
& Entry made
26th Jany. 1837

fees of Office
paid 75

James Adair enters five thousand acres of land in Hamilton County, Beginning at the North west corner of an entry in said County for five thousand acres of land in the name of George Cline and running thence East Nine hundred poles thence North for Compliment excluding prior claims and thence West &c. including the quantity. Located 26th January 1837 by No. 197.

J. A. Lane
Locater

PAGE 257 :

:

No. 198 : Elijah Burdin Enters five thousand acres of land in
E. Burdin : Hamilton County Beginning at the North west corner
enters : of an entry for five thousand acres of land in the
3000 acres : name of James A. Adair thence east Nine hundred
: poles, thence North for Compliment, exc uding prior
: claims -- thence west &c. including the quantity.
Location : Located 26 January by No. 198.
filed and :
entry made : Jacob A. Lane
26 Janry. : Loctr.
1837 :
:
:
:
fees of office :
paid 75c :
:
PAGE 257 :
:
No. 199 : Bryan Sparkman enters five thousand acres of land
B. Sparkman : in Hamilton County Beginning at the North west
enters : corner of an entry in said County for five thou-
5000 acres : sand acres of land in the name of Elijah Burdin
: and running thence East Nine hundred poles thence
: North for compliment excluding prior claims,
Location : thence West &c. including the quantity.
filed and : Located 26th January 1837 by No. 199
entry made : Jacob A. Lane
26th January : Loctr.
1837 :
:
:
fees of office :
paid 75c :
:
PAGE 258 :
:
No. 200 : Henry R. Simmerman enters as General Enterer Six
H. Simmerman : hundred and forty acres of Land in Hamilton County
enters : on the waters of mill Creek, Beginning on a post
640 acres : oak corner to his 250 acres and running North 45
: East 160 poles to a hickory thence South 45 East
: poles to a red oak, then South 45 west poles to
Location filed : a stake, North 45 west 250 to a stake North 45
and entry made : East --- poles to a stake with the lines thereof
29th Febry. : to the Beging, this 20 February 1837
1837 :
:
: Henry R. Simmerman
: Locator
fees of office :
paid 75c : A certified Copy issued the 7th March 1837

Samuel T. Igou, Depty. E. T.

PAGE 258 :

No. 201 : Robert Tunnel Enters 640 acres of Land as General
: Enterer.
:
: Commenst rong on this Page
:
: Samuel T. Igou
: Depty E. T.

PAGE 259 :
:
No. 201 : State of Tennessee} Robert Tunnell enters as Genrel
R. Tunnell : {Entry Six hundred and forty a-
Enters : Hamilton County {cres of land on Wallens Ridge
640 acres : in said County Beginning on Hen-
: ry R. Simmermon line on a stake 30 poles from his
: corner Spanish oak on fowling water, then running
Location filed : with his line North thirty-five East four hundred
& entry made : and Seventy poles to a hickory in said line then
20 Feb. : various Courses so as to include a Spring and white
1837 : oak fot on North Chickamoga, entered this 20th day
: ofFebruary 1837
:
fees of office p: Robert Tunnell
paid : Locator
75c :
: A certified Copy issued the 6th March 1837.
:
: S. T. Igou, D.E.T.
:
PAGE 259 :
:
No. 202 : Peter Helton Enters 640 acres of land on Waldens Ridge
P. Helton : in Hamilton County on the head waters of Waydens Mill
Enters : Creek, Beginning on a Black oak running North 200
640 acres : poles thence East 70 poles, thence South 220 poles,
: thence west poles and to the Beginning so as to in-
: clude the plantation whereon said Helton lives. March
Location filed : 23d. 1837
& entry made :
23 March : B. M. Murphy
1837 : Locator
:
: A certified Copy issued the day and date above.
fees of office :
Paid 75c : S. T. Igou
: Depty. E. T.
:
PAGE 260 :
:
No. 203 : State of Tennessee} James C. Wayland enters as Gen-
J. C. Wayland : {eral Enterer five thousand acres
enters : Hamilton County {of land on Waldens ridge in said

5000 acres	County, Beginning at Peter Heltons East corner and running with the line of Heltons entry of 23rd March 1837, Thence South 360 poles and west 1280 poles,
Location filed and entry made 30th March 1837	thence various courses to the Beginning so as to include five thousand acres entered this 30th day of March 1837
	B. M. Murphy
	Locator
fees of office Paid 75c	A certified Copy issued the day and date above.
	Saml. T. Igou
	Depty. E. T.

PAGE 260

No. 204 P. Helton Enters 4000 acres	Peter Helton Enters 4000 acres of Land on Waldens Ridge in Hamilton County and State of Tennessee Beginning on a corner(?) the North East corner of J. C. Wayland 5000 acer Entry, Thence East to the dadid --lines on the Side of said Ridge, thence South with said lines to the Beginning for Complement 17th August 1837
Location filed and entry made 18 Aug. 1837	Allen White
	Locator
fees of office paid 75c	A certified Copy issued the 28th August 1837
	Saml. T. Igou
	Depty. E. T.

PAGE 261

No. 205 David H. Mathis Enters 5000 acres	David H. Mathis Enters 5000 acres of land in Hamilton County and State Tennessee Waldens Ridge, Beginning on the North East corner of J. C. Wayland 5000 acre Entry thence running Northwardly thence Southwardly thence Round to the Beginning for Compliment 17th August 1837
Location filed and entry made 17th Aug. 1837	Allen White
	Locator
	A certified Copy issued the day and date above
	Samuel T. Igou
Office fees paid 75c	Depty. E. T.

PAGE 261

No. 206 J. H. Wayland	John H. Way and 5000 acres of land in Hamilton County and State of Tennessee Beginning on the North East

Enters 5000 acres	Corner of J. C. Wayland's 5000 acer Entry, thence running Northwardly thence westwardly, thence Round to the Beginning for Compliment 17 August 1837
Location filed and entry made the 7th August 1837	Allen White Locator A certified Copy issued the day and date above.
	Saml. T. Igou Depty. E. T.
Office fees paid 75c	

PAGE 262

No. 207 Wm. C. Roberts Enters 640 acres	William C. Roberts Enters Six hundred and forty acres of Land in Hamilton County on Wallens Ridge and on the waters of Sandy Creek, Beginning on a white oak on the East Side of said Creek running Northwardly— thence Eastwardly, thence Southwardly — thence Westwardly, to the Beginning, so as to include Six hundred and forty acres this 14th November 1837
Location filed and Entry made the 14th Nov. 1837	William C. Roberts Locator A certified Copy issued the day and date above.
Office fees Paid	Saml. T. Igou Depty. E. T.

PAGE 262

Jesse Walker Enters 1000 acres	Jesse Walker Enters One Thousand acres of land in Hamilton County Beginning at or near James Smiths corner running East with Smiths line to the twenty thousand acre line and with the Twenty thousand Acre line & by the Mountain for Compliment entered this 17th day of November in the year 1837
Location filed and Entry made 18th day of Nov. 1837	Jesse Walker Locator A certified Copy issued the 18th November, 1837
Office fees paid 75c	Saml. T. Igou Depty E. T.

PAGE 263

No. 209	Robert Marcum enters 5000 acres of land in Hamilton County, Beginning at a point ner the Line which divides the Hamilton County & Marion County at Eight

Robert Marcum enters 5000 acres	hundred poles Northwardly from the foot of the Ridge nearest the Tennessee River on the North East Side of said River running thence East so far that a line South to the foot of the said Ridge and with the same Bordering on prior
Location filed & Entry made 20 February 1838	claims to the Line of Marion County and with the same to the Beginning for Complainents excluding all prior claims February 20th 1838.
	Joseph G. Smith Locator
Office fees 75c	Certified Copy Issued the 10th Apr. 1838.
	Saml. T. Igou Depty. E. T.

PAGE 263

No. 210 J. Marcum Enters 5000 acres	James Marcum Enters five thousand Acres of land in Hamilton County, Beginning at the North East corner of an Entry in the name of Robert Marcum for 5000 acres of Land and running thence South to the South East Corner of said Entry thence with the foot of the Ridge Eastwardly bordering on pri-
Location filed & Entry made the 20th February 1838	or Entrys so far that a line Northwardly Bordering on prior claims to a point due East to the Beginning, excluding all prior claims and including the quantity. Tennessee, February 20th 1838
	Joseph G. Smith Locator
fees of office paid 75c	A certified Copy issued the 10th Apl. 1838
	Saml. T. Igou Depty. E. T.

PAGE 264

No. 211 James Henderson Enters 5000 acres	James Henderson Enters 5000 acres of land in Hamilton County Beginning at the North west corner of an Entry in the name of James Marcum for 5000 acres of Land in the line of Marion County and running thence East 1260 poles — thence North so far that a line west to the Marion County line and with the
Location filed & Entry made 2 Feby. 1838	same to the Beginning excluding all prior claims will include the quantity. Tennessee Feb. 20th 1838 　　　　J. G. Smith 　　　　Locator

fees of office paid 75c	: A certified Copy issued the 10th April 1838.
	:
	: Saml. T. Igou
	: Depty. E. T.
	:
	:
PAGE 284	:
	:
No. 212 A. Newman Enters 5000 acres	: Alexander Newman Enters 5000 acres of land in Hamilton
	: Beginning at the Beginning corner of an Entry made in
	: the name of James Henderson for 5000 acres of land,
	: running thence East twelve hundred and Sixty poles--
	: thence North so far that a line west to the line of
	: Marion County and with the same to the Beginning for
Location filed &	: Compliment -- excluding all prior claims.
Entry made 20th Feby. 1838	: Tennessee, Feb. 20th, 1838
	:
	: J. G. Smith
	: Locator
	:
	: A certified Copy Issued the 10th Apl. 1838
FEES OF office Paid 75c	:
	: Saml. T. Igou
	: Depty. E. T.
	:
	:
PAGE 265	:
	:
No. 213 J. Billingsley Enters 5000 acres	: Jacob Billingsley Enters 5000 acres of land in Ham-
	: ilton County, Beginning in the line of Marion County
	: at the North East corner of an Entry made in the name
	: of Alexander Newman for 5000 acres of land and running
	: thence East twelve hundred and Sixty poles, thence
	: North so far that a line west to the line of Marion
Location filed &	: County and with the said line to the Beginning for Com-
Entry made 20th Feby. 1838	: pliment excluding all prior claims.
	: Tennessee, Feb. 20th 1838
	:
	: J. G. Smith
	: Locator
	:
fees of Office paid 75c	: A certified Copy issued the 10th April 1838
	:
	:
PAGE 265	:
	:
No. 214 M. Miller Enters 5000 acres	: Michel Miller Enters 5000 acres of land in Hamilton
	: County. Beginning at the North west corner of an
	: Entry in the name of Jacob Billingsley for 5000 a-
	: cres of land and running thence East 1260 poles
	: thence North so far that a line West to the line
	:

Location
filed &
Entry
made the
20th Febry.
1838

of Marion County and with the same to the Beginning
excluding all prior claims will include the quantity.
Tennessee February 20th 1838

J. G. Smith
Locator

A certified Copy issued the 10th 1838

fees of office
paid 75c

Saml. T. Igou
Depty. E. T.

PAGE 266

No. 215
B. H. Throop
enters 5000
acres

B. H. Throop Enters five thousand acres of land in
Hamilton County. Beginning at the North West corner
on the line of Marion County of an Entry in the name
of Michael Miller for 5000 acres and running thence
East 1260 poles, thence North so far that a line
West to the line of Marion County and with the same
to the Beginning for Compliment, excluding all prior

Location filed
and Entry
made 20 Febry.
1838

claims. Tennessee, February 20th 1838

J. G. Smith
Locator

Office fees
Paid 75c

A certified Copy issued the 10th April 1838

Saml. T. Igou
Depty. E. T.

PAGE 266

No. 216
Ashael Hatt
Enters
5000 acres

Ashael Hatt Enters five thousand acres of land in
Hamilton County. Beginning at the North West corner
of an entry in the name of B. H. Thopp for 5000 a-
cres of land on the line of Marion County and running thence East 1260 poles, thence North so far
that a line North and west to the Beginning, exclud-

Location
filed &
Entry made
20th Febry.
1838

ing all prior Claims will include the quantity.
Tennessee Febry. 20th 1838

J. G. Smith
Locator

A certified Copy issued the 10th Apl. 1838

fees of
Office
paid 75c

S. T. Igou
Depty. E. T.

PAGE 267

No. 217	:	Robert Marcum Enters 5000 acres of land in Hamil-
R. Marcum	:	ton Ten. Beginning East of the Marion County Line
Enters	:	running North 20 East 640 poles North 70 west
5000 acres	:	1280 poles South 20 west 640 poles, thence a di-
	:	rect Line to the Beginning for Compliment -- ex-
	:	cluding all prior claims.
Location filed	:	Febry. 20th 1838
& Entry made	:	
24th May	:	Joseph G. Smith
1838	:	Locator
	:	
	:	A certified Copy issued the 24th May, 1838
Office fees	:	
paid 75c	:	Samuel T. Igou
	:	Depty. E. T.

PAGE 267

No. 218	:	James Marcum Enters 5000 Thousand acres of land in
J. Marcum	:	Hamilton County, Tenn. Beginning on the South East
Enters 5000	:	corner of a five Thousand acre entry made in the
acres	:	name of Robert Marcum runing North 20 East 640 poles
	:	South 70 East 1280 poles South 20 West 640 poles
	:	thence to the Beginning for Compliment -- excluding
Location filed	:	all prior claims.
& Entry made	:	Feb. 20th 1838
24th May	:	
1838	:	Joseph G. Smith
	:	LOcator
Office fees	:	A certified Copy issued the 24th May 1838
paid 75c	:	
	:	Samuel T. Igou
	:	Depty. E. T.

PAGE 268

No. 219	:	James Henderson Enters 5000 Thousand acres of Land
James Marcum	:	in Hamilton County, Ten. Beginning at the North East
Enters	:	corner of an Entry in the name of Robert Marcum for 5
5000 acres	:	5000 thousand acres of Land, running North 20 East
	:	640 poles North 70 West 1250 poles South 20 west
	:	640 poles thence to the Beginning for Compliment—
Location	:	excluding all prior claims.
filed and	:	Feby 20th 1838
Entry made	:	
the 24th	:	Joseph G. Smith
May 1838	:	Locator
Office fees	:	A certified Copy issued the 24th May 1838
paid	:	S. T. Igou
75c	:	Depty. E. T.

PAGE 268

No. 220
Alexander
Newman
Enters
5000 acres

Alexander Newman Enters 5000 thousand acres of Land
Beginning on the North West corner of a five thous-
and acre entry made in the name of James Marcum,
running North 20 East 640 poles South Seventy East
1280 poles South 20 West 640 poles, thence to the
Beginning for Compliment -- excluding all prior
claims. Febry. 20th 1838

Location
filed &
Entry made
24th May
1838

Joseph G. Smith
Locator

A certified Copy issued the 24th May 1838

Office fees
paid 75c

S. T. Igou
Depty. E. T.

PAGE 269

No. 221
Jacob Billings-
ley enters
5000 acres

Jacob Billingsley Enters 5000 acres of Land in Ham-
ilton County, Tenn. Beginning at the North East cor-
ner of a 5000 acre Entry made in the name of James
Henderson running North 20 East 640 poles North 70
West 1280 poles South 20 West 640 poles thence to the
Beginning for Compliment -- excluding all prior claims
Feb. 20th 1838.

Location filed
& Entry made
the 24th May
1838

Jos. G. Smith
Locators

A certified Copy issued the 24th May 1838

Office fees
paid 75c

S. T. Igou
Depty. E. T.

PAGE 269

No. 222
M. Miller
Enters
5000 acres

Michael Miller Enters 5000 acres of land in Hamilton County, Tenn. Beginning at the North West corner
of a 5000 acre Entry made in the name of Alexander
Newman running North 20 East 640 poles South 70 East
1280 poles South 20 West 640 poles thence to the Beginning for Compliment -- Excluding all prior claims
Febry. 20th 1838

Location filed
& Entry made
the 24th May
1838

Jos. G. Smith
Locator

A certified Copy issued the 24th May 1838

Office fees
paid 75c

S. T. Igou
Depty. E. T.

PAGE 270 :
:
No. 223 : B. H. Throop Enters 5000 acres of land in Hamilton
B. H. Throop : County, Ten. Beginning at the North East Corner of
Enters : a 5000 acre Entry made in the name of James Billingsly
50000 acres : Running North 20 East 640 North 70 West 1280 poles
: South 20 West 640 poles thence to the Beginning for
: Compliment, Excluding all prior claims,
Location filed : Febry. 20th 1838
and Entry made :
the 24th May :   Jos. G. Smith
1838 :   Locator
:
: A certified Copy issued the 24th May 1838.
Office fees :
Paid 75c :   Samuel T. Igou,
:   Depty. E. T.
:
:
PAGE 224 :
:
A. Hatt : Asahel Hatt Enters 5000 acres of land in Hamilton
Enters : County, Te. Beginning at the North west corner of
5000 acres : a 5000 acre entry made in the name of Michael Miller
: Running North 20 East 640 poles South 70, East 1280
: South 20 West 640 poles, thence to the beginning for
Location : Compliment, excluding all prior claims.
filed and : Febry. 20th, 1838
Entry made :
24th May :   Jos. G. Smith
1838 :   Locator
:
: A certified Copy Issued the 24th May 1838
Office :
fees 75c :   Saml. T. Igou
:   Depty. E. T.
:
:
PAGE 271 :
:
No. 225 : John Kelly Enters 5000 acres of land in Hamilton Coun-
J. Kelly : ty Te. Begin ing on the North East corner of a 5000 En-
Enters : try made in the name of B. H. Throop running North
5000 acres : 20 East 640 poles, North 70, West 1280 poles South 20
: west 640 poles thence to the Beginning for Compliment
: --excluding all prior claims.
Location : Feb. 20th. 1838
filed & :
Entry made :
the 24th May :   Jos. G. Smith
1838 :   Locator
:
: A certified Copy issued the 24th May 1838
Office fees :
Paid 75c :   S. T. Igou, Depty. E.T.
:

PAGE. 271

No. 226
M. Wyout
Enters
5000 acres

Michael Wyout Enters 5000 acres of land in Hamilton County Te. Beginning at the North West corner of a 5000 acre Entry made in the name of Asahel Matt, running North 20 East 640 poles South 70 East 1280 poles South 20 west 640 poles thence to the Beginning for Compliment -- excluding all prior claims.

Location filed
& Entry made
the 24th May
1838

Feby. 20th 1838.

Jos. G. Smith
Locator

Office fees
paid 75c

A certified Copy Issued the 24th May, 1838

S. T. Igou
Depty. E. T.

PAGE 272
No. 227
J. B. Carroll
Enters
5000 acres

State of Tennessee   James B. Carroll enters 5000
                       acres of land in Hamilton Coun-
Hamilton County   ty, Beginning on a Black oak
                       corner of S. B. Hawkins Entry
No. 57 running to the best advantage for compliment -- according to law so as to include 5000 acres of land this 28th August 1838.

Location
filed &
Entry made
the 28th Aug.
1838

J. B. Carroll
Locator

Office fees
Paid 75c

Page 272

No. 228

J. J. Carroll
Enters
5000 acres

John J. Carroll Enters 5000 acres of land in Hamilton County Beginning on the North West corner of James B. Carrolls Entry in H. County. Running to the best advantage according to law so as to include 5000 acres of land, excluding all prior claims.

Location filed
& Entry made
28 Aug. 1838

J. J. Carroll
Locator

28th August 1838

Office rees
paid 75c

PAGE 273

No. 229
R. T. Johnson
Enters
50000 acres

: R. T.(?) Johnson enters 5000 acres of land in Ham-
: ilton County Beginning on S. B. Hawkins 5000 acre
: Entry No. 57 at a Black oak marked S. B. H. -- run-
: ning to the best advantage according to law exclud-
: ing all prior claims so as to include 5000 acres,
: 28th Aug. 1838

Location
filed &
Entry made
28 Aug.
1838

: N. J. Tunnell
: Locator

Office fees
paid 75¢

PAGE 273

No. 230
Wm. C. Tunnell
Enters
5000 acres

State of Tennessee{ Wm. C. Tunnell Enters 5000 Acres
                  { of land in Said County, Beginning
Hamilton County { on the Marion County line on the
                   top of Waldens Ridge of Cumber-
land Mountain at a point near where Suck Creek falls
of said Ridge Running to the Best advantage for Compliment so as to include 4000 acres of land excluding
all prior claims.

Location filed
and entry made
5th Sept.
1838

: N. J. Tynnell
: Locator

Office fees
Paid 75¢

PAGE 274

No. 231
N. J. Tunnell
Enters
4000 acres

State of Tennessee{ N. J. Tunnell Enters 4000 Acres
                  { of Land, Beginning on the North
Hamilton County { West corner of a 200 Acre Entry
                   made by Benj. B. Cannon on or
near the Head of North Chickamauga running to the
best advantage according to law so as to include
4000 acres of land excluding all prior claims.

Location filed
& Entry made
the 5th Sept.
1838

: N. J. Tunnell
: Locator

Office fees
paid 75¢

PAGE 274

No. 232

: Simpson Little Enters 5000 acres of land in Hamilton

Simpson Little
enters 5000
acres

County. Beginning at a point in a line which divides Hamilton County and Marion County at Eight hundred poles Northwardly from the foot of the Mountain nearest the Tennessee river on the South side of said river running thence east so far that a line South to the foot of the Mountain & with the same bordering on prior claims to the line of Marion County and with the same to the Beginning for Compliment -- excluding all prior claims and including the quantity.
Sept. 15th 1838

Location filed
& Entry made
the 15th Sept.
1838

fees of
office
paid 75c

Jas. Simpson
& Doctor Hall
Locators

PAGE 275

No. 233
Harmon Little
enters 5000
acres

Harmon Little Enters 5000 acres of land in Hamilton County Beginning at the North East corner of an entry in the name of Sampson Little for 5000 acres of land and running thence South to the South East corner of said entry thence with the foot of the Mountain Eastwardly bordering on the prior entries so far that a line Northwardly bordering prior claims to a point due East of the Beginning excluding all prior claims and including the quantity.
15th Sept. 1838

Location filed
& entry made
the 15th Sept.
1838

James Simpson
& Doctor Hall
Locators

Fees of
office paid
75c

PAGE 275

No. 234
Thos. Heifner
enters
5000 acres

Thomas Heifner Enters 5000 acres of land in Hamilton County, Beginning at the North West corner of an entry in the name of Harmon Little for five thousand acres of land in the line of Marion County and running thence east 1260 poles, thence North so far that a line west to Marion County line and with the same to the Beginning -- excluding all prior claims, will include the quantity.
Sept. 15th 1838

Location filed
and entry made
15th Sept.
1838

James Simpson
& Doctor Hall
Locators

Fees of office
paid 75c

PAGE 276

No. 235
Joseph W. Bell
enters 5000
acres

Joseph W. Bell enters 5000 acres of land in Hamilton County, Beginning at the Beginning of an entry made in the name of Thos. Heifner for 5000 acres of land Running thence East twelve hundred and sixty poles, thence North so far that a line west to the line of Marion County and with the same to the Beginning for Compliment, Excluding all prior claims.

Location filed
and entry made
the 15th Sept.
1838

15th Sept. 1838

Jas. Simpson
& Doctor Hall
Locators

Fees of
Office
paid 75c

(To S.T.I.)

PAGE 276

No. 236
Ellin Smith
enters 5000
acres

Ellin Smith enters 5000 acres of land in Hamilton County. Beginning at the North west corner of an entry in the name of Joseph W. Bell for five thousand acres and running thence east thence North so far that a line west to the line of Marion County and with the same to the Beginning will exclude the quantity.

Location filed
and made entry
the 15th Sept.
1838

15th Sept. 1838

Jas. Simpson
& Doctor Hall
Locators

Fees of
Office paid
75c

To S.T.I.

PAGE 277

No. 237
Sally H. Simpson
Enters 5000
acres

Sally H. Simpson enters 5000 acres of land in Hamilton County Beginning in the line of Marion County at the North East corner of an entry made in the name of Ellen Smith for 5000 acres of land & running thence East thence North so far that a line west to the line of Marion County and with said line to the Beginning for Compliment -- excluding all prior claims.

Location filed
& entry made
the 15th Sept.
1838

Sept. 16, 1838

Jas. Simpson
& Doctor Hall
Locators

PAGE 277

No. 238 Robt. M. Glenn enters 5000 acres	:	Robert M. Glenn enters 5000 acres of land in Ham- ilton County. Beginning at the North West corner on the line of Marion County of an entry in the name of Sally M. Simpson for 5000 acres, and run- ning thence east, thence North so far that a line west to the line of Marion County and with the
Location filed and entry made the 15th Sept. 1838	:	same to the Beginning for Compliment excluding all prior Claims. Sept. 15th 1838
	:	Jas. Simpson & Doct. Hall Locators
Fees of Office paid 75c To S.T.I.	:	

PAGE 278

No. 239 Mary Little enters 5000 acres	:	Mary Little enters 5000 acres of land in Hamilton County Beginning at the North west corner of an en- try made in the name of Robert M. Glenn for 5000 acres on the line of Marion County Running thence East thence North so far that a line north and west to the line of Marion County and with the same to
Location filed and entry made the 15th Sept. 1838	:	the Beginning excluding all prior claims & includ- ing the quantity. 15th Sept. 1838
	:	Jas. Simpson & Doct. Hall Locators
Fees of office paid 75c To S.T.I.	:	

PAGE 278

No. 240 Albin Shrewsbury enters 5000 acres	:	Albin Shrewsbury enters 5000 acres of land in Hamil- ton County Beginning on the line of Marion County at the Northwest corner of an entry in the name of Mary Little for 5000 acres & running thence east thence North so far that a line to the line of Mar-
Fees of Office paid 75c	:	ion County and with the same to the Beginning for Compliment -- excluding all other claims. 15th Sept. 1838
To S. T. I.	:	
	:	Jas. Simpson Doctor Hall Locators
Location received and Entry made the 15th Sept. 1838		

PAGE 279

No. 241
Moses Scarlett
enters 5000
acres

: Moses Scarlet enters 5000 acres of land in Hamilton
: County. Beginning at the South East corner of an
: Entry for 5000 acres in the name of Albin Shrews-
: bury & running thence East bordering on prior claims,
: west and excluding all prior claims and including the
: quantity.

Location re-
ceived and
Entry made
the 15th Sept.
1838

: 15th Sept. 1838

James Simpson
& Doct. Hall
Locators

Fees of
office paid
75c
To S.T.I.

PAGE 279

No. 242
Sally Roberson
enters 5000
acres

: Sally Roberson enters 5000 acres of land in Hamilton
: County. Beginning at the North West corner of a tract
: of land in the name of Moses Scarlet for 5000 acres
: running thence East, thence Northwardly for Compliment
: West excluding all prior claims.
: 15th Sept.

Location
Received and
entry made
the 15th Sept.
1838

: 1838

Jas. Simpson
& Doctor Hall
Locators

Fees of
Office paid
75c

PAGE 280

No. 243
Jerry Franklin
enters 5000
acres

: Jerry Franklin enters 5000 acres of land in Hamilton
: County. Beginning at the North west corner of an en-
: try in the name of Sally Roberson for 5000 acres and
: running thence east, thence Northwardly with the foot
: of the Mountain so far that a line west and to the

Location re-
ceived & filed
and entry made
15th Sept. 1838

: Beginning on former entries and excluding prior claims
: will include the quantity.
: 15th Septl 1838

Fees of office
75c To S.T.I.

Jas. Simpson
& Doctor Hall
Locator

PAGE 280

No. 244 Hannah Smith enters 5000 acres Location filed and Entry made Sept. 15th,1838 Fees of Office paid 75c	: Hannah Smith enters 5000 acres of land in Hamilton : County. Beginning at the North West corner of an : entry in the name of Jerry Franklin for 5000 acres : and running thence east, thence Northwardly to the : foot of the Mountain for Compliment, bordering all : prior claims for quantity. : 15th Sept. 1838

                                        Jas. Simpson
                                        & Doctor Hall
                                        Locators

PAGE 281

PAGE 245

James Glenn enters 5000 acres Location filed and entry made 15th 1838 Fees of Office paid 75c To S.T.I.	: James Glenn enters 5000 acres of land in Hamilton : County. Beginning at the North west corner of an : entry for 5000 acres in the name of Hannah Smith : and running thence East, Thence Northwardly with : the foot of the mountain so far that a line west : and bordering on prior claims will include the : quantity. 15th Sept. 1839

                                        James Simpson
                                        & Doctor Hall
                                        Locators

PAGE 281

No. 246 William Glenn enters 5000 acres Location filed and entry made the 15th Sept. 1838 Fees of Office paid 75c To S.T.I.	: William Glenn enters 5000 acres of land in Hamilton : County. Beginning at the North West corner of an : entry in the line of Marion County in the name of : James Glenn for 5000 acres Running thence east, : thence North so far that a line West to the line : of Marion County and with a line of the same to the : Beginning for Compliment -- excluding all prior : claims. : 15th Sept. 1838

                                        Jas. Simpson
                                        & Doctor Hall
                                        Locators

PAGE 282

No. 247 Monroe Cox enters	: Monroe Cox enters 5000 acres of land in Hamilton : County Beginning at the North west corner of an : entry of 5000 acres in the name of William Glenn

Location filed : running thence East, thence Northwardly with the f
and Entry made : foot of the Mountain so far that a line West and
15th Sept. 1838 : bordering on former entries excluding all prior
: claims and including the quantity.
: 15th Sept. 1838
Fees of office :
paid To. S.T.I. :
: Jas. Simpson
: & Doctor Hall,
: Locators
:
:
PAGE 282 :
:
No. 248 : John Peterson enters 5000 acres of land in Hamilton
John Peterson : County. Beginning at the North West corner of an
enters : entry for 5000 acres in the name of Monroe Cox &
5000 acres : running thence east, thence Northwardly with the
: foot of the Mountain so far that a line west and
Location filed : bordering all prior claims will exclude the quan-
& Entry made : tity.
15th Sept. : 15th Sept. 1838
1838 :
: Jas. Simpson
: & Doctor Hall
: Locators
Fees of :
office paid :
75c To S.T.I. :
:
:
:
PAGE 283 :
:
No. 249 : James Clenny enters 5000 acres of land in Hamilton
James Clenny : County Beginning on the line which divides the Coun-
enters : ties of Marion and Hamilton at the South west cor-
5000 acres : ner of an entry in the name of John Peterson for
: 5000 acres, Running thence with the County line
: Southwardly thence East for Compliment North and
Location filed : with the lines of former entries to the Beginning
the 15th Sept. : excluding all prior claims, including the quantity.
& entry made : 15th Sept. 1838
1838 :
: Jas. Simpson
: & Doctor Hall
Fees of Office : Locator
paid 75c :
to S.T.I. :
:
PAGE 283 :
:
No. 250 : Willie Crawford enters 5000 acres of land in Hamilton
Willie Crawford : County. Beginning at the North east corner of an en-
enters : try for 5000 acres in the name of James Clenny. Run-
5000 acres : ning thence South, thence east for Compliment — North
: & West with former entries to the Beginning including

Location filed & entry made the 15th Sept. 1838	all former entries. 15 Sept, 1838 Jas. Simpson & Doctor Hall Locators
Fees of Office paid 75c To S.T.I.	

PAGE 284

No. 251 Aron Clement enters 150 acres	Aron Clement of Hamilton County enters One hundred and fifty acres of land on Wallens Ridge adjoining a survey made by said Clement lying in the fork of Opossom Creek, Beginning on the South east line of said Survey, then running one hundred and fifty acres as the law may direct.
Location received & entry made 7th Jany. 1839	I say entered by me 7th January 1839 Aron Clement
Fees of Office paid 75c To	

PAGE 284

No. 252 John Lewis enters 5000 acres	State of Tennessee } John Lewis enters 5000 acres Hamilton County } of land in said County. Beginning on five Maples, on the North east side of a branch that runs into Taliaferro's Mill Creek and on a trace that leads from Suck Creek to Sequachie Valley. Running thence Northwardly 640 poles eastwardly twelve hundred and eighty poles Southwardly 640 poles, westwardly 1280 to the beginning.
Location filed & entry made 1st June 1839	1st June 1839 John Lewis Locator Certified Copy issued 1st June 1839

PAGE 285

No. 253 John Lewis enters 5000 acres	State of Tennessee } John Lewis enters 5000 acres of Hamilton County } land in said County. Beginning on five Maples. Beginning corner to a former entry in the name of John Lewis Running Northwardly 640 poles

| Location
filed &
entry made
1 June 1839 | : | westwardly 1280 poles Southwardly 640 poles Eastward-
ly 1280 poles to the Beginning.
1st June 1839 |

                                    John Lewis
                                    Locator

Fees of Office
paid 75c   :   Certified Copy issued 1 June 1839

PAGE 285

No. 254
John Lewis
enters
5000 acres

State of Tennessee⟨ John Lewis enters 5000 acres of
                   ⟩ land in said County. Beginning
Hamilton County   ⟨ on 5 Maples (beginning corner
                     to a former entry made in the
name of John Lewis) running thence Southwardly 640
poles Eastwardly 1280 poles, Northwardly 640 poles
westwardly 1280 poles to the Beginning.

Location filed
& entry made
1st June
1839
                              1st June 1839

                                    J. Lewis
                                    Locator

Fees of office
paid 75c   :   Certified Copy issued 1 June 1839

PAGE 286

No. 255
John Lewis
enters
5000 acres

John Lewis enters 5000 acres of land in Hamilton
County, Beginning on 5 Maples (beginning corner
to a former entry made in the name of John Lewis)
running thence Southwardly 640 poles, westwardly
1280 poles Northwardly 640 poles Eastwardly 1280
poles to the beginning.

Fees of office
paid 75c   :   1 June 1839

                                    J. Lewis
                                    Locator

                  Certified Copy issued 1 June, 1839

PAGE 286

No. 256X

John Lewis
enters
5000 acres

John Lewis enters 5000 of land in Hamilton County. Beginning on a poplar on the north west side of Middle Creek, above Taleaferro's original line running
thence Eastwardly 1280 poles Northwardly 640 poles
westwardly 1280 poles Southwardly 640 poles to the
Beginning.

Location filed : 1st June 1839
& entry made :
1 June 1839 :
:   J. Lewis
:   Locator
:

Fees of Office : Certified Copy issued 1st June 1839
paid 75c :
:
:
:
:

PAGE 287 :
No. 258 :
  (257?) : John Lewis enters 5000 acres of land in Hamilton Coun-
John Lewis : ty. Beginning on a red oak, corner to an entry in the
enters 5000 : name of John Lewis No. 256 -- dated June 1st 1839.
acres : running thence Eastwardly 1280 poles Northwardly 640
: poles, thence westwardly 1280 poles Southwardly 640
: poles to the Beginning.
Location filed : 1st June 1839
and entry made :
the 1st June :   J. Lewis
1839 :   Locator
:
: Certified Copy issued 1 June 1839
:
Fee of Office :
paid 75c :
:
:
PAGE 287 :
:
No. 258 : John Lewis enters 5000 acres of land in Hamilton
John Lewis : County, beginning on a poplar on the West bank of
enters : Middle Creek Beginning corner to a former entry
5000 acres : in the name of John Lewis No. 256. Running thence
: Northwardly 640 poles, thence Westwardly 1280 thence
: Southwardly 640 poles, thence Eastwardly 1280 poles
Location filed : to the Beginning.
& entry made : 1st June 1839
1st June 1839 :
:   J. Lewis
:   Locator
Fee of :
Office paid : Certified Copy issued 1 June 1839
75c :
:
:
PAGE 288 :
:
No. 259 : John Lewis enters 5000 acres of land in Hamilton
John Lewis : County. Beginning on a Maple marked T. on the South w
enters : west side of Falling Water Creek, abount 2 miles a-
5000 acres : bove the Falls of Said Creek Thence running South-

Location filed & Entry made 1st June 1839	wardly 640 poles westwardly 1280 poles Northwardly 640 poles eastwardly1280 poles to the Beginning. J. Lewis Locator
Fees of office paid 75c	A certified Copy issued the 1st June 1839

PAGE 288

No. 260 John Lewis enters 5000 acres	John Lewis enters 5000 acres of land in Hamilton County on Waldens Ridge of Cumberland Mountain Beginning on a Black oak near a branch that runs into Suck Creek above the falls of said Creek, Running eastwardly 1280 poles, Northwardly 640 thence westwardly 1280 poles Southwardly 640 poles
Location filed & Entry made 1st June 1839	to the Beginning. 1st. June 1839 J. Lewis Locator
Fees of office paid 75c	A certified Copy issued 1 June 1839

PAGE 289

No. 261 X John Lewis enters 5000 acres	John Lewis enters 5000 acres of land in Hamilton County, Beginning on a Maple marked T. Beginning corner of an entry in the name of John Lewis No.259 dated 1st June 1839. Thence Northwardly 640 poles west 1280 poles Southwardly 640 poles Eastwardly 1280 poles to the Beginning.
Location filed & entry made 1 June 1839	June 1, 1839 J. Lewis Locator
Fees of office paid 75c	A certified copy issued 1 June 1839

PAGE 289

No. 262 X John Lewis Enters 5000 acres	John Lewis Enters 5000 acres of land in Hamilton County on Wallens Ridge of Cumberland Mountain Beginning on the South east corner of said John Lewis former entry No. 261, Running thence eastwardly 1280 poles, thence Northwardly 640 poles thence westwardly 1280 poles, thence Southwardly 640 poles to the Beginning.
Location filed & Entry made	

1 June
1839

Fees of Office
Paid 75c

PAGE 290

No. 263
John Lewis
enters
5000 acres

Location filed
and entry made
1 June 1839

Fees of office
paid 75c

PAGE 290

No. 264
John B. Hyatt
enters 5000
acres

Location filed
and entry made
1 June 1839

Fees of office
paid 75cc

PAGE 291

No. 265
William Clift
enters
200 acres

June 1, 1839

J. Lewis
Locator

A certified Copy issued 1 June 1839.

John Lewis enters 5000 acres of land in Hamilton
County. Beginning on a Stake on the North west
bank of Tennessee river in the road that leads
from Dallas to Jasper Thence Northeastwardly thence
Northwestwardly. Thence Southwestwardly, Thence
with the meanders of the river to the Beginning.
1st June 1839

John Lewis
Locator

A certified Copy issued 1 June 1839.

John B. Hyatt enters four thousand four hundred & ten
Acres of land in Hamilton County.
Beginning on a white oak on the N. East Side of a
trace that leads from Tennessee river to Helton Cabbin
Thence Eastwardly 840 poles thence Northwardly 840
poles thence westwardly 840 poles Thence Southwardly
840 poles thence Northwardly 840 poles thence westwardly 840 poles, Thence southwardly 840 poles to the
Beginning.
1st June 1839

(No signature)
Locator

A certified Copy issued 1 June 1839

William Clift enters Ninety Acres of land lying and
being in Hamilton County and State of Tennessee and
bounded as follows, to wit: Beginning on two Black
walnuts lower corner to George W. Williams marked
R.A. thence North eleven Poles to a large Spanish
oak marked B. and continued the same course 80 poles
in all to a stake, thence west keeping the same distance from the Tennessee River to a point 30 poles

Location received and Entry made the 12th day of July 1859	Below the Tumbling Shoals, thence a direct line to the river and extending into the river 20 poles just below the bar at said Shoal, thence up the river keeping 20 poles from the bank of the river to a point opposite the Beginning thence a straight line to the Beginning to contain Ninety Acres be the same more of less and if there is any unappropriated land North of said Survey to include 200 acres and if said
Fees of Office paid 75¢	calls does not cover the Bank and waters of the Tumbling Shoals for 30 poles, above and below a said Shoals the Survey to be so made as to include the bank of the river to original lines and the entire Shoal and bar for twenty poles in the river done in the entry takers Office for Hamilton County this twelfth day of July Eighteen hundred and thirty nine.

William Clift
Locator

A certified Copy issued 12th July 1839.

PAGE 292

No. 266 Jesse Walker enters 640 acres	State of Tennessee{ Jesse Walker enters Six hundred and forty Acres of land in said Hamilton County { County, and on Wallens ridge of Cumberland Mountain on the waters of North Chiccamogga Creek Beginning on a white oak marked J.(?) W. Thence westwardly thence South-
Location received and entry made 6 Sept. 1839	wardly, thence Eastwardly, Thence a direct line to the Beginning, to be an oblong twice the width in length and to include a chalybiate Spring and the number of acres above mentioned. 6th Sept. 1839
Fees of Office paid 75¢	Jesse Walker Locator

PAGE 292

No. 267 Allen White enters 5000 acres	State of Tennessee{ Allen White enters in the entry takers Office in Hamilton County Hamilton County { five thousand acres of land, Beginning at the low water mark on a Maple opposite the lower point of an Island Just above the Town of Chattanooga and above John Cowart's fer-
Location received and filed 31st Sept. 1839	ry. Running North to said Cowart's deeded line, thence westwardly with said line to the Tumbling Shoals, Thence South to the Middle of Tennessee River thence up the river keeping the center of the river

fees paid : as a Boundary Line opposite the Beginning North to
: the Beginning.
:
: Allen White
: Locator
:
:

PAGE 293 :
:
No. 268 : State of Tennessee) William M. Davis enters as Gener-
Wm. M. Davis :) al enteror One hundred and Sixty
enters : Hamilton County (Acres of land, Beginning at the
3000 acres : lower end of a small Island in
: the Tennessee river a short distance above the mouth
: of Chattanooga Creek, thence south eastwardly to the
Location filed : Eastern bank of said river thence up the river with
& Entry made : appropriated lines as it meanders, Thence Northward
3rd Febry. : to a point in the river directly above the upper end
1840 : of said Island, Thence a direct line to the upper
: end of said island. Thence with the western bank
: (at its base) of said island to the beginning so as
fees 75c : to include said Island in One hundred & Sixty Acres
: entered the 3rd day of February 1840.
:
: Wm. M. Davis
: Locator
:
:

PAGE 294 :
:
No. 269 : State of Tennessee) Entry Taker's office March the 25th
Robert N. White :) 1840.
enters 5000 : Hamilton County (Robert N. White enters five thous-
acres : and acres of land in said County.
: Beginning on a Maple, at the low water mark, opposite
: the lower point of the Island just above the Town of
Location re- : Chattanooga, Running North to John Cowarts deeded
ceived & filed : lines, thence Eastwardly up the Tennessee river with
25th March : other lines to the County line of Rhea County then
1840 : Southwardly to the river bank, then down the river
: westwardly keeping the centre of the same as it me-
: anders to the Beginning.
fees paid :
: Allen White
: Locator
:
: Certified Copy issued 25th March 1840
:

PAGE 294 :
:
No. 270 : State of Tennessee) Ephraim Hixson enters One hundred
E. Hixson :) Acres of land on Wallens Ridge in
Enters : Hamilton County (said County Beginning on a stake on
100 acres : Rock House branch, Then Northward-

Location filed and entry made 6th July 1840	ly 200 poles to a stake Thence Eastwardly 150 poles to a stake, then Southwardly 200 poles to a stake, Then Westwardly 150 poles to the Beginning, so as to include a Sulpher Spring, And One hundred acres of land entered this 6th July 1840.
fee 75c	Ephraim Hixson Locator

PAGE 295

No. 271 James Hopper enters 500 acres	State of Tennessee) James Hopper enters five hundred) acres of land in Hamilton Coun- Hamilton County (ty and on Waldens ridge adjoin- ing an entry made by Henry Bra- dens on Hoppers Trace and beginning on the North east corner of said entry made by Henry Braden and now owned by Absolem Deaken's Thence Eastwarsly, Thence westwardly, thence Northwardly so as to Strike the South west corner of the aforesaid entry, Thence with the lines thereof to the Beginning, so as to include a chalybeate Spring and five hundred Acres of land. Entered the 25th day of July, 1840.
Location filed & entry made 25th July 1740	
fee 75c	James Hopper Locator
	Certified Copy issued 25th July 1840

PAGE 295

No. 272 E. Askew enters 1000 acres	State of Tennessee) Elisha Askew enters One thous-) and acres of land on Wallens Hamilton County (Ridge. Beginning at the mouth of Bear Branch on the South side of North Chickamogga Creek Thence up the creek as it meanders, Thence Southwardly, Thence Eastwardly, Thence Northwardly to the Beginning so as to include a Chalybeate Spring that empties into Bear branch and One Thousand acres of land. Entered the 27th day of July 1840.
Location filed & entry made 27th July 1840	
	Elisha Askew Locator
fee 75c	
	Certified Copy issued 27th July 1840

PAGE 296

No. 273 B.B. Cannon Enters 1000 acres	State of Tennessee) B. B. Cannon enters One Thousand) Acres of land on Wallens Ridge Hamilton County (Beginning at the Mouth of Bear branch on the South Side of North Chickamogga Creek

Location filed and entry made 27th July 1840	and corner to Elisha Askew's 1000 acre entry No.272 Thence down said Creek, as it meanders to the North west corner of Cannon & Zimmerman's 1000 acre entry. Thence Southwardly with a line of said last mentioned entry Thence Eastwardly to said Elisha Askew's South East corner, Thence with his line to the beginning.
fee 75c	Entered this 27th day of July 1840

B. B. Cannon
Locator

Copy issd 24th May 1842

PAGE 296

No. 274 Hez. Hughes enters 700 acres	Hezekiah Hughes Enters Seven hundred acres of land on Waldens Ridge of Cumberland Mountain in the County of Hamilton Beginning on the South East corner of a 640 acre entry made by him adjoining Ephraim Hughes--dated the 4th day of November 1833 and No.107
Location received and filed 15th Oct. 1840	Thence South Eastwardly. thence with a line of said entry to the Beginning to include Seven hundred acres of unappropriated lands, entered the 15th day of October 1840

Hezekiah Hughes
Locator

Entry made same day

fees 75c

PAGE 297

275 No. Coleman & Bunch enters 5000 acres	State of Tennessee} Charles Coleman and William Bunch enters five thousand acres of Hamilton County land on Wallens Ridge in said County, Beginning on a Black Oak and chestnut oak on the South east top of Wallens Ridge near Poe's turnpike road, on the North east
Location received and filed and entry made the 23rd day of Jany. 1841	side of said turnpike road, thence Northwestwardly to the North eastern corner of said Charles Coleman's 640 acre entry, thence with his line Northwestwardly to his Northwest corner, thence same course continued to the northwest top of said ridge thence North eastwardly along the extreme top last
fees 75c paid	mentioned to the headwaters of Sale Creek, thence down Sale creek to the Southeast top of said ridge, thence along the Southeast top to the beginning to include five thousand acres of unappropriated land.-- entered the 23rd day of January 1841.

Charles Coleman, Locator

PAGE 297

No. 276

(Blank)

(Blank)

State of Tennessee | Entry takers Office No.276 John
| Brown Jr. Madison Varner & Lew-
Hamilton County | is Varner enters five thousand
acres of land on Waldens Ridge
Beginning where the back line of George R. Cannon
Entry No. 114 crosses Big Soddy Creek, Thence Northeastwardly with said line, Thence Northwestly, thence
Southwestwardly Thence Southeastwardly. thence Northeastwardly to the Beginning, so as to include five-
Thousand acres of unappropriated land in a square or
oblong. Entered February 5th 1841

                    John Brown, Jr.
                    Madison Varner
                    Lewis Varner
                    Locators

PAGE 298

No. 277
Elisha Askew
enters
1000 acres

Location Re-
ceived & filed
and entry made
the 4th day
of March
1841

FEES 75c

State of Tennessee | Elisha Askew enters one thousand
| acres of land on Wallens Ridge
Hamilton County | of Cumberland Mountain, in the
2nd Civil District, adjoining an
entry of 1000 acres heretofore made by said Askew.
Beginning at a stake in a line of the former entry
on the bluff of Chiccamogga creek running thence up
the creek with the meanders of the bluff thereof
thence a Southward course, thence Eastward with a
line of the former entry and thence Northward with
another line of said former entry to the Beginning.

                    Elisha Askew
                    Locator
                    4th March 1841

PAGE 298

No. 278
E. Rogers &
A. Rawlings
enters
1600 acres

Location re-
ceived and filed
and entry made
4th March
1841

State of Tennessee | Elisha Rogers & Asahel Rawlings
| enter Sixteen hundred acres of
Hamilton County | land on Wallens Ridge of Cumber-
land Mountain in the 3rd Civil
District of said County. Beginning at a Black standing near the bluff of rocks on the South east declivity or descent, about a half mile above where Browns
trace from Mountain Creek passes through the Clift
of Rocks at the top of said ridge running thence
Northwestwardly 400 poles, thence Southwestwardly
six hundred & forty poles, thence South Eastwardly
four hundred poles to the bluff of Rocks at the cres-

fees 75¢   cant of said ridge thence up North eastwardly with
the meanders of the Clift of rocks about 640 poles
to the point of beginning.

           Elisha Rogers & Locators
           Asahel Rawlings
           4th March 1841

PAGE 299

No. 279
Charles Coleman
enters
5000 acres

Location re-
ceived and
filed 26 April
1841
entry made
same day

fees 75¢

Charles Coleman enters five thousand acres of land
in Hamilton County and State of Tennessee on Wallens
ridge Beginning at a Black oak and Hickory on the
eastern top of said ridge near Poes turnpike road,
and Beginning corner to an entry made in the name
of Charles Coleman and William Bunch No. 275 for
five thousand acres. Thence Northwestwardly with a
line of said entry No. 275 to the top of said ridge
thence Southwestwardly with the extreme top of said
ridge as a natural boundary, thence Southeastwardly
to the Eastern top thence with the eastern top as
a natural boundary to the Beginning to include the
Cane Creek on Chickamogga Creek and the Creek and
5000 acres of unappropriated land entered the 26th
day of April 1841.

           Charles Coleman
           Locator

PAGE 299

No. 280
G. W. Williams
enters
5000 acres

Location re-
ceived and
filed 30th April
1841

    Entry made
same day
fee 75¢

Gerge W. Williams enters five thousand Acres of
land lying in Hamilton County State of Tennessee
on Waldens Ridge, Beginning at a white Oak just
at the top of the ridge at a place known as "Sciveley's Gap" running thence westwardly thence Southwardly, thence eastwardly, thence Northwardly to the
Beginning so as to include five thousand Acres,
this 30th day of April 1841

           George W. Williams

PAGE 300

No. 281
S. Williams

Samuel Williams enters five thousand Acres of land
lying in Hamilton County State of Tennessee, On Wal-
len's Ridge. Beginning at a white Oak just at the

enters 5000 acres	top of the ridge at a place known as "Scivelly's Gap being the North East corner of a 5000 Acre tract entered by George W. Williams running thence Northwardly, thence westwardly thence Southwardly thence Eastwardly to the beginning, so as to include five thousand Acres. this 30th day of April, 1841.
Location received & filed the 30th day of April 1841 Entry made same Day	
	Samuel Williams
fee 75c paid	

PAGE 300

No. 282 Jesse Walker enters 1000 acres	Jesse Walker enters One thousand acres of land on Wallens Ridge B ginning on three Black Gums near the Beginning corner of James Smiths Ninety Acre entry No. 16 dated 5th July 1824. Thence North 45 west with his closing line one hundred and twenty poles to his corner, thence a direct line to the Beginning corner of an Entry made by Ephraim Hixson No. 270 dated 6 July 1841. Then with his line Northwardly 200 poles same course continued, thence North Eastwardly, thence a direct line to the Beginning, to include said One thousand Acres of land this 11th Sept. 1841
Location received & filed the 11th Sept. 1841 Entry made same day	
	Jesse Walker Locator
fee 75c paid	

PAGE 301

No. 283 J. Coffee enters 500 acres	John Coffee enters five hundred acres of land on Wallens ridge on the head waters of Mill branch. Beginning on two black Gums marked J.C. thence Eastwardly, thence westwardly thence Northwardly to the beginning so as to include said five hundred acres of land and two Springs, one of which is Chalibiate and the other free stone water. this 12th day of October 1841.
Location filed & Entry made 12 Oct. 1841	
	John Coffee Locator
fee 75c	

PAGE 301

No. 284	State of Tennessee} Entry takers office No. 284. John Brown Jr. Madison Varner Hamilton County } & Lewis Varner enters five

J. Brown Jr.
M. Varner
L. Varner
enters
5000 acres

Location
filed &
entry made
the 12th Oct.
1841

fee 75¢
paid

PAGE 302

No. 285
Wm. Cunnungham
enters
300 acres

Location filed
and entry made
30th Decr.
1841

fees

thousand acres of land on Waldens ridge Beginning
where the back line of George R. Cannons entry
No. 114 crosses Soddy Creek, Thence North eastward-
ly with said line, thence Southwestwardly, thence
South Eastwardly to the beginning so as to include
five thousand Acres of unappropriated land in a
Square or oblong.
Entered October 12th 1841

John Brown Jr.
Madison Varner
Lewis Varner
Locators

State of Tennessee William Cunningham enters three
hundred Acres of land on Wallens
Hamilton County ridge in Hamilton County on Wallens ridge in Hamilton County.
Beginning on the North east corner of an entry made
by Hestey Poe of an entry made by Hasten Poe No. 106
Thence Northeastwardly along the top of the Mountain
Thence Northwestwardly, Thence Southwestwardly thence
to the beginning so as to include three hundred acres
of land in a square or oblong.
entered this 30th day of December 1841

William Cunningham
Locator

Certified Copy issued 30th Decr. 1841

B. B. Cannon
D. E. T.

PAGE 302

No. 286
G. Vandergriff
enters
2000 acres

Location filed
and entry
made 31st March
1842

Gilbert Vandergriff enters two thousand Acres of land
in Hamilton on Waldens Ridge of Cumberland Mountain
and on the waters of North Chiccamogga Creek. Beginning on a Spruce pine and Holly tree on the west
bank of the Rock House Creek, and from thence four
hundred poles down the said creek and from thence a
straight line to big Chiccamogga Creek thence up the
same to the mouth of the branch running from Dickens
Cabin from the branch to the Rock house on the same
creek of the Beginning, thence down the creek to the

(No fee mentioned)

Beginning so as to include 2000 acres.
March the 31st day 1842

Gilbert Vandergrift
Locator

Copy 14 Feby.1843

PAGE 303

No. 287
Wm. C. Hixson
enters
5000 acres

Location received & filed
and entry made
26th April
1842

State of Tennessee | William C. Hixson and Washington Hixson enters five thousand Acres
Hamilton County | of land on Wallens ridge of Cumberland Mountain in said County. Beginning where Cozby's Trace crosses North Chiccamogga Creek, thence up the Creek and to Hawkins line, thence with his lines Southeastwardly. Thence North eastwardly, thence Northwestwardly to the beginning so as to include 5000 acres of unappropriated lands as nearly as the boundaries will admit of.
Entered this 26th April 1842

William C. Hixson
Locator

PAGE 303

No. 288
B. B. Cannon
enters
5000 acres

Location received
& filed and
entry made
the 26th
April 1842

fees paid
75¢

State of Tennessee | B. B. Cannon enters five thousand acres of land on Wallens Ridge and
Hamilton County | in Tennessee Valley in said County Beginning on the bank of North Chiccamauga Creek where the line between Hamilton and Marion Counties crosses said creek, Thence South 28° west with said line to a white oak on the bank of Suck Creek marked H. C. & M. C. Thence down Suck creek as it meanders to the Tennessee River up Tennessee river as it meanders to the Mouth of North Chiccamogga Creek thence up said creek as it meanders to the Beginning excluding all prior legal claims and including five thousand acres of unappropriated land.
Entered the 26th April 1842.

B. B. Cannon
Locator

Copy issd 26th May 1842

PAGE 304

No. 289
Ephraim Hixson
Enters 1000
acres

State of Tennessee | Ephraim Hixson enters one thousand Acres of Land on the waters of
Hamilton County | Chickamogga and on Waldens Ridge in Hamilton County. Beginning on the Beginning corner

Location filed and entry made 2nd May 1842	of said Ephram Hixson former entry of 270. Thence Eastwardly with Walkers line to James Smith entry thence with Smiths lines Southwardly and Eastwardly to Smiths Southeast corner thence Southwardly to Hoppers line, Thence westwardly with his line to his Northwest corner thence Southwardly with
Copy 5th Febry. 1849	his line to Dickens corner thence with Dickens line westwardly to Vandgriff's line, thence with his line to his beginning corner, thence up the creek with its meanders to the Beginning including One thousand acres, Entered this 2nd May 1842.

Ephram Hixson
Locater

PAGE 304

No. 290 Wilson Hixson enters 500 acres	State of Tennessee — Wilson Hixson enters as Genl. Enterer 500 acres on Waldens ridge. Hamilton County — Beginning on two Hickereys and white oak corner to George Sawyers Southwardly with John Coffee's line until it strikes Jesse Walkers line then with Walkers line to falling Creek then up the Creek to Puncheon Camp Branch then
Location filed entry made 1st Aug. 1842	Northwardly to a Stock in George Sawyers line then with his line to the Beginning. 1st day of August 1842.

Wilson Hixson
Locater

fee 75 paid	Copy 14th Febry. 1849

PAGE 305

No. 291 Emerson Roberts enters 25 acres	Emerson Roberts enters a tract of land lying in the County of Hamilton, State of Tennessee lying on the East fork of folling Water Creek, beginning on two white oaks thence NorthEastwardly thence Southwardly thence westwardly thence a strait line to the beginning so as to include twentyfive acres.
Location filed & Entry made 26th Nov. 1844	Nov. 26th 1844

Emerson Roberts
Locater
Certified Coppy Issued the 26th Nov. 1844.

Office fees 75 paid	S. T. Igou, E. T.

PAGE 305

No. 292	Janry. 15 1845 Hamilton County, State of Tennessee

R. Qualls
Enters
640 acres

Robert Qualls this day enters Six hundred and forty acres of land lying and being in the County and State aforesaid on Waldens Ridge on the waters of Sale Creek. Beginning at Black oak near the N.West corner of Hickmans 200 acre Survey running thence Southwardly with Hickmans line to bluff of Sale Creek, thence westwardly crossing Lick branch thence Northwardly to Miller line, thence Eastwardly to the beginning, so as to include 640 acres according to law day and date above written.

Location Received and filed 15th day of Janry. 1845

fees Paid

Robert Qualls
Locator

PAGE 306

No. 293
R. Cozby
enters
300 acres

State of Tennessee) Robert Cozby enters three hundred
) acres of land lying in the County
Hamilton County   ) and State aforesaid Beginning on
                       two Sour Wood trees, on the North
Side of a small branch of little Falling water Creek and on the North west Side of the main prong of said Creek nearly opposite and about one mile from Ford's Gap on Waldens ride, Running West 220 poles to a Stake thence South 220 poles to a stake Thence east 220 poles to a Stake Thence North 220 poles to the Beginning. May 1st 1845

Location received AND filed 1st May 1845

Robert Cozby

PAGE 306

No. 294
G. Vandergriff
Enters
2000 acres

Gilbert Vandergriff enters two thousand Acres of land in Hamilton on Wallens Ridge Cumberland Mountain on the waters of North Chicamogga Creek, Beginning on a Sprouce pine & Holly tree on the west bank of the Rockhouse Creek and from thence four hundred poles down the said Creek and from thence a straight line to big Chiccamogga Creek thence up the same to the mouth of the Branch running from Dickens Cabin from the branch to the rock house on the same Creek of the beginning thence down the Creek to the beginning so as to include 2000 Acres July 31st 1845.

Location filed 31st July 1845

Office fees paid 75

                     his
         Gilbert X Vandergriff
                    mark
                  Locator
Test A.G.W. Puckett

PAGE 307

No. 295

John Brown, Allen Walker & William Carr enters two

Brown, Carr & Walker enters 2000 acres

thousand Acres of land in the County of Hamilton County Tennessee on Waldens Ridge on the waters of Soddy Creek, Beginning on a Spruce pine near the mouth of a branch that heads upon the North side of the Round Knob then running West, then South, then East, then North, then around for Compliment so as to include two thousand acres excluding all legal prior rights.

Location filed and entered 10th Decr. 1845

John Brown
Allen Walker &
William Carr
Locators

fee paid 75

Copy Issd 14th April 1846

R. Henderson, E. Taker

PAGE 307

No. 296 Wm. Clift enters 100 acres

State of Tennessee} William Clift enters One hundred Acres of land in Hamilton County County of Hamilton} in the North-west Side of Tennessee river being partly land and partly land covered with water and bounded as follows, to wit: Beginning on a Maple tree on the North west Bank of Tenneeess river thence South 150 poles passing the head of Soddy Island to a stake in Tennessee river, thence East 120 poles to a stake in the river thence North 125 poles to a stake on the North West bank of said river so as to include an Island or tow-head forming in Tennessee river and lying in the 12th Civil District of Hamilton County.

Location filed & entered 24th March 1846

Office fees paid 75¢

Certified Copy 24th March 1846

Located 24th March, 1846.

Wm. Clift
Locator

fee paid 75 Copy issued same date

R. Henderson
Entry Taker

PAGE 308

No. 297 Jesse Walker Enters 5000 acres land

State of Tennessee} Jesse Walker enters five thousand acres of land in Hamilton County Hamilton County { aforesaid, on the waters of Soddy Creek, Beginning on a Black Gum or Chestnut oak, near William Cunningham Corner, Running East to John Brown Jrs. and Varners line thence Northwardly to John Brown Srs. line thence with said line to the west corner, thence a straight line to the County line then with said line to Chickamauga

Location filed and entered 6th April 1846

A True Copy
of this entry
issued to
Jesse Walker.
This the 20th
of June 1855
F. G. Blackwell
E. T.
fee 75c paid

Creek so as to include five thousand Acres, excluding all prior entries.
This 6th April 1846.

his
Jesse X Walker
mark
Locator

Test.
S. T. Igou   R. Henderson, E.T.

PAGE 308

No. 298
Lewis Former
Enters 3000
acres of
land

filed &
entered
22nd Sept.
1846

fee paid
& Copy Issd
same day

R. T. Henderson
E. T.

State of Tennessee | Lewis Former enters 3000 acres of
                   | land in Hamilton County, Tennessee
Hamilton County | lying on Waldens ridge. Beginning
                      near the Bluff on McGills Creek
running with the Bluff up to the Creek to the County
line with said line to the Bluff on Rock Creek thence
down the Bluff of said Creek to Parks line, thence
with Parks line to the beginning, excluding all prior
legal entries.

Lewis Parks
E. T.

Sept. 22nd 1846

PAGE 309

No. 299
George Levi
enters
five hundred
acres of
land

Location filed
26th Nov. 1846
entered same
day

George Levi Enters five hundred acres of land in Hamilton County Tennessee. Beginning on two white oaks
& a Hickory the corner of the big Survey between John
Rogers and himself, it being a twenty thousand acre
Survey of Charles McClung running thence North Easter-
ly to the corner of Cozby's land near the standing
rocks thence North Westwardly to the top bluff of the
Mountain thence with said bluff Southwestwardly to
Van De Griffs Gap, thence to the Beginning. Excluding all prior legal entries.

George Levi, Locator
R. Henderson, E. T.

PAGE 309

No. 300
James Gothard
1280 Acres of
land

James Gothard enters twelve hundred and eighty Acres
of land Beginning on the South side of Rocky Creek
on the bluff near Yarnells line, running West then

Location filed 10 Febry. 1847 & entered same day fee 75c paid Copy 20 Febry. 1847	South, then Eastwardly to the beginning so as to Contain 1280 acres. James Gothard Locator R. Henderson, E. T.

PAGE 309

No. 301 G. R. Cannon 5000 acres 3rd April 1847 Copy 31 July 1848	George R. Cannon enters five thousand acres of land lying in Hamilton County, Tennessee, Beginning on the bank of Tennessee river at the Rhea County line running with the meanders of the Tennessee river to the foot of Waldens ridge to a point opposite the beginning thence to the beginning so as to include five thousand acres excluding all prior legal entries 3rd April 1847 G. R. Cannon Locator R. Henderson, E. T.

PAGE 310

No. 302 Stat (Blank) (Blank)	State of Tennessee } Elisha Rogers enters 1000 Acres of land in Hamilton County aforesaid. Beginning on a red oak tree on the Spur of Waldens ridge, running with Jacob Hartman's line to John Fousts line then to the top of the Bluff of rocks at the top of the Mountain at Fousts Gap, then along the top of the Mountain to a Pine tree at Scivleys Gap, then to the beginning so as to include One thousand Acres excluding all prior legal entries. Elisha Rogers Locator
	Hamilton County

PAGE 310

No. 303 (Blank)	State of Tennessee } Elisha Rogers & James Rogers enters Sixteen hundred acres of land on Waldens ridge of Cumberland Mountain in the 3rd Civil District of said County. Beginning at a Black oak standing near
	Hamilton County

(Blank)

the bluff of rocks on the Sout East Declivity or descent about a half mile above where Brown's trace from Mountain Creek passes through the Clift of rocks at the top of said ridge running thence Northwestwardly 400 poles thence Southwestwardly Six hundred & fortypoles thence Southeastwardly four hundred poles to the bluff of rocks at the ascent of said ridge, thence up NorthEastwardly with the meanders of the Clift of rocks about 640 poles to the point of beginning.

Elisha Rogers &
James Rogers
Locators

Entered 11th Oct. 1847

PAGE 311

No. 304

(Blank)

State of Tennessee, Hamilton County. Thomas W. Spicer Enters five thousand acres of land in said County lying on Waldens ridge of Cumberland Mountain, Beginning on a Black oak tree on the bluff of Chickamauga Creek about one hundred yards from the South East corner of a large pool of Water near what is called the Wild Cat trace, leading up the Mountain. Thence N. 20° East, thence 640 Six hundred and forty poles thence N. 70° west 1280 poles, thence S. 20° West 640, thence S. 70° East to the beginning, so as to include the large pool of Water.
Entered 18 Oct. 1847

J. G. Smith
Locator

PAGE 311

No. 305

(Blank)

State of Tennessee R. Henderson enters three thousand Acres of land in said County lying on the South East Side and top of Waldens ridge of Cumberland Mountain Beginning on a Black oak marked R. on the right hand side of Poes turnpike road near a small drean in a flat where there is a pole bridge in the road running N. E. thence N. W. thence S. W. thence South East to the beginning so as to include three thousand Acres of unappropriated land.

Hamilton County

R. Henderson
Locator

Entered 18th Oct. 1847

PAGE 312

No. 306

(Blank)

State of Tennessee} William Clift enters five thousand
Acres of land lying and being in
Hamilton County | the County of Hamilton aforesaid
in the 2nd & 3rd Civil Districts
of said County and bounded as follows, to wit: Beginning on a stake on the North Bank of Tennessee river at the Mouth of North Chicamauga Creek, thence West
with the due west line of the twenty thousand acres,
Survey to the top or highest bluffs of rock on Waldens
ridge of Cumberland Mountain, the same Course continued to the line between the Counties of Hamilton & Marion, then with said County line to Tennessee river then
with the River as it meanders to the beginning, excluding all prior legal claims.
June 27, 1843

William Clift
Locator

R. Henderson
Entry Taker

PAGE 313

No. 307

(Blank)

State of Tennessee} Jesse Walker enters two thousand
Acres of land in said County. Be-
Hamilton County | ginning at a Black oak in Smith's
reservation line, Thence N. 31½
E. 180 poles to a stake at the foot of Waldens ridge
Thence No. 5° E. 230 poles to a Black oak in the Cave
of Chicamauga Creek, thence westwardly to the Beginning so as to include two thousand acres of unappropriated land.
Aug. 22nd 1848

R. Henderson, E. T.

Copy 22 Aug. 1848

PAGE 313

No. 308

(Blank)

State of Tennessee} Samuel Brison enters three hundred
Acres of land in said County lying
Hamilton County | on top of Waldens ridge on the wat-
er of Chicamauga Creek, Beginning
on a Spruce pine near where the Weaver branch empties
into Chicamauga Creek, running up said creek a west
course to the Cozby trace then with said trace a South
Course to the line of entry No. 75 in the name of Henry Braden with the line of said entry to the weaver
branch, then down the branch a North Course to the

(Blank)

beginning so as to include three hundred acres, exclusive of prior legal claims.
Jany. 30, 1849

                    Samuel Brison
                    Locator

Copy same day.

                    R. Henderson
                    E. T.

PAGE 314

No. 309

John A. Minnis enters five thousand Acres of land in Hamilton County, Tenn. on Waldens ridge, Commencing on a Black oak, on the bluff of said Mountain about one half mile from where the New turnpike called Marion & Hamilton Turnpike goes up on the East Side of said Mountain and about one half mile from where said road goes up said Mountain, thence Northwestwardly with the line of Asahel Rawlings & Elisha Rogers and on in the direction of said line so as to include five thousand acres by running thence North westwardly direction to the bluff of the Mountain and then with the bluff of the mountain to the beginning.
Feby. 5, 1849

Copy issued
13th August
1853

                    John A. Minnis
                    Locator

PAGE 314

No. 310

James C. Connor enters five thousand Acres of land lying in Hamilton & Marion Counties, or Waldens ridge Beginning on a White oak and two Dogwoods and a Sourwood pointer on the North Side of North Chicamauga Creek, and near where the Cozby trace crosse North Chicamauga- thence West nine hundred poles, thence North Nine hundred poles, East nine hundred poles, thence South to the Beginning.
This 5th Debry. 1849

                    James C. Conner
                    Locator

PAGE 315

No. 311

William Rogers enters five thousand acres of land on Waldens Ridge in Hamilton and Marion Counties, Beginning on a chestnut on the head Waters of Falling Water in Hamilton County run then Southwestwardly Nine hundred poles to a stake, then Northwestwardly Nine hundred poles to a stake then North Eastwardly

Nine hundred poles to a stake then to the beginning
so as to include five thousand Acres of unappropriated land, This 5th Febry. 1849

William Rogers
Locator

Copy isd
13th Aug.
1853

PAGE 315

No. 312

Joseph Rogers & Absolam Selser enters Six hundred acres
of land lying on Waldens ridge in Hamilton County East
Tennessee. Beginning on a Dogwood in a line, of Jesse
Walker entry No. 282 near a large rock, thence South
Sixty Six East four hundred poles to a Stake in Roberts
line, Thence South 40 West three hundred and ten poles
with said Roberts line to a stake, thence West one hundred and Sixty poles to a stake and pointers corner to
said Entry No. 282 thence North four hundred poles to
the Beginning.
This March 5th 1849

Joseph Rogers
A. Selser
Locators

R. Henderson
E. T.

PAGE 316

No. 313

(Blank)

State of Tennessee) Samuel Williams and Company enters four thousand eight hundred
Hamilton County   Acres of Land in Hamilton County
on Waldens Ridge of Cumberland
Mountain Beginning on a stake and double white Oak
in the line between the Counties of Merrion an Hamilton on the South Side of Poes turnpike Road, thence
Southward with the line of said Counties Seven hundred poles to a stake in said line thence Eastwardly
at right angles with said line of 20000 acre Survey
at the foot of Wallens ridge then North East with
the line of the 20000 Acre survey fourteen hundred
poles to a stake in said line, thence westwardly to
the line of the Counties of Marrion and Hamilton
thence with the line of said Counties to the beginning to include four thousand eight hundred Acres of
vacant and unappropriated land if there be so much
after platting out all better Grants entered this
7th day of September, 1849.

William Clift
Locator
The survey and description of the above entry is

recorded on Page 161 of this book.

James Lamon
C. S. & E. T.

PAGE 317

No. 314

State of Tennessee | Richard Henderson and James W. W. C.
Henderson enter three hundred and
Hamilton County | twenty Acres of land in said County
Beginning on the North Bank of Tennessee river at a point North west from what is called
the Lowhead in said river below Chattanooga thence South
west 600 poles to the South bank of Tennessee river
thence North East 320 poles to a stake, thence North
west 600 poles to the North bank of Tennessee river,
thence a direct line to the beginning, including said
Low head April 25th 1850

(Blank)

Richard Henderson
Jas. W. C. Henderson
Locators

R. Henderson
E. T.

PAGE 317

No. 315

State of Tennessee | Jesse Walker enters five hundred
acres of land on North Chicamauga
Hamilton County | Creek in said County. Beginning on
a Black Oak corner on the North
East side of said Creek Corner of a 2000 Acre entry
made by said Walker No. 307, running North Eastwardly
along the line of a 122 Acre tract granted to said
Walker One hundred poles, then North then West, then
South, then to the beginning so as to include five hundred Acres September 2nd 1850

(Blank)

Jesse Walker
Locator

R. Henderson
E. T.

Copy same day.

PAGE 318

No. 316

State of Tennessee | Elisha Rogers enters One thousand
(of land in Hamilton County on Wal-
Hamilton County | dens Ridge Beginning on three black
oaks and chestnut in a line of
Washington and William Hixson entry where William entry

Elisha Rogers
1000 acres
Land

General
Entry

: of No. 311 crosses said line, thence running with said
: William Rogers line a South west Course to a line of
: an entry of Daniel Scivily thence along said line to
: a line of an entry and survey made by Asahel Rawlings
: and Elisha Rogers of Sixteen hundred Acres and thence
: along said line a North east course until it crosses
: Washington and William Hixson line and then along said
: line a North west course to the beginning.
: This 24 day of February 1851

:   Elisha Rogers
:   Location

: Test F. S. Blackwall
: Entry Taker for Hamilton County

PAGE 318

No. 317
Hezikiah
Hughs
Enters 500
acres Land
General entry

fee paid
75 cts.

: State of Tennessee) Hezekiah Hughs Enters Five hundred
:   ) Acres of Land in Hamilton County
: Hamilton County | Tennessee on Waldens Ridge on Over
: | Rock--house creek in said County.
: Beginning on a black oak on said Creek runing thence
: North to the County line, thence west with said line,
: then South parralel to the first line, thence to the
: beginning, so as to include five hundred acres.
: This 29 day of July 1851

:   Hezekiah Hughs
:   Locator

: Certified Copy issued
: F. G. Blacknall
: Entry Taker

PAGE 319

No. 318
Ephraim Hughs
322 Acres
Land

Location
received
1 Nov. 1851

: Ephraim Hughes Enters three hundred and twenty two acres
: of Land, lying in Hamilton County Tenn. lying on the head
: waters of Opossom Creek, Beginning on a white oak about
: one pole west of York Spring, thence South 31 degrees
: west 280 poles to a Maple tree thence South 55 degrees
: East 160 to a black Gum and Mountain Oak, Thence North
: 40 degrees East 282 poles to a stake, thence North 55
: degrees West 208 poles to the beginning, including three
: hundred & twenty two acres of Land.
: This 1 Nov. 1851

:   Ephraim Hughs
:   Locator

F. G. Blacknall
Entry Taker for Hamilton County, Tenn.

PAGE 320

No. 319
John A. Minnis
Enters
5000 Acres
of
Land General
Entry Re-
ceived and
filed May 3
1852

State of Tennessee| John A. Minnis enters five thous-
and Acres of Land in Hamilton
Hamilton County | County Tennessee, on the Top and
sides of Waldens Ridge Beginning
on a chestnut oak on the North Side of Anderson's
Turnpike road standing in a drean about 8 or 10 steps
from the Cliff of the Mountain where said road goes
up the Mountain and about forty or fifty yards from
the Toll gate, thence along the upper Cliff of the
Mountain in a Northerly direction two hundred poles
to a stake on the top cliff of the Mountain then east
three hundred poles to a stake thence South with the
lines of unappropriated Lands, thence westwardly, thence
North to the beginning so as to inc ude five thousand
Acres unappropriated land. May 3--1852

                    John A. Minnis
                    Locator

Copy issued 6 May 1852
F. G. Blackwell Entry taker for H. C.

PAGE 320

No. 320
John A. Minnis
Enters 5000
Acres of land
General Entry
received and
filed May 3
1852

State of Tennessee| John A. Minnis enters five thous-
and Acres of Land in Hamilton
Hamilton County | County, Tennessee on the side of
Waldens Ridge Beginning at the
North west corner of a five thousand Acre entry made
on the 3 day of May 1852 by John A. Minnis running
thence East with the line of said Entry three hundred
poles to the North East corner of the same hence North
about thirty East along the range of the Mountain and
with the line of appropriated lands, thence West about
three hundred poles to a stake on the top of the Mountain then with the Mountain Cliff Southwardly to the
Beginning so as to include five thousand acres excluding all prior valid claims.
May 3, 1852

                    J. A. Minnis
                    Locator

Copy Issued 8 May 1852

                    F. G. Blacknall
                    Entry Taker for Hamilton Co.

PAGE 321

No. 321
J. A. Minnis
enters

State of Tennessee| John A. Minnis enters five thous-
and Acres of Land in Hamilton Coun-
Hamilton County | ty Tennessee on the side and top

5000 acres
of Land
General
Entry
Received
and filed
May 5
1852

Copy Issd
5 May
1852

PAGE 322

No. 322
Location
received
and filed
4th Jan.
1853

Office fees
paid 75¢

PAGE 323

No. 323
R. C. McRee
Enters 5000
Acres of
land

of Waldens Ridge Beginning at the North west Corner of an entry No.— in the name of John A. Minnis on the uper Cliff of said Mountain running then East with the line of said Entry about three hundred poles to a stake thence Northwestwardly with the line of appropriated land and excluding the same thence west and thence South to the beginning so as to inviude five thousand acres excluding all prior valid claims.

     J. A. Minnis
     Locator

F. G. Blacknall
E. T. H. C.

State of Tennessee) George R. Cannon enters Sixteen hundred Acres more of less of
Hamilton County | land which entry is bounded as follows, to wit: —
Beginning on Cornett's old reservation line, west corner thence to the due west line, thence due west with said line to Ford's corner, and thence South with Ford's line to More's line and with it to Stringers line and with it to Simmerman's corner and thence with his line to Cowarts corner, thence with his line to Becks corner thence with Beck's line to the Tennessee river, and thence up said river to Cornetts survey where Whitehead lives, thence with said Survey to Smiths Ninety Acre tract and with it to the reservation line and thence due North with said line to the beginning this the 4th of Jan. 1853

     G. R. Cannon
     Locator

     F. G. Blacknall
     Entry Taker

Certified Copy issued the same day
     F. G. Blacknall
     Entry Taker

State of Tennessee) Robert C. McRee Enters 5000 Acres of land in said State and County
Hamilton County | on Waldings Rige of Cumberland Mountains, Beginning on the corner of an Entry made by Clift & Mc Ree No. 152 the 26 Sept. 1835 and one hundred and Sixty poles from

General Entry

the Beginning corner of Clift & McKee's entry and in the line of the twenty thousand Acres of land below the waters of Opossom Creek, thence with Clift & McRees line Northwardly 1400 poles to the County line thence Southwardly with the County line 800 poles to a stake in sd. line Southwardly about 1400 poles to the line of the 2000 acres thence with sd. line North 20 East to the beginning to contain 5000 Acres of unappropriated Land done in the Entry Takers Office in the town of Harrison this 9th March 1853

Robert C. McRee
Locator

Certified Copy issued this the 9th day of March 1853 to R. C. McRee.

F. G. Blacknall
Entry taker for H.C.

PAGE 323

No. 324
Entry
-- Acres
of Land

State of Tennessee | Elizabeth Pearson's Entry 5000 acres more or less of land in said State and County on the side of Lookout Mountain on Lookout Creek Beginning at Back line of Jesse Smith Entry on a white oak and thence running North 340 poles on the line of Parke's heirs land to a stake and thence East a little South 160 poles to a stake and thence South west to the Georgia line 900 poles to stake and thence along the Georgia line 240 poles to stake, and thence to the beginning corner North 640 poles be the same more or less, Containing 5000 acres, more or less and unappropriated lands done in the Entry Takers Office in the town of Harrison. This the 23rd day of March 1853.

Hamilton County

General
Entry

her
Elizabeth X Pearson
mark
Locator

Certified Copy issued this the 23rd day of March, 1853 to Elizabeth Pearson, Locator

T. M. McCrary D. P.
Entry Taker for H.C.

PAGE 324

No. 325
D.S. Jones
Madison Varner
Enters
500 of land

Daniel S. Jones and Madison Varner Enters five Hundred acres of land in Hamilton County and State of Tennessee. Beginning on a double white Oak & big rock at the foot of Waldens Ridge in the line of the twenty thousand Acre tract of land known as the

General
Entry

Mc Clung & Cozby tract and also the corner to D. S. Jones and Ephraim Hughs lands on which they now live running thence Northwardly to Browns & Varners five thousand Acre Grant on the line of the same, thence Southwestwardly with the meanders of said Creek to the 20,000 Acre line, thence with said line to the beginning so as to include 5000 Acres more or less. April 4th 1853.

D. S. Jones
Madison Varner
Locators

Certified Copy issued this 4th April 1853

F. G. Blacknall, E. T.

PAGE 325

No. 326
Brown & Varner
Enters 2000
acres of
land

General Entry

State of Tennessee } John Brown & Lewis Varner enters Two thousand Acres of land in the

Hamilton County } County and State aforesaid, beginning on a black Gum a corner of a two hundred Acre entry made in the name of William Cunningham. Then Southwardly with said line to a certain branch known as the Luster branch then East to the line of a twenty thousand Acre line near the foot of Waldens Ridge then Northwardly with said line of a five Thousand Acre Survey of Brown & Varner then S, Wardly with said line to the South East Corner of said survey Seven hundred poles to a stake in said line then South to a stake in line of a five thousand Acre Survey made in thename of Jesse Walker then Eastwardly with said land around to the beginning.

John Brown, Jr. &
Lewis Varner

Q F. G. Blacknall Entry Taker for Hamilton County, Tenn. Certified Copy issued this the 4th of January 1854, to John Brown, Jr. & Lewis Varner, locators

F. G. Blacknall E. T. for E.C.
By T.M. McCrary D. E. for E.C.

PAGE 326

No. 327

State of Tennessee } Samuel H. Hunter Enters Twentyfive Acres of land in said County in 1st

Hamilton County } Civil District, Beginning on a chestnut oak on the North East bank of

Samuel H. Hunt r:
Enters
25 Acres
General
Entry
Entered 12 day
of May 1853

North Chickamoga in the line of a thousand Acre Tract in the name of Jesse Walker in the Gulf below S. H. Hunter's Mill, thence up the bank of said Creek on the North side 250 poles, thence Southwestwardly crossing said Creek to said Walkers 1000 Acre line thence down said line to the beginning Corner. This 13th day of May 1853.

Samuel H. Hunter
Locator

Test.
F. G. Blanknoll Entry Taker
of said County

PAGE 326

No. 328
P. R. Lomerick
Entry
180 Acres
General Entry

Entered 5th day
of Sept.
1853

State of Tennessee | P. R. Lomerick enters one hundred and eighty Acres of land in Hamilton County, Tenn., on Waldens Ridge on the waters of Middle Creek, beginning on a post oak and two hickories corner to Wm. R Rogers, J. C. Conner, Levi Green and J. A. Minnis 3.5000 Acre entries of No. 311. Beginning with the line of the same North Eighty nine Degrees west three hundred and ninety poles to a stake in Scarby's eight thousand acres line then South 67 East with scarby's line four hundred and twenty poles to the post oak and white oak thence North one degree East One hundred and fifty two poles to the beginning. This the 5th day of September, 1853

Hamilton County

P.R. Lominick
Locator

Test:
F. G. Blacknell Entry Taker for said County & State
A certified Copy issued this the 5th day of Sept./53
to P. R. Lominick

F. G. Blacknell
E. T.

PAGE 327

No. 329

State of Tennessee | George R. Conner & Samuel H. Hunter enters 500 Acres of land more or less in the state and County aforesaid, lying in a narrow string on the side of Waldens ridge, beginning on Joshua Johnsons South East corner on a chestnutt tree a short distance below the poe Road at the top bluff of said Ridge

Hamilton County

G. R. Connor
&
S. H. Hunter
500 Acres
General
Entry

thence Southwesterly with said top bluff Six hundred and fifty poles thence Southerly course to the foot of the Mountain, thence Northeasterly with said Mountain to Sody Creek, thence up said Creek to the topmost bluff, thence with said bluff crossing the Poe Road to the beginning corner.

George R. Cannon
Samuel H. Hunter
Locators

F. G. Blacknall Entry Taker for said County & State.

A certified Copy issued this the 5th day of Sept. 1853 to G. R. Connor & S. H. Hunter

F. G. Blacknall
Entry Taker

PAGE 328

No. 330
G. R. Cannon
Enters
1
Acre of Land Entered 9 Aug.
1854

State of Tennessee
Hamilton County

George R. Cannon Enters One Acre of Land Lying in Hamilton County Tennessee on the North Side of the Tennessee River including the old ferry known as Brown of old Ferry on the bluff between John Johnson corner and N. Pendergrass Land and thence with their lines and the meanders of the river so as to include One Acre of Land more or Less. This 9 day of August 1854.

G. R. Cannon
F. G. Blacknoll Entry T. for H. C.

PAGE 328

No. 331
G. R. Cannon
&
F. G. Blacknall
Enters
50 Acres
more or less
Made 9 Aug.
1854

State of Tennessee
Hamilton County

George R. Cannon and F. G. Blacknoll enters Fifty Acres of Land in Hamilton County, Tennessee, including a large Pond situate on the North side of the Tennessee River adjoining the Lands entered by Joshua Johnson Entry No. 22 entered 6 July 1824. Beginning on a poplar corner to said Joshua Johnson Entry-- thence S 16 W. 110 poles to a Hickory & Sweet gum on the side of said pond, then South 27° East 150 poles to James Smith line, then South 45° W. Crossing the pond to James Smith corner on a line of the R. G. Waterhouse land then to the old reservation line known as John Brown Reservation line thence along said reservation line to the beginning. Entered 9 Aug. 1854

F. G. Blacknall
George R. Cannon
Locator
F. G. Blacknall Entry Taker For H. C. E. Tennessee

PAGE 329

No. 332
W. Mason
Enters
200 Acres
Land

Entry filed
this 9 day
of Sept.
1854

State of Tennessee | Walker Mason enters Two hundred
Acres of land in said County Ly-
Hamilton County | ing in said County on the North
Side of the Tennessee River, Be-
ginning on a white Oak on the North Bank of the Ten-
nessee River about a half mile above the Suck, thence
North to the bluff at the top of Waldens ridge thence
westwardly with said bluff to Suck Creek thence down
Suck Creek to where it enties into Tennessee River
thence to the Beginning, running with said Tennessee
River containing two hundred Acres, more or less.
Entered this 9 Sept. 1854

Walker Mason
Locator

Witness,
F. G. Blacknall
Entrytaker

PAGE 330

No. 333
James S. Edwards
Enters
1 Acre Dec. 7
1854

State of Tennessee | James S. Edwards Enters One Acre
of land more or less, beginning
Hamilton County | in said County on the North side
of Winton Island in Tennessee
River at the lower end of said Island immediately
below the Mouth of North Chickamauga Creek known
as the Chickamauga Low Head all in the County and
State aforesaid.
This 7 day of December, 1854

James S. Edwards
Locator

Certified Copy issued same day Entry made

F. G. Blacknall
Entry Taker for
Hamilton County
Tennessee

PAGE 330

No. 334
R. G. Jack
John A. Minnis
R. C. McKee
Enters
5000 Acres

State of Tennessee | Robert G. Jack, John A. Minnis
and R. C. McKee enters Five
Hamilton County | thousand Acres of land beginning
on the North bank of North Chick-
amauga Creek and at a point where the Old McClung
LINE CROSSES SAID creed thence with said old line to

of Land
Entered on
the 3rd day
of April
1855

Location
filed 3 April
1855

the Rhea County, thence along the Rhea County line up and to the Top Cliff of the Mountain known as Waldens Ridge, thence with the Top Cliff of the Mountain with its various meanders to said North Chickamauga Creek, thence down the same to the Beginning, Being in Hamilton County, Tennessee.

                    Robert G. Jack
                    Locator

This 3rd of April 1855

                    F. G. Blacknall, E. Taker

PAGE 331

No. 334
Isaac Roberson
Enters 5000
Acres of Land

Entered
7th May
1855

State of Tennessee | Isaac Robinson Enters Five Thousand Acres of Land in Hamilton

Hamilton County | County, Tennessee, Lying on Waldens Ridge in said County Beginning on the County line between Bledsoe and Hamilton Counties where said County Line crosses Rock Creek thence along said Line North Eastwardly to where said Line crosses Owens or McGills Creek, thence down the center of said creek to the main bluff of the Mountain thence Southwestwardly with the said bluff to Center of Rock Creek thence along there centre up said Creek to the Beginning Corner, including Five Thousand Acres.
May 7, 1855

                    Is aac Robinson
                    Locator

F. G. Blacknall Entry Taker for Hamilton County, Tenn.
Certified Copy issued same day.

PAGE 332

No. 335
A. G. W. Puckett
William Johnson
F. G. Blacknall
Enters
5000

Location
Filed
8 day
of May
1855

State of Tennessee | A. G. W. Puckett, William Johnson and F. G. Blacknall enters Five

Hamilton County | thousand Acres of Land in said County lying on Waldens Ridge on the Waters of North Chickamoga, Beginning on County line between the Counties of Marion & Hamilton where the same crosses North Chickamoga Creek at a stake on the North East side of said Creek, on the top of said Mountain then to the center of said Creek then down the Center of the Creek, to the Line of the Doak Entry where the said creek runs through the Mountain then North Eastwardly One mile and a half to a stake & Pointers, then Northwestwardly parralel with the General

corse of the said Creek including the Main Bluff of
the Mountain to a stake in said County Line One mile
and a half from the beginning, then to the Beginning
so as to include Five thousand Acres of land.
May 8, 1855.

        A. G. W. Puckett
        William Johnson
        F. G. Blacknall
        Locators

Certified Copy iss'd. same day

PAGE 333

No. 336

State of Tennessee | A. G. W. Puckett, William Johnson
                  | & F. G. Blacknall enters Five
Hamilton County | Thousand Acres of land in said
                  | County lying on Waldens Ridge on
the water of North Chickamauga Creek Beginning on the
County line between the Counties of Marion and Hamilton where the said line crosses North Chickamoga Creek
on a Rock in the Centre of said Creek then down said
creek along the line of Entry N 335, this day made by
the said Puckett, Johnson & Blacknall to the Line of
the old Doak Entry where said creek runs into said Entry then in a westwardly course with the said One Mile
and a half to a stake on the top of the Mountain and
points then Northwestwardly paralel to the General
Course the said Creek including the main bluff of the
Mountain to a stake in the line between said County
One Mile and a half Of the beginning thereto along said
line to the beginning so as to include Five Thousand
Acres. May the 8th 1855.

        A. G. W. Puckett
        William Johnson
        F. G. Blacknall
        Locator

PAGE 334

No. 337
J. G. Smith
Enters 5000
Acres of Land
Entry made
May 11th
1855

State of Tennessee | Joseph G. Smith Enters five Thous-
                  | and Acres of Land in said County
Hamilton County | (Lying on Waldens Ridge of Cumber-
                  | land Mountain, Beginning on Black
oak marked S. B. H. beginning corner to an entry made
by S. B. Hawkins N. 57, thence N. 70° W. One Thousand
& five hundred poles to a stake near a black Oak pointer thence S. 20° W. 500 poles to a black oak, thence
S. 70° E. one thousand & five hundred poles to a stake

near a black Oak pointer thence S. 20° W. 500 poles
to a black oak, thence S. 70° E. one thousand &
five poles to a stake thence to the Beginning so
as to include Five Thousand acres of Land. Entry
made May 11th 1855

                    Joseph G. Smith
                    Locator

Attest.
F. G. Blacknall E. T.

(This entry No. 337 and the following numbers 338 to
 340 inclusive were crossed out with pen and ink.
 They were copied for the names and locations given)

PAGE 334

No. 338
J. G. Smith
enters
5000 Acres
of Land

Entry made
May 11th
1855

State of Tennessee| Joseph G. Smith Enters Five Thou-
                  | sand Acres of Land in said County
Hamilton County | Beginning on a stake first corner
                  | from the beginning Entry No. 337,
Thence N. 20° East 500 poles to a white oak, thence
S. 70° E. 1500 poles to a stake, thence S. 20 W. 500
poles to the Beginning corner of Entry 337 then with
the line of the same to the beginning so as to include
five thousand acres of Land. Entry made May 11, 1855.

                    J. G. Smith
                    Locator

Attest.
F. G. Blacknall Entry Taker.

PAGE 335

No. 339
Joseph G. Smith
Enters
5000 Acres
of Land

Location filed
May 11th
1855

State of Tennessee| Joseph G. Smith Enters Five Thou-
                  | sand acres of Land in said County
Hamilton County | Beginning on a stake the N. W.
                  | corner of Entry No. 337 thence
S' 20° W. 500 poles to stake, thence S' 70 E. 1500
poles to Black Oak thence N. 20° E. 500 poles to the
time of Entry No. 337 then with the line of the same
to the beginning so as to include five thousand acres
of land. Entry made May 11th 1855

                    Joseph G. Smith
                    Locator

F. G. Blacknall Entry taker.

PAGE 335

No. 340
J. G. Smith
Enters 5000
Acres of
Land

Entry made
May 11
1855

State of Tennessee) Joseph G. Smith enters five thous-
and acres of Land lying partly in
Hamilton County (Hamilton and Marion Counties Beginning on the N. E. Corner of En-
try No. 338 thence N. 70 W. 800 poles to a black oak
thence S. 20 W. 1500 poles to a chestnut Oak, thence
S. 20° E. 800 poles to Entry No. 339 thence with the
line of the same & Entry N. 337 & 338 N. 20° E. to the
beginning encluding 5000 acres of Land.
May 11th 1855

J. G. Smith
F. G. Blacknall, E. T.

PAGE 336

No. 341
J. G. Smith
Enters
500 acres
of land

Entry made
May 11th
1855

State of Tennessee) J. L. Smith Enters Five Thousand
acres of land in said County Begin-
Hamilton County (ning on --
(Remaining part of entry missing)

PAGE 337

No. 337
A. G. W. Puckett
W. Johnson
F. G. Blacknall
Enters five
Thousand acres
of land

Location in
said---
Recd. May 12
1855

State of Tennessee) A. G. W. Puckett, William Johnson
and F. G. Blacknall enters five
Hamilton County (thousand Acres of Land in said
County, Lying on Waldens Ridge of
Cumberland Mountain Beginning on the North East corner
of an Entry made in the name of Puckett, Johnson & Blacknall of Entry No. 335 then South with said Line to the
South East corner of said Entry thence East three hundred & fifty poles, thence to a point on the line between the Counties of Marion & Hamilton three Hundred
and fifty poles from the beginning-thence to the Beginning so as to include Five Thousand Acres.
May 12 1855

A. G. W. Puckett
Wm. Johnson
F. G. Blacknall
Locators

PAGE 338

A. G. W. Puckett
William Johnson
F. G. Blacknall

State of Tennessee) A. G. W. Puckett William Johnson
and F. G. Blacknall Enters Five
Hamilton County (Thousand Acres of Land, Lying in

Entered 5000 Acres of Land	said County partly in Hamilton & Marion Beginning in Hamilton County Tennessee on a Black oak marked S.B.H. corner to Samuel B. Hawkins Entry No. 57 thence N. 70° W. 1280 poles thence South 20° West 1280poles, thence South 70° East 1280 poles Thence to the Beginning so
Entry made 12 May 1855	as to Enclude Five Thousand Acres of Land. Entry made May 12th 1855

A. G. W. Puckett
Wm. Johnson
F. G. Blackwell
Locators

PAGE 339

No. 339
Joseph G. Smith
F. G. Blacknall
Enters
five Thousand
Acres of
Land
Entry made
12 day of May

State of Tennessee Joseph G. Smith, F. G. Blacknall
                    enters Five Thousand Acres of
Hamilton County   land in said County on Waldens
                    Ridge of Cumberland Mountain Be-
ginning on a Black oak corner to same marked S.B.H.
corner to an Entry made by Samuel B. Hawkins of No.
57 dated August 1851 thence N. 20° E 680 poles, thence
S. 70° E. 1500 poles, thence S. 20° W. 680 poles,
thence to the Beginning including Five thousand Acres
of Land.
Entry made May 12, 1855

J. G. Smith
F. G. Blacknall
Locator

F. G. Blacknall, E. T.

PAGE 339

No 340

State of Tennessee Joseph G. Smith F. G. Blacknall en-
                    ters Five Thousand Acres of Land in
Hamilton County   Said County Beginning on the North
                    West corner of Entry this day made
in the name of the said Smith of No. 339 thence N. 20°
East 680 poles thence South 70° East 1500 poles thence
S. 20° W. 680 poles thence to the Beginning including
Five Thousand Acres of Land.
Entry made May 12, 1855.

Joseph W. Smith
F. G. Blacknall
Locator

F. G. Blacknall
Entry Taker

PAGE 340

No. 341
J. G. Smith
F. G. Blackwell
Enters 5000
Acres of Land

Entry made
May 12
1855

State of Tennessee | Joseph G. Smith & F. G. Blackwell
Enters Five Thousand Acres of Land
Hamilton County | in said County Commencing on the
North West corner of an Entry this
day made in the name of the said Smith of No. 340
thence North 20° East 680 poles, thence South 70° East
1500 poles to the N. North East corner of said Entry
N. 340 thence along the line of the same to the Beginning so as to include Five Thousand acres of Land.
Entry made this May 12, 1855

                              Joseph G. Smith
                              F. G. Blackwell
                              Locator

F. G. Blacknall Entry Taker.

PAGE 340

No. 342
J. G. Smith
F. G. Blacknall
Enters 5000
Acres of Land

Entry filed
May 12th
1855

State of Tennessee, Hamilton County, Joseph G. Smith
Enters Five Thousand Acres of Land in said County,
Commencing on his former Entry No. 341 this day made
this day by the said Smith on the North West corner
of the said Entry thence N. 20° E. 680 poles thence
S. 70° E. 1500 poles thence S. 20° W. 680 poles,
thence to the Beginning along the line of Entry No.
341 so as to include 5000 Acres of Land.
May 12, 1855

                              J. G. Smith
                              F. G. Blacknall
                              Locator

Attest.
R. G. Blacknall E. T.

PAGE 341

No. 343
J. G. Smith
F. G. Blacknall
Enters
5000 Acres
of land
Entry made
May 12, 1855

State of Tennessee | Joseph G. Smith enters Five Thous-
and acres of Land in said County
Hamilton --- | Beginning on his former Entry,
thus made of No. 342 on the North
West corner of said Entry, thence N. 20° East 1280
poles thence --- 1500 poles thence S. 20° W. 1280 poles
to the line of his said No. 342 Entry then to the Beginning so as to include Five Thousand Acres of Land.
Entry made May 11th 1855

                              J. G. Smith
                              F. G. Blacknall
                              Locator

F. G. Blacknall, E. T.

PAGE 341

No. 344
Joseph G. Smith
F. G. Blacknall
Enters
5000 Acres
of land
Entry
made
May 12
1855

State of Tennessee | Joseph G. Smith, F. G. Blacknall
enters Five Thousand Acres of
Hamilton County | Land in said County on Waldens
Ridge commencing on his former
Entry No. 339 this day made on the Beginning corner
of said Entry on a Black oak marked S.B.H. corner
to S. B. Hawkins Entry No. 57, thence N. 20° E. 680
poles thence N. 70° West 1500 poles thence S. 20 W.
680 poles, thence to the Beginning so as to include
5000 acres.
Entry made May 11th 1855

    Joseph G. Smith
    F. G. Blacknall
    Locator
F. G. Blacknall Entry Taker
    E. T.

PAGE 342

No. 345
J. G. Smith
Enters
5000 Acres
of Land
Entry made
May 12th
1855

State of Tennessee | Joseph G. Smith enters Five Thou-
sand acres of Land in said County
Hamilton County | Commencing on the N.E. corner of
his former Entry this day made of No. 344 thence N. 20°
E. 680 poles thence N. 70° W. 1500 poles thence S. 20°
W. 680 poles thence to the Beginning so as to include
Five Thousand acres of Land.
Entry made May 11th 1855.

    J. G. Smith
    F. G. Blacknall
    Locator

F. G. Blacknall Entry Taker.
    H. C.

PAGE 342

No. 346
J. G. Smith
Enters
5000 acres
of Land

May 12
1855

State of Tennessee | Joseph G. Smith Enters Five Thou-
sand Acres of Land in said County
Hamilton County | Beginning on the N. E. corner of
his former Entry this day made
of No 345 thence N. 20° E. 680 poles thence N. 70° W.
1500 poles thence S. 20° W. 680 poles thence to the
Beginning including Five thousand Acres of Land.
Entry made May 12, 1855.

    J. G. Smith
    F. G. Backnell
    Locator
F. G. Blacknall, Entry Taker for H. C.

PAGE 343

No. 347
J. G. Smith
F. G. Blacknall
Enter
5000 acres
of Land

Entry made
May 11
1855

State of Tennessee Joseph G. Smith enters Five Thousand Acres of Land in said County Commencing on the N. E. Corner of his former Entry this day made of No. 346, thence N. 20° E 680 poles, thence N. 70° W. 15 W. 1500 poles thence S. 20° W. 680 poles thence to the beginning, including Five Thousand Acres of Land. Entry made May 12th 1855.

Hamilton County

      J. G. Smith
      F. G. Blacknall
      Locator

F. G. Blacknall Entry Taker H.C.T.

PAGE 343

No 348
J. G. Smith
Enters
5000 acres
of Land

May 12
1855

State of Tennessee--Hamilton County, Joseph G. Smith enters Five Thousand Acres of land in said County, Commencing of his former entry, this day made of Entry No. 347, thence N. 20° E. 1280 poles thence No. 70° W. 1500 poles thence S. 20°W. 1280 poles, thence to the Beginning so as to include five Thousand Acres of Land May 12-1855.

      J. G. Smith
      F. G. Blackwell
      Locator
F. G. Blacknall Entry Taker
      H.C.Tenn.

PAGE 344

No. 349
G. B. Cannon
F. G. Blacknall
Enters
150 Acres
Land

State of Tennessee G. R. Cannon and F. G. Blacknall Enter One hundred and fifty acres of Land in said County on Walden Ridge of Cumberland Mountain Beginning on a Bluff of North Chickamoga Creek on a black oak near the North East corner of a large pool of water about One hundred yards from said pool thence North 20° E. 640 poles to Joshua Johnson's line thence South Eastwardly with his line to a sassafras corner of said Johnson land then to the beginning including One hundred & fifty Acres. Entry made May 12-1855

Hamilton County

      G. B. Cannon
      F. G. Blacknall
      Locator

PAGE 344

No. 350
G. R. Cannon
&
F. G. Blacknall
Enters
5000 acres
of Land
May 12
1855

State of Tennessee--Hamilton County. George R. Cannon
& F. G. Blacknall Enters Five Thousand acres of land
on Waldens Ridge in said County commencing on a Chestnut and Sassafras trees on the Bank of Roaring Creek
opposite the yellow Bank near the County line of Hamilton & Bledsoe County thence Northwardly with said
line to the highest Bluff of Waldens Ridge--thence
Southwestwardly along the highest Bluff of Wandens
Ridge crossing Rocky & Oppossom Creeks to Sody Creek
and down Soddy creek to the line of 20,000 acre Survey of McClung & Cosby, thence with said line North
Eastwardly to the 19,000 acre Survey in the name of
McClung & Cozby--thence with said line to the beginning including Five Thousand acres of unappropriated
Land. May 12-1855

                    G. R. Cannon
                    F. G. Blacknall
F. G. Blacknall Entry Taker for H. C. Tenn.

PAGE 345

No. 351
G. B. Cannon
&
F. G. Blacknall
Enter
1000 Acres
of land

Entry made
May 15
1855

State of Tennessee) George R. Cannon & F. G. Black-
                   nall Enters One Thousand acres of
Hamilton County | Land in said County on Waldens
                   Ridge Beginning on a bluff of
North Chickamoga Creek on a black oak stading about
100 yards from the SouthEast corner of a large pool
of water thence North Eastwardly to Joshua Johnson
South East corner of his 100 Acre Entry, thence Northwardly with his line to Jacob Reynolds line thence
 with his line the same corse To Fryer's Entry with
said Entry to the Bluff thence with the Bluff to the
Beginning so as to include One Thousand Acres of land.
Entry made May 15, 1855.

                    F. R. Cannon
                    F. G. Blacknall
                    Locators

F. G. Blackwell Entry Taker

PAGE 346

No. 352
G. R. Cannon
F. G. Blacknall
Enters
500 acres
Land

State of Tennessee) G. R. Cannon and F. G. Blacknall
                    Enters Five hundred Acres of Land
Hamilton County | on Walden Ridge of Cumberland Moun-
                    tain lying on the waters of North
Chickamoga Creek, Beginning on an ash tree standing
about thirty feet South West of a Mineral Spring on the
land entered by B. B. Cannon near the Cabin built by
Shoemaker & others thence along said Cannons line SO

Entry made
16 July 1855

Fees of Office
Paid

Certified Copy
issued
same day

POLES to his North West corner then the same corse continued 320 to a stake, then South 50 W. to the bluff of Chickamoga Creek then South Eastwardly along said Bluff to the Beginning so as to include Five hundred Acres of land.
Entry made this 10 July 1855

G. B. Cannon
F. G. Blacknall
Locator

Attest.
F. G. Blacknall Entry Taker H. C.

PAGE 347

No. 353
G. R. Cannon
&
F. G. Blacknall
Enters
2000 acres
Land

Entry made
23 August
1855

State of Tennessee} George R. Cannon and F. G. Blacknall Enters Two thousand Acres of
Hamilton County { Land in said County lying on Waldens Ridge a part of Cumberland
Mountain Beginning on an Maple tree Standing near the top Bluff of the Mountain on the East side of North Chickamoga and about fifty feet South west of a Mineral Spring which is on the Land entered by B. B. Cannon, thence Southeastwardly with the top bluff of the Mountain with the line Puckett(?) Johnson & Blacknall Entry No. 355 thence to the line of Cannon & Blacknall Entry No. 357, thence with the closing line of said Entry where the same leave the Frye Entry then with the Frye line, thence with Cannon Entry to the beginning encluding two thousand Acres more or less, entered 23 August 1855

F. G. Blacknall
G. R. Cannon
Locators
F. G. Blacknall Entry Taker of Hamilton County.

PAGE 348

No. 354
F. G. Blacknall
&
G. R. Cannon
Enter
5000 Acres

State of Tennessee} F. G. Blacknall & G. R. Cannon
Enters Five Thousand Acres of
Hamilton County { Land in said County, lying on
Waldens Ridge of Cumberland Moun-
tain Beginning on the North East corner of an Entry made by Packett Johnson & Blacknall No. 357 made 12 May 1855, thence Southwardly with the line of the same 1280 poles, thence North 20 East 640 poles, thence North to the County line between Between Marion & Hamilton thence to the Beginning so as to include Five Thousand Acres Entry made 23 day of August 1855.

No. 354 (cont'd) :   F. G. Blacknall
of Land   :   G. R. Cannon
General Entry   :   Locator

                   : Attest.

Location filed : F. G. Blacknall Entry Taker of Hamilton County.
August 23
1855

PAGE 349

No. 355   : State of Tennessee   F. G. Blacknall & G. R. Cannon
F. G. Blacknall   :   Enter Five thousand Acres of
G. R. Cannon   : Hamilton County   land lying on Waldens Ridge
Enter   :   of Cumberland Mountain in said
5000 acres   : County beginning on the North East corner of an En-
of Land   : try No. 354 this day made in the name of F. G. Black-
                   : nall and G. R. Cannon then Northwestwardly with the
                   : with the County line between Marion and Hamilton
Entry made   : 1280 poles to a stake, thence west to the line of
23 August   : their entry No. 354, thence to the beginning enclud-
1855   : ing five thousand acres.
                   : Entered Augst. 24, 1855

                   :   F. G. Blacknall
                   :   G. B. Cannon
                   :   Locators

                   : F. G. Blacknall
                   : Entry Taker of Hamilton County.

PAGE 350

No. 356   : State of Tennessee   Lewis Patterson Enters Two Thou-
Lewis Patterson :   sand Acres of Land in said Coun-
                   : Hamilton County   ty Beginning on an oak marked
                   :   L. P. in the line of James Goth-
                   : ards Entry running thence westwardly 640 poles to a
Enters 2000   : stake thence North to the Beginning so as to include
acres   : 2000 Acres of land, Entry made 1Oct. 1855
Entry made   :
Oct. 1, 1855   :   Lewis Patterson
                   :   Locator

                   : Attest.
                   : F. G. Blacknall Entry Taker, H. C.

PAGE 350

No. 357   : State of Tennessee   William C. Thatcher enters Fifteen
                   :   hundred Acres of Land in said Coun-
                   : Hamilton County   ty Beginning on an oak in the South
                   :   line of Lewis Pattersons, Entry No.
                   : 356 made 1 October 1855 running South Eastwardly to

THE top of the Gulf of Middle Creek, thence Northward-
with James Gothard line to Pattersons, beginning corner of Entry No. 356 thence to the Beginning.
Entry made 51 Oct. 1855.

W. C. Thatcher
Locator

Attest.
F. G. Blacknall Entry Taker
Fees of Office paid.

PAGE 351

No. 358
F. G. Blacknall
&
G. R. Cannon
Enters 5000
Land
Entry made
19 Dec.
1855

State of Tennessee | F. G. Blacknall & G. R. Cannon
| Enters five thousand Acres of
Hamilton County | land in said County on Waldens
Ridge, Beginning on the North-
east corner of F. G. Blacknall & G. R. Cannon, Entry
No. 355 then South 640 poles, thence West 1280 poles
then North 640 poles to the South West corner of entry No. 355 then with the line of the same to the Beginning Containing Five thousand Acres of Land.
This 20 day of Dec. 1855

F. G. Blacknall
G. R. Cannon
Locator

F. G. Blacknall
Entry Taker for H. C. Tennessee

PAGE 352

No. 359
S. W. Robertson
5000 Acres

State of Tennessee | Samuel W. Robertson Enters Five
| thousand Acres of land in said
Hamilton County | County, Beginning on the East cor-
ner of an Entry made in the name
of Isaac Roberson on the 7 May, 1855 No. 334 on Mc-
Gill Creek thence up the main Bluff of the Mountain
to Walkers Turnpike Road thence with said Road westwardly to Harts line thence with Harts line & said
Road to the Bledsoe County line, thence with the
county line of Bledsoe and Hamilton to Isaac Roberson North corner on McGills or Owens Creek, thence
down said Creek with said Roberson line to the beginning to include Five thousand Acres. Ent. this 22 Oct. 1856

Samuel W. Roberson
Locator

Attest.
F. G. Blacknall, Entry Taker of Hamilton County, Tenn.

PAGE 353

:
No. 360 : State of Tennessee) Jesse Walker Enters Four thousand
Jesse Walker :) and five hundred Acres of land in
Enters : Hamilton County (said County, Beginning on the North
4500 acres : West Corner of a tract of Land
of Land : owned by Haster Poe the same of which the said Poe now
: lives on Thence North forty five degrees East 640 poles
: with said Poe's Northern Boundary line of said Tract,
Entry made : thence North 1200 poles to a stake then West 640 poles
29 Nov. : to a stake, then South to the beginning containing
1856 : four thousand & five hundred Acres
: Entered on 29 Nov. 1856
:
:
: Jesse Walker
: Locator
:
: Attest.
: F. G. Blacknall
: Entry Taker of H. C.
: Copy Issued the same day.
:
:
:
PAGE 354 :
:
No. 361 : State of Tennessee) Isaac Roberson and C. E. Shelton En-
Isaac Roberson :) ters Five thousand Acres of Land in
& : Hamilton County (said County lying on Waldens Ridge
S. E. Shelton : of Cumberland Mountain. Beginning
Enters : on the County Line between the Counties of Hamilton
5000 Acres : & Bledsoe where Walker Turnpike Road crosses said Line
of Land : with the said County line Eastwardly to the corner of
Rhea and Hamilton Counties then Eastwardly with said
line to a point opposite to the East top of the Moun-
tain, thence down the Mountain along the Moun. bluff
General Entry to Walkers Turnpike Road to the Corner of Samuel W.
made 7 Feb. Roberson Entry No. 359 thence with the Road & said
1857 Roberson Line to the beginning Including Five Thousand
Acres of Land.
Entry made 7 Feb. 1857 then to the Beginning March 3,
1858.

Jesse Walker
Locator

Attest.
F. G. Blacknall
Entry Taker

Certified Copy Issued 7 Feb. 1857.

(There is a line drawn through names Walker, Trewitt
& Blacknall)

PAGE 355

No. 362 Charles C. Walker Enters 500 Acres Land 20th of Feb. 1857	State of Tennessee Charles C. Walker enters Five hundred Acres of Land in said Hamilton County County and State Commencing on the 20,000 Acre Land of McClung & Cozby to where the same crossed North Chickamoga Creed on the South side of said creek on a pine & Hickory thence up & with the Creek so as to include the said Creek Three hundred & twenty poles to a stake, then North East Four hundred poles to a stake, then South eastwardly three hundred & twenty poles to a stake, thence to the beginning so as to include Five hundred Acres. Entry made 20 Feb. 1837 (1857(?) Charles C. Walker, Locator Attest. F. G. Blacknall Entry Taker

PAGE 355

No. 363 (blank)	State of Tennessee Hamilton County, Jessee Walker & D. C. Trewitt Enters Three hundred & twenty acres of Land in said County on Waldens Ridge of Cumber- land Mountain, Beginning on a Hickory corner & Black oak Pointer on the water of Little Soddy Creek the second corner to the said Jessee Walker 5000 Acre tract, thence East 110 poles then South 320 poles, the n South 320 poles, thence west to Joshua Johnson line thence along his line to the Survey of Elisha Rodger line then with said line to William Cunningham line then to the beginning, March 3, 1858. Jesse Walker Locator F. G. Blacknell, Entry Taker Copy issued same day.

PAGE 356

No. 363 Hezekiah Hughs & F. G. Blacknell 1000 General Entry made July 27 1857	State of Tennessee Hezekiah Hugh &F. G. Blacknall Enters One Thousand Acres of Hamilton County (Land Lying on Waldens Ridge in Hamilton & Bledsoe Counties, Be- ginning on the East Corner of Samuel Roberson one thousand Acres tract where lyes on the water of Little Posson Creek, then with said Roberson line to William Hixson line then with Hixson line to Hezekiah Hughs line then with Hughs line to the beginning so as to include One thousand Acres of Land. Entry made July 27-1857.

No. 363 (cont'd)   Hezekiah Hughs
                              F.G. Blacknall
                              Locators

Entry Taker fees
paid   Attest.
               F. G. Blacknall Entry Taker

PAGE 356

No. 364   State of Tennessee Anderson Roneyls Enters a small
Anderson   Island in said County lying in the
Roneyls   Hamilton County   Tennessee River between McCalln
Enters   Mill & Lookout Mountain opposite
7 acres   John L. Divine from below Chatta-
an Island   nooga Containing about Seven Acres lying at the lower
end of said Island then running North east along the
edge of Low water mark to the uper end of said Island
then South west with the low water mark on the west
Entry made   side of said Island to the beginning, in the same.
14 Sept.   Entry made 14 Sept. 1857
1857

                            Anderson Roneyls
                            Locator
fees of
Office paid
75   Attest.
           F. G. Blacknell
           Entry Taker

PAGE 357

No. 365   State of Tennessee Able Kesterson Enters five Thou-
                       sand acres of Land in said County
          Hamilton County   Beginning on a Sycamore tree stand-
                      ing near the Marion line on the
South side of the Tennessee River at the Suck thence
across said River to a stake on the South side 20 poles
thence up the South side with the meander of said River to a Walnut Stump Standing on the bank of said River near the Warehouse of M. R. Allen the corner to the
said Allen Land & then North 70° West to the North
(blank)   bank of said River to a stake thence to the beginning
containing Five Thousand Acres.
Entry made 26 Nov. 1857

                            Able Kesterson
                            Locator

          Attest
          F. G. Blacknall, Entry taker
          Copy issued 26 Nov./57

PAGE 357

No. 366

(blank)

State of Tennessee) Able Kesterson Enters Five Thou-
                  (sand Acres of land in said County--
Hamilton County (Beginning on a Walnut stump stand-
                      ing on the South Bank of the Tenn-
essee River corner of his former Entry No. 365 thence
North 70° west with the line of said Entry to a stake
the corner of said Entry standing on the north bank
of said River, thence Northeastwardly up with the
meanders of said River to the County line between
Bledsoe and Hamilton County to a stake standing in
said line on the bank of said River then South 70°
East to a stake on the South bank of said River thence
down the same with its various meanders to the beginning containing Five thousand Acres.

                            Able Kesterson
                            Locator

Attest.
F. G. Blacknall Ent.
Copy Issd. 26 Nov./57

PAGE 358

No. 367

State of Tennessee) Jesse Walker & D. C. Trewitt
                  (Enters Three hundred & twenty
Hamilton County (acres of land in said County on
                    Waldens Ridge of Cumberland Moun-
tain, Beginning on a hickory corner & Black oak pointer
on the water of Little Soddy Creek the second corner
to the said Walker 5000 Acre tract then East 160 poles
then South 320 poles thence West to Joshua Johnson
line then along his line to the Survey of Elisha Rodg-
er line then with said line to William Cunningham line
then to the beginning.
March 3rd 1858.

                        Jesse Walker
F. G. Blacknall Entry Taker Copy issued & fee of office
paid same day.

                      F. G. Blacknall, E. T.

PAGE 358

No. 368

State of Tennessee-- Hamilton County. Jesse Walker
Enters Two hundred Acres of Land in said County on
Waldens Ridge of Cumberland Mountains. Beginning
on a Chestnut oak standing at the bluff marked W
standing on the east side of the old line between
the Counties of Marion & Hamilton on the North
side of Coop Creek near George Fletcher, then North

: eastwardly with the County line 200 poles to a
: stake then South 70° east to the line of the 5000
: Acre Entry made in the name of said Watkins then
: South westwardly with said line to Coop Creek then
: up the creek with the meander thereof to the County
: line then with County line to the beginning.
: Entry made this 3 March A. D. 1858.

:   Jesse Walker
:   Locator

: Attest. F. G.Blacknall E. T.
: Fee paid.Copy issued sand day.

PAGE 359

No. 369   : State of Tennessee) Peter Bolton Enters Five Thousand
Peter Bolton   :   (Acres of Land in Hamilton County
Enter   : Hamilton County   ) Beginning on a rock in the line of
5000   :   Judson Coundry(?) boundary at the
                   : foot of Walden Ridge in the 11 district of said Coun-
                   : ty running then due west to Isaac Roberson line on the
Entry made   : Mountain then with said line to McGill Creek, then with
3 April   : said Creek to the foot of said Mountain, then with the
1858   : foot of said Mountain to the beginning, Containing 5000
                   : Acres.
                   : April 3, 1858

:   Peter Bolton
:   Locator

: Attest:-
: F.G. Blacknall
: Entry Taker

PAGE 359

No. 370   : State of Tennessee) A. L. Anderson enters two Thous-
A. L. Anderson   :   ) and Acres of Land in Hamilton Coun-
Enters 2000   : Hamilton County   ) ty on the North side of Tennessee
Entry   :   River, Beginning on a white oak
made   : standing in Thomas Laymans line at the foot of the ridge
Apr. 10   : running thence with Lamons line Eastward to Laymans
                   : corner thence same course continued to the public Road
                   : leading from Johnsons ferry to Dallas, thence with said
                   : Poe road to where Anderson back line crosses said Road
                   : know as the Churchill line, thence with the Churchill
                   : line Southward, thence with Andersons call to the be-
                   : ginning.
                   :   A. L. Anderson, Locator
                   : April 10, 1859

PAGE 380

No. 371
B. F. Clark
Enters
5000 Acres
Land

State of Tennessee) B. F. Clark Enters Five Thousand
              () Acres of Land in said County Be-
Hamilton County () ginning on a hickory corner to
              Clift & McRee Entry on North Side
of Rocky Creek, then with Clift & McRee's line N. 80½
W. 1000 poles, thence N. 20 E. 600 poles to a stake,
thence S. 70 E. to the foot of Waldens Ridge thence
to the Beginning. Entered this 1st day of December
1859.

                    B. F. Clark
                    Locator

Attest. F. G. Blacknall Entry Taker H.C. Tennessee

Copy Issued 1st Dec./59

PAGE 360

No. 1.-372
William Clift
Enters
1000 Acres

Entry made
June 3rd
1867

State of Tennessee) William Clift enters One Thousand
              () Acres of land in Hamilton County
Hamilton County (and lying in the 11 Civil Dist.
              thereof on the face of Waldens
Ridge of Cumberland Mountain and on the waters of Sale
Rocky Creeks and is bounded as follows, to wit:- beginning on a black Gum and Ash trees in the line of
the 20,000 Acre Survey and at the old indian Boundary
line at the foot of Waldens Ridge thence South Seven
degrees west 170 poles to a black Gum and poplar thence
South twenty two degrees west four hundred poles to a
white oak, thence South Eighteen degrees west to the
North East line of a Grant for 5000 Acres of land belonging to Clift & McRee, thence East with this line
to the line of the 20,000 Acre Survey at the foot of
Waldens Ridge--thence with the line of the 20,000 Survey to the beginning to contain 1000 acres of land
after pedling out all better Claims.
Located June the 3 day A. D. 1867.

                    William Clift
                    Locator

S. A. McKenzie Entry Taker
Copy issd same day

PAGE 361

No. 373
A. G. W.
Puckett
Enters
200

State of Tennessee) A. G. W. Puckett enters two Hundred
              () Acres of land on Wallens Ridge of
Hamilton County () Cumberland Mountain on waters of
              Bear Branch, and on the South side
of North Chickamauga Creek in Hamilton County, Begin-

Entry made Jany. 8 1870	NWG on a stake where Puckett, Blacknall & Johnson's entry No. 385 crosses the line of B. B. Cannon entry No. 273 thence Southwardly with said line two hundred poles to a stake in said line--thence westwardly two hundred poles to a Stake in the line of the lands belonging to the heirs of Houston Hixson known as the
fees Office paid 75c S. A. McKenzie E. T.	Entry of Elisha Askew No. 272 thence with said line Northwardly (175) one hundred & Seventy five poles to a stake in the line of said Puckett, Blacknall & Johnson--thence with said line Eastwardly to the beginning so as to include Two hundred Acres.

This 8 day Jany. 1870

          A. G. W. Puckett
          Locator

S. A. McKenzie E. T.

PAGE 362

No. 374
Geo. Walker
John Walker
1½ acres
TowHead
near
Chickamauga
Isl
	State of Tennessee George Walker & John Walker Enters
	                    One & a half Acres of land called
	Hamilton County a Tow Head lying in the Tennessee
	                    River at the Northwest Corner of
	the Chickamauga Island near the Mouth of North Chickamauga Creek. Entry made this 2nd May 1870.

          George Walker
          Locator

Entry made 3nd May 1870	A certified Copy issued this 2 May 1870

          S. A. McKenzie
          Entry Taker

PAGE 363

No. 375
2000 Acres
	State of Tennessee J. M. Reilly and J. E. Teague
	                    enters two thousand acres of land
	Hamilton County more or less in Hamilton County
	                    Tennessee on Waldens Ridge waters
	of Suck Creek Beginning at a Stake in the Center of said Creek opposite the mouth of the west fork of Suck Creek running thence down the main creek to the granted land near the mouth thence Eastward and North Northeastwardly and Northwardly with the line of other Surveys to a Maple the Northeast corner of the tract on which John Burnet formerly lived at Graysons Gap said Maple corner is on the bank of Main Suck Creeknear the head, thence down the Same as it mean-

TO THE South east corner of a 3469 Acre Survey belonging
to Haley & Long, thence with a line of the same west to
the west fork or little Suck Creek thence down the
same to the beginning this 9 day of January 1871 so as
to include all the vacant land adjoining Such Creek.

J. M. Reilly
Locator

S. A. McKenzie E. T.

PAGE 364

No. 376 : State of Tennessee William Clift enters Three thousand
acres of vacant and unappropriated
Hamilton County land in said County, Bounded as
follows to wit:- Beginning on a stake at the foot of
Waldens Ridge of Cumberland Mountain in the line of
the 20,000 Acre Survey where a line of an entry made
by Samuel Williams & Co. William Clift comes at the
foot of Waldens Ridge as it meanders with the line of
the 20,000 Acre Survey to the due west line to a corner of the 20,000 Acre Survey--thence west with a line
of a Grant of the State of Tennessee to William Clift
or William H. Stringer to the line of Marion and Hamilton Countues--thence North East with said County
lines to another line of Samuel Williams and Co. Thence
with said line to the Beginning Given under my hand
this 14th day of March 1871

William Clift
Locator

R. L. McNabb E. T.

PAGE 365

No. 377 : State of Tennessee J. S. Wilse & Nash H. Burt Enters
One Thousand Acres of land lying in
Hamilton County Hamilton County and Bledsoe on Waldens Ridge beginning on what was
the East corner of Samuel Roberson's Old Entry made July 27th 1857, which lies on the waters of little Soddy

(blank) : Creek--Thence with said Robersons line to what was William Hixons Old line thence with said Hixons old line
then with said Hughes old line to the Beginning, so as to
to include One thousand acres excluding all former entries. This 10th day of July 1871

Fee 50¢ paid. R. L. McNabb E. T.

PAGE 366

No. 388 (378(?)) : State of Tennessee, Hamilton County, J. S. Wilse and

Nash E. Burt enter five thousand acres of land in
s id County on Waldens Ridge: - Beginning on the S
South east corner of what was known as F. G. Blacknall
and G. R. Cannon Entry--thence South Six hundred and
forty poles--thence West 1280 poles--thence N. 640
poles to a line of F. G. Blacknall and G. R. Cannon's
Old entry thence with said line to the Beginning so
as to contain five thousand acres excluding all valid
former Entry.
July 10th 1871

> J. S. Wiltse &
> Nash H. Burt
> Locator

R. L. McNabb E. T.

PAGE 367

No. 389

State of Tennessee} J. S. Wiltse and Nash H. Burt
enter five thousand acres of land
Hamilton County } lying on Waldens Ridge of Cumberland Mountain in said County
Beginning on the North east corner of what was known
as F. G. Blacknalls and G. R. Cannons entry. Thence
North west wardly with the County lines between Marion and Hamilton 1280 poles. Thence South 640 poles
to a stake Thence West to the line of the above old
Entry made by Blacknall and Cannon to the Beginning
so as to include 5000 Acres of land excluding all
former valid Entries.
This 10th day of July 1871

> J. S. Wiltse and
> Nash H. Burt
> Locators

R. L. McNabb E. T.

PAGE 368

No. 390

State of Tennessee} J. S. Wiltse & Nash H. Burt Enter
5000 acres of land in said County
Hamilton County } lying on Waldens Ridge of Cumberland Mountain. Beginning on the
North east corner of an old Entry made by Puckett,
Johnson and Blacknall Thence Southwardly with the line
of the same 1280 poles, thence No. 20° E. 640 poles,
thence N. to the County line between Marion and Hamilton Thence to the Beginning--so as to include five
thousand acres excluding all former valid Entries.
This 10th day of July 1871.

> J. S. Wiltse &
R. L. McNabb E.T.   Nash H. Burt, Locators

PAGE 368

No.----

State of Tennessee) J. S. Wiltse & Nash H. Burt enter
)   two thousand acres of land in
Hamilton County   ) said County lying on Waldens Ridge
                        a-part of Cumberland Mountain Be-
ginning on a Maple tree standing near the top Bluff
of the Mountain on the East side of North Chickamogga
and about 50 feet South West of a Mineral Spring which
is on the land entred by B. B. Cannon

(blank space)

No. 391

thence Southeastwardly with the top Bluff on the Mountain with the line Puckett Johnson & Blacknall Old Entry. Thence with the Closing line of said Entry where
the same leaves the old Fryer Entry. Thence to the Beginning including two thousand Acres more or less excluding all former valid Entries.

                        J. S. Wilse &
                        Nash H. Burte
                        Locator

R.L. McNabb
   E. T.

PAGE 370

No. 392

State of Tennessee) J. S. Willse & Nash H. Burt Enters
)   five hundred Acres of land on Wal-
Hamilton County   ) dens Ridge of Cumberland Mountain o
                        on the waters of North Chickamauga
Creek, Beginning on an ash tree standing about thirty
feet South West of a Mineral Spring on the land entered
by and known as B. B. Cannons Old Entry, near the Cabin built by Shoemaker and others--thence along said
Entry line of B. B Cannon 80 poles to his North West
corner then the same course continued 320 poles to a
stake Thence South 50° W. To the Bluff of Chickamauga Creek. Thence Southeastwardly along said Bluff to
the Beginning so as to include five thousand acres excluding all former entries.

                        J. S. Wiltse &
                        Nash H. Burt
                        Locators
July 10th 1871
R. L. McNabb E. T.

PAGE 371

No. 393

: State of Tennessee- Hamilton County J. S. Wiltse &
: Nash H. Burt Enter One Thousand Acres of land in
: said County on Waldens Ridge. Beginning on a bluff
: of North Chickamauga Creek on a black oak standing
: about one hundred yards from the Southeast corner
: of a large Pool of water. Thence Northeastwardly to
: Joshua Johnsons old South corner of his hundred acre
: entry. Thence Northwardly with his line to Jacob
: Reynolds old line. Thence with his line the same
: course to Fryers old entry with said Entry to the Bluff
: Thence with the bluff to the Beginning so as to in-
: clude one thousand acres of land, excluding all former
: valid Entries

                    J. S. Wiltse &
                    Hash H. Burt
                    Locators
: This 10th day of July 1871
: R. L. McNabb, E. T.

PAGE 372

No. 394

: State of Tennessee| J. S. Willse & Hash H. Burt enter
: | 5000 acres land on Waldens Ridge
: Hamilton County | in said County commencing on a
: | chestnut and Sassafras trees on
: the Bank of Roaring Creek opposite Yellow Bank near
: the County line of Hamilton and Bledsoe Counties
: thence Northwardly with said line to the highest
: Bluff of Waldens Ridge crossing Rocky Creek and O-
: possom Creek to Soddy Creek and down Soddy Creek to
: the line of Old 20,000 Acre Survey of McClung and
: Cosby Thence with said lint Northeastwardly to the
: old 19000 Acre Survey of McClung & Coesby Thence
: with said line to the beginning so as to include
: five thousand Acres of land.
: Excluding all former valid Entrees.

                    J. S. Wiltse &
                    Hash H. Burt
                    Locators
: This 11th day of July 1871
: R. L. McNabb E. T.

PAGE 373

No. 395

: State of Tennessee| J. S. Wiltse & Nash H. Burt Enter
: | one hundred and fifty Acres of
: Hamilton County | land in said County on Waldens
: | Ridge of Cumberland Mountain Be-

ginning on a Bluff of North Chickamauga Creek near
the N. E. corner of a large Pool of water about one
hundred yards from the said Pool. Thence North 20°
E. 640 poles to Joshua Johnsons Old line. Thence
Southeastwardly with his line to a Sassafras corner
of said Johnsons farm. Thence to the Beginning including one hundred and fifty acres ecluding all
former valid entries.

J. S. Wiltse and
Nash H. Burt
Locators

This 11th day of July 1871
R. L. McNabb E. T.

PAGE 374

No. 396

State of Tennessee) J. S. Willse & Nash H. Burt enter
                     five thousand acres of land in
Hamilton County   said County on Waldens Ridge of
                     Cumberland Mountain. Beginning
on Black oak corner markes S. B. H. corner entry
made by Samuel B. Hawkins, dated August 1st, 1831.
Thence South 70° E. 1500 poles. Thence South 20°
West 680 poles thence to the Beginning including
five thousand acres of land excluding all former
entries.
This 11th day of July 1871

J. S. Wiltse and
Nash H. Burt
Locators

R. L. McNabb E. T.

PAGE 375

No. 397

State of Tennessee) J. S. Wiltse and Nash H. Burt
                     enter five thousand acres of
Hamilton County   land lying in said County. Partly
                     in Hamilton and Marion Counties. B
Beginning in Hamilton County Tennessee on a Black oak
marked S. B. H. corner to Samuel B. Hawkins Old En-
try. Thence N. 70° West 1280 poles, thence South 20°
West 1280 poles. Thence South 70° East 1280 poles
Thence to the Beginning so as to include five thou-
sand Acres of land excluding all former valid Entries.

J. S. Wiltse and
Nash H. Burt
Locators
This 11th day of July 1871. R. L. McNabb E. T.

PAGE 376

No. 398

State of Tennessee} J. S. Wiltse & Nash E. Burt Enter
                   } 5000 acres of land in said County
Hamilton County   } on Waldens Ridge of Cumberland
                     Mountain. Beginning on the North
East corner of an Entry made in the name of Puckett
Blacknell and Johnson. Thence South with said line
to the Southeast corner of said Entry. Thence East
350 poles, Thence to a point between the Counties
of Marion and Hamilton three hundred and fifty poles
from the beginning so as to include fivethousand Acres.
Excluding all former valid Entries.

                        J. S. Wiltse &
                        Nash E. Burt
                        Locators

This 11th day of July 1871

                        R. L. McNabb E. T.

PAGE 378

No. 399

State of Tennessee} J. S. Wiltse & Nash H. Burt enters
                  } 5000 acres of land in Hamilton Coun-
Hamilton County   } ty lying on Waldens Ridge on the
                    waters of North Chickamauga Creek
Beginning on the County line between Marion And Hamilton where the said line crosses North Chickamauga Creek
on a rock in the center of said Creek Then down said
Creek along the line of Entry 5 5 to the line of the
Doak Entry were said Creek runs into said entry thence
in a Westwardly course with the said xxxx -- one mile
and a half to a stake on the top of the Mountain.
Thence North Westwardly parallel to the general course
of said Creek, including the main Bluff of the Mountain to a stake in the line between said Counties one
mile and a half of the Beginning said side to the beginning so as to include five thousand acres, excluding all valid Entries.
This 11th day of July 1871

                        J. S. Willse &
                        Nash H. Burt
                        Locators
R. L. McNabb E. T.

PAGE 379
No. 400

State of Tennessee} J. S. Willse & Nash H. Burt enter
                  } 5000 acres on Waldens Ridge Begin-
Hamilton County   ning on the waters of North Chick
                    amauga beginning on the County

lines between the Counties of Marion and Hamilton where the same crosses North Chickamauga Creek at a stake on the North east side of the said Creek on the top of said Mountain Thence to the centre of said Creek Thence down the centre of said Mountain Thence to the centre of said Creek Thence down the said Creek to the line of the Dock Entry where the said Creek runs through the Mountain, then North eastwardly one mile and a half to a stake thence Northwestwardly parallel with the General course of the said Creek, including the main bluff of the Mountain to a stake in the said County line one m mile and a half from the Beginning. Thence to the Beginning so as to include five thousand Acres, excluding all former valid entries.
This 11th day of July 1871.

J. S. Wiltse
Nash H. Burt
Locators
R. L. McNabb E. T.

PAGE 380

No. 401

State of Tennessee) J. S. Wiltse and Nash H. Burt
Enter fifty Acres of land in
Hamilton County Hamilton County Tennessee including a pond situated on the
North Side of the Tennessee River adjoining the land entered by and known as Joshua Johnson's Entry Beginning on a poplar corner to said Joshua Johnson's old entry. Thence South 6° West 110 poles to a hickory and Sweet gum on the side of said pond. Thence South 27° East 150 poles to James Smith's old line thence South 45° West crossing the pond to James Smith's old line, thence to the old Reservation line, known as John Brown Reservation. Thence along said Reservation line to the beginning, excluding all former valid entries. This 11th day of July 1871.

J. S. Willse and
Nash H. Burt
Locators
R. L. McNabb E. T.

PAGE 381

No. 402

State of Tennessee) Henry S. Jones enters three hundred
and ninety nine acres of land on
Hamilton County Waldens Ridge in Hamilton County
State of Tennessee. Beginning at
the N. E. corner of said lot on a stake corner to ah

Entry made by A. G. W. Puckett, William Johnson and
F. G. Blacknall thence with their line S. 20½° W. 320 rods
rods to a stake and post oak Pointer--thence N. 69½
West 224 rods to a stake on the County line Thence with
said line N. 29½° West to a stake on the South bank of
Coopers Creek. Thence S. 69½ E. 175 poles to the be-
ginning so as to include three hundred and ninety nine
Acres.
Excluding all former valid entries.

                Henry S. Jones
                Locator

This 13th day of September 1871.

              R. L. McNabb E. T.

PAGE 382

No. 403

State of Tennessee   Nash H. Burt & J. S. Wiltse enter
                     Jointly eighteen hundred & eighteen
Hamilton County   acres of land jointly in Hamilton
                     County, Tennessee. Beginning at the
Northeast corner on a stake, Post oak pointer, it being
Southeast corner of an entry made by Henry S. Jones No.
402. Running thence South 20½° West with the line of an
Entry made by A.G. W. Puckett, Blacknall & Johnson 960
rods Southwest corner of their said Entry to a stake
and pointer. Thence North 69½° West to a stake on the
County line between Marion & Hamilton 374 rods, Thence
North 29½° East 980 rods with said County line to a
Stake to a corner of an Entry made by Henry S. Jones
No. 402. Thence with the line of said Jones South 69½
East 224 rods to the Beginning.
September 20th 1871

              Nash H. Burt &
              J. S. Wiltse
              Locators

R. L. McNabb E. T.

PAGE 383
No. 404

State of Tennessee   Emerson Roberts Entry beginning
                     on a hickory and black oak bush
Hamilton County   at the foot of the impassible
                     bluff on Waldens Ridge in Hamil-
ton County and State of Tennessee. In a line of an
entry made by Jessie Walker--Thence North 40° W. passing over said bluff and along a line of said Roberts
former Entry 62 poles to a white oak and black oak in
a line of Allen Pickett. Thence North 45° E. 318 poles
along said picketts Milwood and Moses line to a stake
two hickory --black gum chestnut and chestnut oak pointers in a line of A. Selcer and Joseph Rogers heirs,
Thence South 45° E. about 25 poles along their line

passing over the bluff of said Mountain to the foot
of bottom of South bluff to said Walkers entry line,
thence South west along said bluff and line as it
meanders. Supposed to be 400 poles to the Beginning.
This 14th of November 1872.

> Emerson Roberts
> Locator

James Lamon
Entry Taker & Surveyor

PAGE 384

Number 405

State of Tennessee{ O. S. Green and J. G. Bias enter
two hundred and twenty five Acres
Hamilton County { of land jointly in Hamilton County
Tennessee. Beginning on a double c
chestnut Oak in Stanleys line on the North end of the
Round Nob, thence South 6° West one hundred and forty
poles to a stake and pointers Thence West 240 poles to
a stake and pointers near the bluff of Suck Creek,
thence North 20° West one hundred and forty five poles
to two pines in Conners Green, and Minnis'es line,
thence with said line South 89° East two hundred and eit
eighty poles to the beginning. This fifth day of Dec-
enber 1874.

> O. S. Green and
> J. G. Bias
> Locator

James Lamon
Surveyor and E. T.
    Run out by Alfred Conner

PAGE 385

Number 406

State of Tennessee{ Pursuant to an Entry made in the
Entry Takers Office of said Coun-
Hamilton County { ty on the 9th day of September 1849
and Numbered (313) Three hundred and
thirteen by Samuel Williams and William Clift under the
firm name and style of Samuel Williams & Co. and by
virtue of authority in me vested by James Lamon Survey-
or for said County of Hamilton endorsee on said Cer-
tifice of Entry appointing me a special Deputy to survey the lands mentioned in the within entry and to make
plat and map of the same for grant to issue upon, and
I have surveyed for the said Samuel Williams and William Clift Four thousand Eight Hundred acres of land
on Waldens Ridge of Cumberland Mountain. Beginning on

a white oak in the line between the Counties of Hamilton and Sequatchie formerly Marion on the South
Side of the Turnpike road and running thence South
29° West with said County line Seven hundred poles to
a stake and hickory pointer. A short distance below
Rells(or Rills) Creek and on the side of a ridge
Thence South 61° East thirteen hundred and twenty
poles to a small Walnut at the corner of a field at
the foot of the Mountain. Thence North 44° East
crossing Chickamauga Creek at Eighty three poles.
Two hundred and fifty four poles to a stake, Thence
North 60° East Four hundred and Sixty poles to a
Stake thence 35° East three hundred and four poles to a
stake. Thence North 11° East Three hundred and eighty
two poles to a pine and pointers -- thence North 61°
west Fifteen hundred and twenty poles to the County
line. Thence with the County line South 29° west Six
hundred poles to the beginning, Surveyed the 29th day
Of November 1875.

> J. W. Clift
> Special Deputy
> for H.C.

James Lamon
E. T. & Surveyor

PAGE 387

Number 407

State of Tennessee⟩ John Cummings enters the North
　　　　　　　　　⟨ East Half of Section Twenty Six and
Hamilton County   ⟨ all other parts of said Section men-
　　　　　　　　　　tioned previous to this date. In
the Second Fractional Township, Range five west of basis line in the Ocoee District. Also the South west half
of Section Twenty three and all other parts of said
Section unentered up to this date in the Second Fractional Township Range five West of the Basis line in
the Ocoee district Hamilton County Tennessee this 6th
day of January 1875.

> James Lamon E. T.
> & Surveyor for
> Hamilton County, Tenn.

PAGE 387

No. 408

State of Tennessee⟩ William Clift and M. E. Clift enter
　　　　　　　　　⟨ 500 Acres of unappropriated lands
Hamilton County   ⟨ in said County of Hamilton bounded
　　　　　　　　　　as follows to wit:- Beginning on
two pines of a stake in the North East line of the S.W.Doak

Grant: thence North 30° East to the line of the 20,000
Acre Survey thence South west with the line of said
20,000 Acre Survey & the lines of the lands formerly
belonging to Haston Poe to the Beginning.

William Clift
Locator

Entry made this June 27th 1881

E. C. Beck
Register & Ex. Office
Entry Taker

PAGE 388

No. 409

State of Tennessee) P. D. Sims & R. C. McRee Enter 500
) acres of unappropriated land in
Hamilton County   ) said County of Hamilton & State of
                     Tennessee & Bounded as follows--
Beginning on Stake on Middle Creek or Cain Creek the
North Fork of North Chickamauga Creek, and the North
East corner of the Layton H. Smith Grant--Thence South
27½ West with the line of said Layton H. Smith Grant
to McInturff Creek or Standefres Creek the South Fork of
North Chickamauga Creek--thence with the meanders of
said Creek to its Junction with Middle or Cain Creek --
the North Fork of North Chickamauga Creek, Thence up
said Creek to the beginning--known as the Toe of the big
Horse Shoe--

R. C. McRee
Locator

Entry made this May 25, 1887

E. C. Beck
Register & Ex.
Officio Entry Taker

PAGE 389

No. 410

State of Tennessee) O. S. Green & Lewis Shepherd enter
) 60 Acres of unpossessed land in
Hamilton County O) said County of Hamilton & State of
                     Tennessee & Bounded as follows:-
Beginning on a stake one pole East of the line between
Hamilton & Sequachee and in Hamilton County and allso
near a double chestnut corner to said Green & Wilder
& & Stratton, then N. 88° west 125 poles to a stake then
South 2° west one pole to a stake in said Greens line

Then N. 87½ west along a line of Henry Grayson and others 110 poles to the center of Suck Creek, then down Suck Creek as it meanders about 125 poles to a stake in said Creek with a beach & Spruce pine and two Maples pointers then South 85½ East about 83 poles to a stake in Zion Crows line then N. about 16° west 115 poles along said Crows line to two pines, then South 88°E. along said Crows North line 121 poles to a stake one pole East of said County line, then N. 31 East one pole to the Beginning.

O. S. Green

This 23 April 1888

E. C. Beck
Reg. & Ex. Office
Entry Taker

P GE 390

(?)

State of Tennessee { I. H. F. Rogers, Register and Ex. Officio Entry Taker of Hamilton
Hamilton County { County, Tenn., do hereby certify that I have carefully collated the foregoing transcript of the Original Entry Takers Books Nos. 1&2 from page One to page Three Hundred and Ei Eighty Nine (389) both inclusive) with said Original Entry Takers Books. That this transcript contains a full true and complete Copy or transcript of the Record in said Original Books.

Witness m y hand this June 19th 1895.

E. F. Rogers, Register &
Ex. officio Entry Taker
Hamilton County, Tenn.

PAGE 391

No. 411

State of Tennessee { Henry Barker enters 9 acres of un-possessed land in said County of Ham-
Hamilton County { ilton and State of Tennessee and bounded as follows--
Beginning at a stake-- the South East corner of Henry Barkers home place. Thence N. 37° 5' E. 3009 feet to a stake and pointers--corner to H. Johnsons land--thence S. 56° E. 79 ft. to apost Oak corner to E. F. Hixsons land- Thence with E. F.(or Ephraim) Hixson's line along the top of ridge about 2979 ft. to B. F. Hollands line Thence with B. F. Hollands line about 231 ft. to J.M. Longs corner. Thence with Longs line about 235 ft. to

the beginning.

H. F. Rogers Register and
Ex. officio Entry Taker

"Survey to entry of 9 acres of unpossessed land by Henry
Barker in Second Civil District of Hamilton Co. Tenn.
----- ---- (Small drawing)

PAGE 392

No. 412

State of Tennessee Ransom Rogers and Henry Johnson
Enter 500 acres of unpossessed
Hamilton County land in said County of Hamilton
and state of Tennessee and lo-
cated on top of Waldens ridge and in the 16th Civil Dist.
of said county and Near North Chickamauga Creek and
bounded on the North and East by the land of the Chattanooga Company Limited. and on the South and west by the
land of Hale, Selcer and Hixson.
This January 28 1895

Ransom Rogers Locators
Henry Johnson

Filed this August 31st 1897

H. F. Rogers Register &
Ex.officio Entry Taker

(The end)

www.ingramcontent.com/pod-product-compliance
Lightning Source LLC
Chambersburg PA
CBHW080607270326
41928CB00016B/2960